WOMEN
❧ AND THE ❧
AUTHORITY
of SCRIPTURE

A Narrative Approach

SARAH HEANER LANCASTER

TRINITY PRESS INTERNATIONAL
HARRISBURG, PENNSYLVANIA

Copyright © 2002 Sarah Heaner Lancaster

Trinity Press International, P.O. Box 1321, Harrisburg, PA 17105

Trinity Press International is a division of The Morehouse Group.

Cover art: *Three Peasant Women,* Camille Pissarro. Christie's Images/SuperStock.

Cover design by Corey Kent

Library of Congress Cataloging-in-Publication Data

Lancaster, Sarah Heaner, 1956-
 Women and the authority of Scripture : a narrative approach / Sarah Heaner Lancaster.
  p. cm.
Includes bibliographical references and index.
  ISBN 1-56338-356-X (pbk. : alk. paper)
  1. Bible—Evidences, authority, etc. 2. Bible—Feminist criticism. I. Title.
  BS480 .L33 2002
  220.1'3—dc21

                                                    2002005400

Printed in the United States of America

02 03 04 05 06 07   10 9 8 7 6 5 4 3 2 1

WOMEN
AND THE
AUTHORITY
of SCRIPTURE

Contents

Acknowledgments

A Christian woman inescapably faces questions about the authority of the Bible. In a sense I have been working on this issue in some way throughout my life. When I began formal academic study in preparation for ordination, I had the opportunity to think about the authority of the Bible in light of what feminists were beginning to say about it. My attention to this issue took a more focused form when I began my dissertation as a Ph.D. student at Southern Methodist University. I concentrated on the work of Hans Frei partly because his approach to the Bible was so different from other approaches that I had encountered. I wanted to understand what he was up to. Not initially sympathetic to his ideas, I was intrigued by using narrative as a category for understanding the Bible. I brought my feminist questions to that project, and the resulting dialogue illuminated issues that I wanted to pursue further. I should acknowledge here the contributions of my dissertation committee, the members of which were Charles M. Wood, William S. Babcock, and Jouette M. Bassler.

In the years that have passed since I wrote that dissertation, I have expanded my research into areas that go well beyond the idea of narrative that Hans Frei used. His name is mentioned only rarely in what follows, and his influence on my thinking at this point is indirect. I started down this path because of studying his work, but the path has taken me ultimately to unexpected places. Although I worked out some fundamental approaches to certain problems in that dissertation, this book is very different from it.

I am grateful to those who have contributed their time to helping me think through the issues that surround this topic. While at Methodist Theological School in Ohio (MTSO), I have twice taught a course entitled "The Authority of Scripture," and the students have been willing and eager participants in discussion. I have also taught a course on revelation for the Theological Consortium of Greater Columbus, to which MTSO belongs, and I learned a great deal from the ecumenical nature of the student body in that class. Robin Knowles Wallace, Lisa Withrow, Kevin Smith, Tyron Inbody, and Randy Litchfield have all read portions of this book and offered comments. Charles M. Wood has read almost the entire manuscript, and he graciously made time to do so despite other pressing work.

On the eve of my one-term sabbatical, during which time I was to do the major writing of this book, my mother was diagnosed with a terminal illness. The months in which I had planned to give birth to this project were mostly spent helping her through her illness and death. I am grateful to Henry Carrigan, my editor at Trinity Press, for allowing me the extra time I needed to finish writing. When I came back from sabbatical, I also received the support of my school in the form of a course release so that I could make up for some of my lost writing time. My husband, Kermit Lancaster, made many sacrifices and picked up extra responsibilities so that I could work on this project. I am, as always, grateful to him for his constant support of my work.

I wrote this book for all women who struggle with the authority of the Bible, but I especially would like to offer it in memory of my mother, Dorothy Bearden Heaner, and for my daughters, Jocelyn and Kendra. I hope her past and their futures are honored here.

Introduction

Feminist theology was born struggling with Scripture. From the beginning, feminists recognized how the situation of women was bound up with certain understandings about women (and men) that were rooted in the Bible. To find patriarchal ideas in sacred writ gave those ideas the appearance of being permanent and unquestionable. As more and more women grew in feminist consciousness of their oppression, women faced the question of how to respond to the Bible and to the traditions that called it sacred. The varied responses have been shaped largely by the question of whether women believe the Bible to have authority for their lives in some way. Women's struggle with the Bible certainly extends beyond Christianity, but among Christians have been at least these responses. Some women have continued to accept the authority of the Bible without question, and they remain in the church without change in attitude or action. Others leave Christianity completely in the belief that the Bible and Christian tradition are irredeemably patriarchal. They deny, then, that the Bible has any authority for them. Still others both recognize that Scripture is to a large extent patriarchal and yet choose to remain participants in Christianity. The decision to stay implies their acceptance of Scripture as in some sense authoritative for Christian life, despite its problematic character. Usually, though, "staying" involves much more than acceptance. The decision is often grounded in the hope for transformation of the church and of the way it understands its sacred text. The heart of the struggle with Scripture for reformist Christian feminists lies here, at the intersection between the life-affirming and life-degrading power that Scripture has for women. This particular struggle is the one I want to explore in this book.

Those who choose to stay and struggle do so in very different ways. In this book, I will look at some of the major approaches that feminists have taken in the past twenty-five years toward understanding the authority of the Bible. Toward the beginning of that period, feminist theology was so new that it was possible to be thoroughly familiar with feminist writings as well as other major thinkers. More recently, though, feminist works abound to the extent that keeping up with this literature alone could be a career in itself. As women have increasingly found voices to speak, the category "feminist" has undergone considerable redefinition. Whereas once those who called themselves "feminist" sought to speak for all women, now it is clear that the experiences of white, middle-class, educated women are quite different from the experiences of women in other situations and other parts of the world. While in its broadest sense "feminist" can include any struggle for the full humanity of women, that struggle has different accents, for instance, those expressed in womanist and *mujerista* theologies. In comparison to these other perspectives, "feminist" has come to specify one among many voices that call for justice for women. While I recognize that other perspectives are important for understanding the entire scope of the reformist struggle, in this book I will confine myself to discussion that can now be properly called "feminist." I am also confining my discussion specifically to Christian feminism. Jewish feminists have been very important for bringing to light problems not only with the Bible itself but also with certain formulations of Christian feminist responses to those problems. I am situated, though, within the church, and my immediate concern is with the canon that has been collected as the Christian Bible (when I use the term "Bible," I am referring to this canon). My own questions arise in this context with this book. My intent is, not to deny the significance of any of these other perspectives, but to focus on one strand of the discussion, which has within it its own variations. I hope I have learned from these other views, but I cannot speak for them. My hope is that the insights gained by examining the struggle from the perspective I have will also be useful to women of other perspectives. They will, of course, have to discover for themselves what is helpful in their own contexts.

Reformist feminist theology, though, cannot accomplish its purpose with feminist ideas alone. The very nature of the struggle—to transform a faith tradition—requires that the tradition itself be examined. Toward that end, I will include in this book a discussion of the doctrine of Scripture developed during the time of Protestant orthodoxy because it lies behind many of the assumptions Christians have today about the authority of the Bible. This doctrine relies heavily on the notion of verbal inspiration, to which many (not simply feminists) object. To say that the very words of Scripture come directly from God is to make those words immune to criticism. Feminist theologians, though, know that many things the Bible "says" need to be criticized. To reject this doctrine of Scripture outright may seem more helpful than to take it seriously enough to study it, but there is good reason to examine it carefully. Although the context of the discussion in which the idea took shape has largely been lost to us, the notion of verbal inspiration lingers on through assumptions that are brought to discussions about biblical authority. The frequency with which feminists have had to denounce it indicates the staying power that it has had in the minds of many. It is useful, under the maxim of "Know your enemy," for feminists to examine this concept in its proper context in order to know how to address properly the problems that it raises.

Positive reasons for studying this doctrine of Scripture also exist. In contrast to the popular versions most of us encounter, the doctrine of Scripture developed by Protestant scholastic theologians is highly nuanced and sophisticated and helpfully brings out many issues that must be addressed in any proposal about Scripture's authority. Furthermore, despite great differences that exist between Protestant orthodoxy and feminism, there are some similar impulses. Protestantism was itself a reform movement, and the orthodox theologians who elaborated Reformation ideas into formal doctrines stood in great continuity with those ideas. It is instructive for feminists to see how the impulses behind the Reformation played themselves out. An examination of the Protestant orthodox doctrine of Scripture can be useful to feminists to see what the doctrine was trying to safeguard as well as how it ultimately fails. The legacy of the Protestant doctrine of Scripture is a sad one for women, and not simply for Protestant women. Roman Catholic feminist theologians have had to fight vigorously against the notions that came out of Protestant orthodoxy because they have been so pervasive. Much needs to be challenged and changed. Still, we may be able to learn something from the attempts that were made in that time so that we can better understand the role and authority of Scripture in our own.

One of the concepts that has to be examined in light of the way that Protestant orthodoxy developed its understanding of Scripture is revelation. What is often at stake in certain understandings about Scripture that have been harmful to women is the question of Scripture's reliability when it speaks about God. Revelation is taken to be the disclosure of supernatural truth, of specific knowledge about God that can be gained in no other way. To understand revelation as "content," and to say that Scripture is the sole source of this content, is to make Scripture the key to saving knowledge of God. Scripture is understood to have authority because it reveals God's word to us as nothing else can. Attempts to indicate human errors in Scripture, then, threaten the trustworthiness of Scripture as revelation. For women to challenge the Bible's description of our situation is to challenge potentially much more than cultures, either the cultures that produced these passages or our own. Under this particular understanding of revelation, it is to challenge the security of salvation itself.

In order to counter the problems that biblical passages present for women, feminists need to provide an alternative account of revelation. Feminists have begun to address this need, typically arguing that the locus of revelation is in women's experience, not in the words of the Bible itself. Rather than being locked in the text, revelation takes place when God's word is heard anew, and specifically for feminists when it is heard in a transforming and reforming way. Revelation as experience discloses not only a certain understanding of God but also an understanding of the world and ourselves that allows us to be critical of oppressive structures in the world. Revelatory experience, far from being a once-and-for-all event of the past with a specific and unchanging content, is ongoing as God constantly calls us forward into a new and better future. This shift from propositional content to experience in understanding revelation is not limited to feminist theology. Many theologians have worked to conceive of revelation in a way that avoids the problems of a propositional approach and that highlights the personal encounter we have with God. Feminist identification of "women's experience" as the locus of revelatory experience is not identical to the more general discussion about the experience of revelation but depends in many ways on the insights of that discussion. It is important for feminists to participate in that broader discussion in order to offer a more complete description of what we mean when we talk about a revelatory experience of God. In this book, I will explore some of the ways in which that experience has been described and how that description intersects with feminist concerns.

Sandra Schneiders's work *The Revelatory Text* is helpful for seeing the complex way in which Scripture is involved in disclosing God to us.[1] She argues that the "locus" of revelation is neither the mere words of the Bible nor simply some internal experience of the reader but rather a complex interaction of Bible, reader, and community. This approach allows one to acknowledge both the value of past testimony about knowledge of God and the need for ongoing appropriation of that knowledge. One may build on this more complex interaction to begin to address a problem that has been raised recently within feminism itself regarding what we mean by "women's experience." Rather than simply speaking of an internal, prelinguistic experience of God that is independent of any other experience, feminists now largely recognize how all our experiences, even our experiences of God, are shaped by our social locations.[2] We never have knowledge of God apart from the communities in which we participate. Given this situation, we have to think in a new way about what counts as reliable, saving knowledge of God. No longer is the question simply whether Scripture is trustworthy. Truth cannot be guaranteed by proposing a unique production process for the Bible, and neither need it be completely threatened by challenging that special production process. Reliable knowledge of God rests neither on how Scripture was recorded nor on the truth of every detail that it contains. If it is possible to have reliable knowledge of God, that knowledge will be the product of how God works in us individually and communally. The real question about Scripture's authority is how it contributes to this work of God in us.

Understanding the Bible as narrative helps illumine the way that Scripture may be used by God as an instrument for revelation. The Bible invites us to see the world as God's and to live accordingly. Through the many individual narratives and other kinds of literature in the biblical texts, Scripture offers us a multifaceted understanding of how God is present to us and interacts with us. In a very general way, the Bible works as a narrative or story; that is, all these materials are somehow together involved in a sort of "telling." I am not suggesting that a single line of plot runs from beginning to end, although the canon is loosely shaped to indicate some movement from creation through problematic human existence to the restoration of all things. Rather, the "telling" is something like the way families share stories with children. Although those family stories are told over time by different people in different ways with varied levels of accuracy and detail, together they provide for the children a sense of identity and purpose. Biblical "telling" involves more, of course, than simply sharing memories. It also involves calling us to attend to the ultimate context for our lives, which in traditional Christian language may be called "testimony" and "proclamation," in everything we do. We are challenged to understand, accept, and live according to the reality of God's involvement in the world and in our lives. Part of the "formation" that takes place lies in how we respond. To a large extent, we become who we are as we appropriate the story we have heard in the way we live. Some appropriations may be so significant (such as moving from unbelief to belief) that we may in fact be transformed from what we were before. Narrative, then, moves us from simply remembering to creatively and imaginatively appropriating what we have heard in a way that can truly liberate us.

Although we cannot expect to find utter consistency in the Bible, we can discern a certain kind of "coherence." The varied materials that one finds in the Bible have not simply come together by chance. The shape of the canon indicates the way that the Christian community has understood these materials to "hold together" (cohere). Although the connection is in many ways loose, the canon does provide a pattern for the direction in which we are to understand them.³ The canonical shape is not itself sacred, and certainly variations regarding the collection persist among Christian churches. There is, though, very broad agreement about the core of this collection. That agreement indicates something very important about the "story" that the community wants to tell; it is a "story" that is not simply textual but is remembered and told liturgically and catechetically as well. The Christian community has been sharing its memories and passing them on longer than it has had a written record of those memories, and it has told its story quite effectively to countless Christians who have had no access to the written materials even after they had been produced. Narrative "coherence," then, involves much more than textual consistency. One can discern a narrative even among disparate written materials when one is attentive to the story that the church is trying to tell in many ways. Another aspect of coherence is equally important, namely, the way that this Christian story "hangs together" with our lives. Feminists have often said that they continue to acknowledge Scripture's authority in some way, despite all the problems it presents for women, because it continues to "ring true" in some way with their experience.⁴ Feminists who remain Christian seek integrity between their experiences as feminist women and their religious faith. Any discussion of the authority of Scripture that wants to take feminist insights seriously will have to attend to the ways in which the Bible does and does not exhibit this kind of coherence.

If the Bible discloses God through narrative, then what kind of authority does it have and exercise? Answering that question requires examining the concept of authority itself. Letty Russell set the stage for feminist conversation about authority by calling for a shift in paradigms, from conceiving authority as "domination" to conceiving it as "partnership."⁵ This approach highlights the need to see that authority is properly exercised in and through community relationships, not in an individual's or group's control over a community. Feminist insight that authority is fundamentally relational accords well with certain philosophical analyses of authority. In this book, I hope to show how those analyses can deepen and expand the central feminist conviction about authority. With a fuller understanding of authority itself, it will be easier to see the ways in which Scripture has been misused with regard to women, and also the ways in which it may properly authorize liberation for women.

Toward that end, the work of Richard De George is enlightening. In *The Nature and Limits of Authority*, De George examines the varied ways authority is held and exercised in social life.⁶ Whether it is found in the sphere of the family or government or religion, authority is relational. A normal and necessary part of life, authority has common features that cut across the varied ways in which it is held and exercised. De George both analyzes the structure that pertains to any instance of authority and describes multiple types of authority, each of which has distinct purposes and requires distinct responses. Although one may talk about general features of authority itself, there is no authority in general. Authority is held and exercised only by particular individuals in particular realms or fields and in particular contexts. De George's analysis brings to light the fluidity of authority relations in society. Given the various types of authority that exist, the various situations in which we find ourselves, and the various kinds of expertise that we all have, each of us bears authority and is subject to authority at different times. Furthermore, even when we are subject to authority, the authority relation itself exists for the benefit of the one who is subject to it, not for the one who bears it. Both these insights can help to address the very serious problems that feminists have raised regarding the typical understanding of authority as domination. In the first place, the purpose of authority properly understood and exercised is, not to control others, but to enrich those others in some way. Second, this understanding of authority can help women claim the valid ways in which they have authority that largely go unrecognized. This analysis will have important bearing on the role that Scripture plays in the lives of women and also on the ability and responsibility that women have to read Scripture in light of their own experiences. A common objection to feminist theology is that it supplants Scripture's authority with the authority of women as interpreters. As we shall see, pitting these two expressions of authority against each other is unnecessary. Both the authority of Scripture and the authority of women can be maintained together.

If the Bible's role in our lives is indeed as multifaceted as I have described above (and perhaps even more so), then the way that it exercises authority in our lives will be equally multifaceted. Given the many types of authority that De George identifies, the Bible may have and exercise its authority in different ways. Equally important is specifying the domain in which the Bible's authority holds. Toward this end, it is helpful to recall that feminists are not the first to wrestle with questions of Scripture's authority in the face of serious challenges. In earlier generations, theologians sought to come to terms with the way in which modern historical and scientific methods made the Bible's propositional claims problematic, and it became important to distinguish in some way between the message that Scripture was trying to convey and the words in which it attempted to convey that message. In various ways, theologians argued that Scripture's point is, not to tell about history or science, but to tell about God, and through this distinction they were implicitly indicating the appropriate domain in which Scripture exercises its authority.[7] Challenges to the truth of Scripture's apparent claims regarding history or science are not fatal to Scripture's authority because historical and scientific matters do not fall within its proper domain. Rather, Scripture exercises its proper authority when it speaks to us about its own proper subject.

Like the challenge of historical consciousness for previous generations, the challenge of feminist critical consciousness calls for distinguishing the domains in which the Bible does and does not properly have authority. The problem for feminist theologians, though, is somewhat different than it was for theologians who dealt with the historical and scientific problems because much more than credibility is at stake. One cannot simply address feminist concerns by distinguishing between the "medium" and the "message." The "medium" itself—patriarchal language, images, and concepts—does damage to women. Still, if we want to be able to continue to acknowledge Scripture's authority, we must be able to say that the good news of the Bible can be distinguished from patriarchal language, images, and concepts. Thinking in terms of narrative provides one way to begin to make this distinction. The medium and message are not easily separable in a story, but a story does not simply function as a report either. One becomes engaged in a narrative, and one's engagement can take many forms, including discomfort and struggle. We are shaped not merely by hearing it but by becoming involved with it. Our involvement may be diverse and take place on a number of levels, but a narrative does try to communicate something to us. The Bible's point is not to tell about patriarchy; it is to tell about our salvation, that is, how God is present to us and interacts with us in order to bring us to fullness of life. Its genuine authority is not exercised in defending and maintaining a patriarchal world. Women may criticize those things in Scripture that appear to do so without invalidating Scripture's authority in its proper domain. In fact, women are obligated to engage in such criticism since those patriarchal elements actually hinder the Bible's ability to speak to women and thus exercise its proper function to bring us to an encounter with God. To speak accurately and adequately of women's salvation requires listening to what women say regarding the ways in which our lives are diminished and enriched. The questions and protests women raise regarding the ways in which biblical texts have been used and misused against us as well as the testimonies women bear regarding the ways in which biblical texts have set us free to live fully are equally important for helping identify the way that Scripture appropriately enables God's work in us.

Narratives are not merely experienced but are also interpreted, and feminist theology acknowledges the need and calls for multiple interpretations of Scripture. Especially in recent years, feminist theologians have recognized that women are shaped in different ways, that we bring different experiences to the texts we interpret, and that we need to hear what each voice is saying. I hope to show that the narrative approach to Scripture I have in mind allows for these multiple interpretations. To see the Bible as a narrative that invites us to understand the world as God's eliminates the possibility of a single "correct" interpretation. The word "canon" in one of its senses means a "rule" or "measure," and at times this sense of the word has been invoked to say that Scripture serves as a norm to establish which interpretation is "right" and which is "wrong." Indeed, Scripture does act as a norm or standard in some way, but it is important to ask what kind of a standard it actually is. One might ask, What is it a standard for? How does it properly exercise its normative authority? If the Bible functions as a narrative that calls forth our imaginations to see the many ways in which God's presence is known to us, then it does not serve as a standard for a single, right interpretation. There may be many ways of being "right." There also may be many ways of being "wrong." Recognizing that the narrative does provide some limits for our work means that we are not left adrift in complete relativism. Furthermore, imaginative interpretation will necessarily take into account the situation of the interpreter. If Scripture is to illumine the way in which God is present for me and for my community, I will have to make use of what I understand about my community and myself. The Bible functions as more than a memory precisely when these other elements are taken into account. The role of Scripture as canon, then, has to be understood in light of its own function as a resource for innovative reflection.

Reading the Bible as narrative provides a way of bringing out the nuances of the problem of Scripture's authority. The question, Does Scripture have authority? is misleading because it implies that one can give a simple "yes" or "no" answer and because it suggests that authority resides in the Bible and nowhere else. To say, though, that women have authority to interpret Scripture in light of their own experiences does not deny Scripture's authority. Properly understood, the two are not in conflict. Both the Bible itself and the concept of authority are complex enough to allow for nuanced interaction with the text. What reformist feminists need is a way to affirm the authority of the Bible without at the same time denying the authority of women to speak truly about the problems that the Bible presents for them. It is to that task that I direct this project.

NOTES

1. Sandra M. Schneiders, *The Revelatory Text: Interpreting the New Testament as Sacred Scripture* (San Francisco: HarperSanFrancisco, 1991).

2. See, e.g., Mary McClintock Fulkerson, *Changing the Subject: Women's Discourses and Feminist Theology* (Minneapolis: Fortress, 1994).

3. Despite the fact that as a Protestant I acknowledge in principle that the canon is open, and despite the fact that as a feminist I understand that feminist theologians have sometimes employed that principle to suggest changing the canon in fact, I take the established Christian

canon seriously for two reasons. First, I am concerned with women who remain in the church and who consequently read the Bible as it has already been shaped in Christian tradition. While it may be that someday the canon will be shaped quite differently than it is now, women need to find a way to think about the authority that the Bible as we know it now may have for them. Second, acknowledging an already established canon does not eliminate the possibility of reading and learning from other sources in very significant ways. Christian theologians have always made use of extracanonical writings. One only has to remember how Augustine used Greek philosophy to see how significantly other sources can impact Christian thought.

4. See, e.g., Margaret A. Farley, "Feminist Consciousness and the Interpretation of Scripture," in *Feminist Interpretation of the Bible* (ed. Letty M. Russell; Philadelphia: Westminster, 1985), 43.

5. See Letty M. Russell, *Household of Freedom: Authority in Feminist Theology* (Philadelphia: Westminster, 1987).

6. Richard T. De George, *The Nature and Limits of Authority* (Lawrence: University Press of Kansas, 1985).

7. Theologians with very different commitments engaged in this task. For instance, Rudolf Bultmann distinguished between the mythological worldview of the New Testament and its intent to proclaim truth that could not be described adequately in mythological language. Hans Frei also attempted to make a distinction, although he worked within a Barthian framework that contrasts in many ways with Bultmann's concerns. Frei argued that despite the apparent historical and scientific statements found there, the Bible is, not "about" history or science, but "about" God's presence to the world in Jesus Christ, the understanding of which is unfolded for us in a cumulative narrative. In their own ways and without explicitly using this terminology, both Bultmann and Frei identified the way in which the Bible exercises its authority appropriately, for Bultmann when it discloses to us authentic human existence in light of God's love and for Frei when it portrays for us a world in which God is present through Jesus Christ.

CHAPTER ONE

Feminist Theology and the Bible

Early in its development, feminist theology pursued two related tasks: working out methods for reading the Bible in a way that supported women's full humanity and wrestling with the authority of the Bible. Women who undertook feminist theology in some form recognized the authority of the Bible as a central issue that needed to be addressed. For one thing, feminists saw clearly that women's full humanity was regularly undermined by appeals to the authority of the Bible. For another, feminists who resisted a complete break with their religious heritage had to come to terms with the scriptural aspect of that heritage in some way. And furthermore, despite the very real problems that the Bible presented to women, many feminists continued to find it to be a source of life and liberation in some way. Wrestling with the authority of Scripture was at the center of feminist theology.

More recently, however, the emphasis among feminists has shifted somewhat. While discussion regarding the authority of Scripture has not entirely disappeared, it has receded into the background. Instead, methodological questions often center on strategies for reading biblical texts or on the nature of "canon" itself.[1] These questions certainly deserve examination, and I do not want to deny their importance. Direct discussion about the authority of Scripture, though, often gets eclipsed by these other concerns so that this topic gets brief treatment, perhaps a single essay in a collection.[2] The issue of the authority of the Bible lies behind all these other discussions, though, and it still needs sustained attention for a number of reasons. First, some of the intellectual assumptions in earlier attempts to provide an account of the authority of the Bible are no longer widely held. Theological conversation has shifted in important ways, and those shifts should be taken into account in order to produce an account of the Bible's authority that incorporates the insights of current scholarship. By referring to "earlier attempts" to work on the problem of the authority of the Bible, I do not intend to discount the work of the women who developed them.[3] Indeed, I am indebted to them, and I think that the tendency to disregard the question they worked so hard to address is a problem. This book is an attempt to return to an issue that they identified as having crucial importance. My goal in this chapter is simply to take note of the obvious: the terms of academic discourse are continually changing. Feminist inquiry must take account of the discussion as it has developed and cannot be content to rest on what has been said before. Second, while academic questions regarding reading strategies and the nature of canon are important, they are also at a considerable remove from the questions women ask in churches in this country. Women who struggle to understand the Bible as Christians still need a way of approaching this particular canon. Women who remain in the church know that this book has had a positive impact on their lives, and even sophisticated reading strategies need to be grounded somehow in the affirmation that this book is worth reading in the first place. Finally, Christians continually face the need to respond to concrete questions that arise both in the church and in the world, and how we do respond in large part depends on how we understand the authority of the Bible. As we face a growing number of divisive issues, the need to engage in dialogue about the authority of the Bible is great, and feminists have something important to say in that conversation. Rather than relying on what has been said before, feminist theologians should renew the investigation in order to make a contribution to the larger church at a crucial time.

In this chapter, I will first review some of the early insights and explorations about the authority of the Bible for women. Then, I will indicate some of the issues that have influenced feminist theology in recent years and explore how they bear upon the discussion of the Bible's authority. With this background, we can begin to examine the questions at hand with the specific concerns of feminism in mind.

EARLY FEMINIST INSIGHTS ABOUT THE BIBLE

No simple way to characterize the early stages of "second-wave" feminism exists, because every woman found herself in her own situation and made her own discoveries.[4] In the first chapter of *Sharing Her Word*, for instance, Elisabeth Schüssler Fiorenza recounts how her immigrant status, academic research, and Roman Catholic background contributed to the difference in her viewpoint from that of other women participants at a landmark conference sponsored by the National Council of Churches on "Women Doing Theology" held in 1972 at Grailville, Ohio.[5] Because women were learning to speak for themselves and to speak out of their own experiences, it is not surprising that a variety of understandings about feminism flourished. Some women worked with ideas about male/female complementarity, others with female ascendancy, and still others with a male/female equality that reconceived human nature itself.[6] Although no uniformity in the ideas and experiences of the women who lived through that time emerged, feminists had a common purpose: to claim full humanity for women who have been considered derived from and subordinate to men.[7]

Second-wave feminists recognized, as first-wave feminists had before them, that the Bible was a major barrier to accomplishing this purpose. In fact, the Bible could rightly be charged with having provided resources for women's oppression for millennia. Subtle exclusions as well as outright prohibitions against women's full participation in society and religion helped shape the attitudes, expectations, and practices that kept women in a subordinate position to men. Much early feminist work focused on pointing out the ways that the Bible set up, reinforced, and was used to justify women's inferior status. To make the matter worse, the Bible was not just any book—it was the "word of God." These attitudes, expectations, and practices, then, seemed to have divine sanction. So severe was the problem that many women rejected the Bible altogether. Others, though, recognized that the same book that had helped to create the problem also had helped them in some ways to see the problem, and it even gave them some resources for overcoming it. Between the same covers, one could find depictions of women as manipulative and unimportant alongside depictions of women as powerful and influential. One could find household codes that narrowly restricted women's behavior alongside statements that in Christ there is "neither male nor female." If God seemed to be sanctioning women's oppression through the words in the Bible, God also seemed to be calling for the liberation of all people from oppression. Many feminists recognized the deep ambiguity of the Bible itself and found themselves, as Mary Ann Tolbert has said, "on the horns of a dilemma."[8] As necessary as it was to bring to light the ways that the Bible has been harmful to women's well-being, it was just as necessary to acknowledge how it had given us a vision of the way things ought to be. The problem for feminists who wanted to reform the tradition, rather than leave it behind, was to discern how to use this double-messaged text so that it supported, rather than defeated, their concerns.

Since historical criticism was the dominant interpretive method at the time, many feminists undertook historical work of various sorts. Some dealt with the Bible by setting problematic passages in historical context. Showing, for instance, that the injunction for women to be silent in church was written with a particular setting in mind, or with outdated assumptions, calls into question the appropriateness of applying that injunction to different situations

in a different time. Other feminists used the Bible as a source for reconstruct-
ing the history of women in Christianity and early Judaism, or "herstory."
Imagining the actual situations of women, bringing to light "invisible" women,
and identifying the contributions that women made were all ways of recover-
ing a past that had been lost to us. Reclaiming our heritage became a high priority in feminist interpretation of the Bible.

These attempts to interpret the Bible historically, though, often led to
greater questioning of its value for women. After all, references to women are
few and those not entirely positive. Little has been recorded about women in
the first place, and what has been retained in history has been written from a
decidedly male perspective. Even if one successfully finds useful information
about women in the past, one cannot help but long all the more for what cannot be retrieved. What would the women have said if they could have spoken
for themselves? What did they do that we will never know? What comfort did
they find in their religious faith? What struggles did they have? Not merely the
absence, though, but even the presence of women presented a problem. Whatever the women did and said took shape in a patriarchal world. No amount of
reconstruction could change that context, and the assumptions, values, and
practices apparent in the biblical texts cannot all be explained away. The
"dilemma" that reformist feminists faced had no easy solution.

All these discoveries and problems had bearing on how feminists ap-
proached the issue of the authority of the Bible. If feminists had to acknowledge that the Bible was patriarchal through and through, how could women
possibly account for the other side of our experience with it, namely, that
through it we somehow found a liberating encounter with God? How could
women understand the Bible so that, instead of functioning as an authoritarian rule to keep us in our place, it could be seen as authorizing our full
humanity? The issue of the authority of the Bible could not be ignored but
had to be addressed head on. A number of feminist theologians began to take
on the task.

FUNDAMENTAL FEMINIST CONCEPTS

As feminists began to explore the problem of the authority of the Bible, certain concepts emerged as important for describing the specifically feminist
way of approaching the Scriptures. Of particular importance for this discussion are "women's experience" and "feminist critical consciousness." Each of
these categories has bearing on how feminists reconceived some traditional
theological categories.

One of the clearest discussions about "women's experience" as a category
for feminist interpretation occurs in Rosemary Radford Ruether's contribution to *Feminist Interpretation of the Bible* in 1985.[9] There, Ruether sets the

concept "women's experience" within the context of human experience itself in order to show the legitimacy of using it as an interpretive category and how it is unique. Human experience, she explains, is both the starting and the ending point of all interpretation. What we now take to be Scripture or tradition first arose out of human experience, and both must continue to illuminate human experience in order to remain relevant to us. Although they are often regarded as external standards with their origin directly in God, religious symbols, formulas, and laws arose as interpretations of some breakthrough revelatory experience. These codified elements of tradition must themselves be authenticated by new generations, or they "die" and are discarded. By appealing to women's experience as a category of interpretation, feminists are in one sense doing the inevitable—testing received tradition against their experience in order to see whether it does, in fact, prove illuminating.

In another sense, though, appealing to *women's* experience is both novel and radical. What is different about the feminist approach is that it appeals precisely to women's experience, which has a specific shape and function. By "women's experience," Ruether does not mean all the varied life experiences that women may have in their different contexts. Nor does she mean primarily the experience of being biologically different from men, which might provide women with a distinctively "feminine" way of thinking about and interpreting Scripture. Biological differences between men and women are not irrelevant to her discussion, she says, and experiences of menstruation or bearing children may indeed be important for interpretation. However, Ruether has most in mind "women's experiences created by the social and cultural appropriation of biological differences in a male-dominated society."[10] In other words, she is focusing on how women's biological experiences, such as menstruation, are understood in a male-dominated society in ways that alienate women from our bodies and minds and place us in lesser, more derivative, and more dependent positions than males hold in society. The experience that becomes crucial for interpreting the Bible, then, is the experience of recognizing that this understanding of our bodies and minds—of our biological differences and our viewpoints—is false and imposed on us by male-dominated culture. Women see "what is" (according to male-dominated culture) as false in light of the truth of "what ought to be." Women's experience understood in this sense is, for Ruether, a "grace event" and leads to a "conversion experience" through which sexism is named and judged.[11]

Similarly, Schüssler Fiorenza intends a specific meaning when she speaks of women's experience, and that meaning is related to her understanding of patriarchy. For her, patriarchy is not simply a male perspective or even male domination but a "social, economic, and political system of graded subjugations and oppressions."[12] Patriarchy can be imagined as a pyramid with God on top, the most exploited people on the bottom, and a complex layering of hierarchical relationships in between. Thus, women toward the top of the pyramid will be subordinate to men toward the top of the pyramid, but those same women will stand over both men and women toward the bottom of the pyramid. This system of exploitation is so pervasive that it shapes every aspect of our lives, and we do not even see the effect it has on us. Within this system, women are socialized to identify with men, and the result is self-alienation. Women's experience as a critical principle, then, is defined with respect to patriarchy. Like Ruether, Schüssler Fiorenza does not mean simply the experience of being a woman, or the individual life experiences we have as women. While these experiences may be important, they must be seen in light of something else. For Schüssler Fiorenza, women's experience means fundamentally "the experience of women (and all those oppressed) struggling for liberation from patriarchal oppression."[13] She recognizes the need to attend to particular experiences of women, but what matters for feminist interpretation are particular experiences of marginalization, victimization, and oppression. Only when these experiences are brought to light and become the norm for our interpretation will we be able to dismantle the oppressive structure that binds us all.

Understood in this special way, women's experience began to shape feminist critical consciousness. The awareness of oppression in society at large and for women in particular is one side of that consciousness. The other side is the awareness "that women and men are fully human and fully equal."[14] With these two things in mind, feminists brought a critical bearing to every enterprise, including biblical interpretation. Feminists based the practice of "criticism," that is, of making sound judgments or evaluations, on convictions about oppression and liberation so that women's experience becomes normative for critical evaluations. Negatively stated, those things that promote or perpetuate oppression are judged to be bad. Positively stated, those things that promote liberation are judged to be good. With the recognition of oppression and the goal of liberation, women have crucial insights for making evaluations and judgments about what they see around them and thus gain a new understanding of themselves as decision-making subjects.[15]

By claiming the right to exercise feminist critical judgment in making these kinds of evaluations, women are claiming to have a certain kind of authority. In doing so, though, women often find themselves in conflict with other "authorities," namely, the persons and structures that have had the power to promote and perpetuate oppression. The convictions that feminists hold are so basic that, as Margaret Farley says, "contradictory assertions cannot be accepted by feminists without violence being done to their very understandings and valuations."[16] Exercising feminist critical consciousness, then, is not simply a distant, intellectual enterprise but instead places women in a "fight for their lives." In order for the integrity of women's experience to be honored, women have to be able to ask these critical questions.

When these questions are addressed to the Bible, though, the conflict becomes truly impassioned because another issue of integrity is at stake: the Bible's status as revelation. Feminists have pointed out that in making judgments about the relevance and truth of certain passages in the Bible, they are not really doing anything different from other critical readers of the Bible.[17] Still, a common objection to feminist critical interpretation and theology has been that it places some external norm (women's experience) above the Bible itself. The fundamental concepts and practices embraced by feminists raised equally fundamental issues about the Bible. Did the authority of women as interpreters directly challenge the authority of the Bible? Did the "grace event" that constitutes women's experience function as an alternate revelation? Was there any way to bring the fundamental commitments of feminist theology into dialogue with an equally fundamental commitment to the Bible as the word of God? Answering these kinds of questions became a dominant task for feminist theology, and reformist feminists attempted to undertake the task in such a way that they did not set up an invidious relationship between their feminist convictions and their faith heritage. Typically, reformist feminists argued that in some way the Bible provided a basis for their feminist insights.[18] But how? Although they shared many common convictions about women's situation, feminists began to develop different approaches to addressing the pressing problems that those convictions raised. I will look below at three approaches that have shaped feminist conversation about the authority of Scripture in important ways.

THREE FEMINIST APPROACHES TO THE AUTHORITY OF THE BIBLE

First, Ruether developed a "method of correlation" for dealing with the problems that feminist theology raised regarding the Bible. In this approach, she attempts to identify a principle of Scripture that is normative and correlates with an identified critical feminist principle. By identifying a normative scriptural principle for one side of the correlation, Ruether does not deny the thoroughly patriarchal character of the Bible but recognizes within the Bible itself the presence of a powerful and pervasive critique of religion that can be a source for feminist criticism of patriarchy. The Bible contains, she suggests, two religions: a religion that provides a "sacred canopy" for the social order (i.e., that validates the existing human order by attempting to show it is sanctioned by the divine order) and a religion that denounces this sacred canopy as idolatry and apostasy and seeks to overthrow it in favor of an alternative society and true faith. This second "religion," which Ruether more often calls "prophetic faith," shows how far removed the current social order is from the divine order and denounces the injustice that it finds there.[19] This second religion is the normative one, not simply because it serves feminist purposes but because it has been the standard that biblical religion has applied to itself. In fact, Ruether sees this tradition of criticism at the heart of the gospel, present in the countercultural vision of the Jesus movement. Since it draws from a vision of God's reign, prophetic faith has been able to provide a basis for self-criticism when biblical religion has failed to be what it ought to be. Ruether turns to this tradition of prophetic criticism (which she sometimes calls the "prophetic-liberation tradition," the "prophetic-messianic tradition," or simply the "prophetic tradition") in order to find the principle for the biblical side of the correlation.[20]

But Ruether does not mean by the word "principle" a static set of ideas. What she finds in this prophetic tradition is a perspective that recognizes and denounces exploitation whenever and wherever it occurs. Constant discernment is necessary because even the language used by prophets to criticize exploitative relationships in one context may itself need to be criticized in another (as when conflicts with Jewish religious leaders in the New Testament later serve to support anti-Semitism).[21] As a result, this "prophetic tradition" cannot be simply identified with any specific set of texts in the Bible. It is, rather, a process by which biblical religion reevaluates itself in new contexts in order to know what truly is the word of God in this time and place. The process of reevaluation becomes of central importance, and, in fact, it becomes the location for revelation. Rather than being a property of the text itself, so that the Bible contains a deposit of revealed truths, revelation occurs in the experience of seeing what *is* in light of what *ought to be.*

Certain "breakthrough experiences" shed light on events so that they become "paradigms of ultimate meaning," and those experiences get passed on and interpreted through symbols.[22] New symbols, though, are needed in new times and places. The Bible provides us with a record of our memory of the revelatory experiences of the community and of how those experiences have been interpreted in the past, but that memory is not binding on interpretation in the future. We continually reinterpret our roots in order to open up a life-giving future for the people in the present community. In fact, the value of the past seems to be that it points to the future, the future in which justice will be done for all. "It is this redemptive future, not past events," says Ruether, "which is ultimately normative."[23] Scripture is normative, then, as an account of our past that records a process of continuing reform in the direction of a particular vision for the future.

To this biblical principle, a process of criticism based in revelatory vision, Ruether correlates a feminist principle. In this time and place, the recognition of women's exploitation even by biblical religion is a fundamental need. Women's experience is indeed revelatory in exactly the same way that other prophetic experiences have been revelatory, for it identifies an androcentric bias in religious tradition, a bias that has appealed to divine authority for justification, on the basis of a different vision of the divine order. In this way, feminist criticism follows the prophetic tradition in denouncing a religion of the "sacred canopy." Ruether states the critical principle of feminist theology as "the promotion of the full humanity of women," and this principle has both positive and negative implications: negatively stated, "Whatever denies, diminishes, or distorts the full humanity of women is . . . to be appraised as not redemptive," but also positively stated, "What does promote the full humanity of women is of the Holy, does reflect true relation to the divine, is the true nature of things, is the authentic message of redemption and the mission of redemptive community."[24] Like the prophets of the Bible, women have a vision of what it means to be authentically human in light of God's reign, and in seeking full humanity *for women* that vision leads to criticism of the present social and religious order. Like the prophetic tradition, feminism names injustice and points toward an alternative, just society. In the continuing need to speak out against injustice, whatever its form, and to speak for justice in the ongoing redemptive struggle against oppression, feminist theology takes its place alongside other prophetic movements in biblical tradition.

Ruether is explicit about what this correlation implies about the authority of the Bible. She has found the normative principle by which biblical religion has always judged itself and by which feminists now judge biblical religion. Because the prophetic norm is a perspective rather than a body of texts, any previous statements recorded in the Bible can be tested and reinterpreted with regard to the current critical judgment. In light of the egalitarian vision of the normative prophetic tradition, Ruether claims, "To the extent to which Biblical texts reflect this normative principle, they are regarded as authoritative. On this basis many aspects of the Bible are to be frankly set aside and rejected."[25] As radical as this claim may sound, Ruether denies that she is suggesting anything new. She points out that such rejection has taken place before in Christian history, for instance, when Christianity set aside Hebrew ritual law as no longer normative in light of a new principle of ethical interiority or when Christians reject texts that justify slavery as normative. Though nonnormative texts have not been physically removed from the canon, there has never been a time when all parts of the Bible have been considered as equally authoritative. Feminists have merely shifted the ground for what is to be considered normative and authoritative and what is not.

Ruether does not, however, rule out a change in the canon itself. *Woman-guides: Readings toward a Feminist Theology* is her attempt to begin the process of making a new "canon" for feminist theology that would provide a usable tradition for women. In it, she offers a collection of material from the Bible, from alternative Christian writings, from pagan resources, and from materials—such as poetry and parables—newly written by women, all of which may be used to make women's experience visible. Although intended as an initial proposal rather than a definitive list, Ruether's effort in *Woman-guides* points to the seriousness of the problem of the Bible's authority for women. Despite her attempt to find a correlation between the biblical principle and the feminist principle, Ruether sometimes despairs of the value of the Bible for women, even saying, "Feminist theology cannot be done from the existing base of the Christian Bible."[26] If a correlation between the biblical principle and the feminist principle does indeed exist, the correlation itself may call for a radical reformulation of the very tradition out of which that biblical principle comes.

Second, Letty Russell, like Ruether, seeks a correlation between a biblical principle and a feminist principle.[27] Russell pursues this correlation, though, in a distinct way as she examines the nature of authority itself. Because the people in authority have almost always been men, and because appeals to male authority have often been used to limit women's freedom in a variety of areas of life, the notion of authority itself is problematic for many feminists.[28] Still, feminist emphasis on women's ability to make good judgments about everything from biblical interpretation to physical well-being implies that women have a certain authority. Feminists, then, both criticize authority and claim it. In consequence, the meaning of authority itself becomes an important question, and that is the question that Russell addresses in much of her work.

Russell defines authority as "legitimated power," a definition that she borrows from Jo Ann Hackett. In this understanding, authority, like power, is an ability to accomplish desired ends, but it is power that has further become legitimated by the structures of society. Authority accomplishes its end by evoking assent from the respondent, who accepts it as legitimate. Authority and power, she says, are involved in the dynamics of all human relationships. Those relationships may be established in different ways, for instance, through a political or economic structure or through charismatic influence of one person on another. Authority may even involve knowledge or wisdom that one person has and another person values enough to assent to or follow. For Christians, the source of authority in our lives is God. God's self-revelation in Jesus Christ through the Holy Spirit makes the authority of the Bible or the church legitimate. Unfortunately, authority has been distorted in the

Christian tradition so that it has been legitimated instead by social structures that are patriarchal.[29]

Since the structure of society has been patriarchal, the prevailing paradigm of authority in Christianity and Judaism has been shaped by patriarchy. In this paradigm, authority is understood as domination, in that high rank usually brings with it the authority to control other people, events, and so on. Patriarchy itself has to do with hierarchical orderings that set one class, race, and so on, above another, and this paradigm of authority as domination perpetuates this hierarchical ordering. Russell observes that some kinds of authority are not explicitly based on rank, such as the authority of knowledge or of charisma, but the paradigm of domination is so pervasive that even these kinds of authority may be exercised in dominating ways. In the patriarchal paradigm, authority is exercised over community, the proper response to authority is submission to whoever is "on top," and certain ideas or people who disagree with the hierarchy are shut out of the system or the discussion. One finds "truth" by ordering ideas and doctrines into a system that makes sense in its coherence. The price of this tight coherence is the exclusion of views, quite often the views of women, minorities, and groups of Third World people. To be admitted to the system, these groups pay the price of giving up their unique views. The paradigm of authority as domination is inadequate, says Russell, "because it provides a religious rationale for the domination and oppression of the weak by the oppressive political, economic, and religious power elites" and also because the world is simply so diverse that it makes no sense to force people into a single, rigid view of theological and social truth.[30]

In place of a paradigm of authority as domination, Russell proposes a paradigm of authority as partnership, which is more fitting to the insight of feminist and other liberation theologies that knowledge is standpoint dependent. A person's context (including class, culture, and gender) shapes that person's experience, so what one person knows from experience will be different from another's. Attending to all the various experiences of Christians, including especially those who are considered nonpersons, expands our understanding of the ways in which God's word is believed and lived out.[31] Authority that is conceived as partnership can take all these standpoints into account. In this paradigm, ordering does not involve prioritizing some positions and excluding others but instead takes place in "participation in the common task of creating an interdependent community of humanity and nature." Instead of being exercised *over* community, authority is exercised *in* community. Instead of a single, monolithic authority, "multiple authorities" cooperate with and contribute to one another so that all are enriched. As differences are valued and respected, those who have found themselves marginalized because they are different will learn to value themselves as human beings. Instead of allowing inclusion on the basis of assent to one neat system of theological truth, the Christian community welcomes and includes "all who are willing to share in building a community of human wholeness that is inclusive of women and men of every race and class." The discussion is framed in terms of communal search rather than rightness of doctrine.[32]

Because search and cooperation are primary, the concern over whether the norm or the key to interpreting Scripture should come from within the biblical tradition or outside it in the feminist community is for Russell no longer a relevant question. When authority is exercised in community, people are not coerced into consenting to a single, unchanging principle. Instead, a configuration of sources of faith enriches our experience of God. Consent to the Bible's authority, then, comes when the Bible helps make sense of personal experience or experiences. She says, "The Bible has authority in my life because it makes sense of my experience and speaks to me about the meaning and purpose of my humanity in Jesus Christ." For Russell, the interpretive key is "the witness of scripture of God's promise for the mending of creation on its way to fulfillment. That which denies this intention of God for the liberation of groaning creation in all its parts does not compel or evoke my assent (i.e., it is not authoritative)." In the feminist paradigm of authority, the issue of norm is no longer "understood as a competition between feminist critical principles drawn from within and from outside of the canon. . . . Rather, the issue is how stories and actions of faithfulness can help us to celebrate and live out signs of God's justice and shalom for all humanity." Authority, ultimately, is located in the future, beyond canon or feminism, in the vision that God has for the world.[33]

Finally, while Ruether has concentrated on finding a correlation between principles, and Russell has focused on the notion of authority itself, Schüssler Fiorenza directs her attention to the community of women as interpreters of the Bible. Feeling the full force of the androcentric character of the Bible, Schüssler Fiorenza is critical of Ruether's attempt to correlate the feminist critical principle with a biblical one. In order to find a biblical principle that can correspond to feminist concerns, Ruether has created an idealized view of the prophetic tradition, when instead feminists should recognize that even this tradition repressed and oppressed women.[34] To insist, as Schüssler Fiorenza does, that the Bible is patriarchal through and through does not mean that one should not try to reclaim the Bible. She recognizes that even though the Bible has legitimated patriarchy, it has also authorized women to reject oppressive powers.[35] But because no pristine principle can be uncovered and correlated with feminist concerns, the effort to reclaim the Bible has to lie elsewhere. Furthermore, locating a norm in any single perspective in the Bible is reductionistic because it cannot do justice to the pluriform character of the

Bible. Schüssler Fiorenza is looking for an approach that allows us to reclaim the whole Bible, but in such a way that its patriarchal character can be rejected and its liberating power can be affirmed.[36]

To find this approach, one first has to eliminate a deeply embedded understanding of the Bible as mythical archetype, that is, as an ideal form that establishes a binding, unchanging pattern to which instantiations of the archetype must conform. In this understanding, the Bible provides a unitary and universal standard by which interpretation may be tested. For instance, a doctrinal version of this approach would take the Bible to be revelation, and as such it provides infallible answers to questions or dogmatic guidelines for theological reflection. A historical version of this approach would take texts to be reliable when they report "what really happened," and interpretations are "right" when they conform to this accurate report. Both approaches treat the Bible as a timeless archetype because both identify something in or about the Bible that is normative for all times and places. No matter what is identified as normative, when the Bible is considered to be an archetype, there is a standard to which subsequent Christianity must conform. This approach is not helpful to feminists, though, because any standard found in the Bible cannot help but be shaped significantly by the patriarchy in which it was produced. Feminist theology needs to find a way of understanding the Bible that can admit change, not merely continue the way things have been.

Fortunately for feminists, recent biblical scholarship has called into question the very idea of an archetypal understanding of the Bible by showing just how dependent biblical texts are on the life setting in which they took shape. Materials and traditions were selected and reformulated, not merely transmitted, in order to speak to different communal contexts. The Bible consists, not of revealed timeless ideas or neutrally reported (or neutrally accessible) historical events, but of faith responses to historical situations. It bears witness in itself to a process of cultural adaptation. Taking this insight into account, Schüssler Fiorenza suggests replacing the idea of archetype with that of prototype. A prototype denotes an original model that is open to its own transformation.[37] For example, when the Wright brothers invented the first successful flying machine, they did not build an archetype to which subsequent flying machines had to correspond. Rather, they built a prototype that was later improved and developed in a variety of ways.[38] To understand the Bible as prototype, then, means that it is "the model of Christian faith and life." Moreover, rather than being uniform, it is a "multiform" or "pluriform" model, made up of vastly different kinds of materials with different theological understandings for different situations. In Schüssler Fiorenza's view, Christian faith and life are still under development. Instead of looking only to the past for guidance, as in an archetypal understanding, one must look also to the present and even to the future to see in what way this model should be developed. As a model of Christian faith and life, the Bible provides a sense of history and identity rather than timeless norms. As we examine our history, we can see the likely trajectory of a culture shaped by the Bible, and feminists assess the alternatives to a trajectory marked by patriarchy and take steps to redirect it.[39] To understand the Bible as prototype makes it possible to evaluate and transform biblical tradition, to understand and interpret the Bible "in such a way that its oppressive and liberating power is clearly recognized."[40]

This new understanding of the Bible calls for a new paradigm for biblical interpretation that acknowledges not only the communally shaped character of biblical texts but also the need for communally shaped interpretations of those same texts. Just as the concrete pastoral situations of the community determined what was selected, transmitted, and created by authors of the Bible, the concrete pastoral situations of the community ought to determine how the Bible is interpreted and preached today. New Testament writers did not consign revelation to the past even though for them revelation took place decisively in Jesus Christ. They could use traditions about Jesus freely because they believed that Jesus still spoke to them through the Holy Spirit. Schüssler Fiorenza wants to reclaim the creative tension between past and present that existed in the New Testament communities and to affirm that inspiration did not end with them. Interpretation does not consist simply in repeating what has been said before but in attending to what the Holy Spirit wants to say here and now. The meaning of a text is not completely disclosed until one finds the connection between the experience of God that originated the text and the experience of God now.

The new paradigm for interpretation preserves the Bible as a whole, with its pluriform character, as a record of the past, but it does not consider every text to be equally relevant to any given situation. The task of preaching involves discernment about the texts that this community needs to hear and about the way in which it needs to hear them. The criterion for evaluation does not derive from the Bible itself, nor does it derive from the validity that any text had in the past within the community for which it was written. Instead, the criterion is drawn from the present community to which the text speaks. The Bible, then, does not have authority in and of itself but only insofar as it has relevance for the salvation of the present community.[41] Because the Bible is a prototype instead of an archetype, and because it is a pluriform rather than a uniform model, room exists both for evaluating texts critically and for transforming them.

The interpretive community that is responsible for this evaluation and transformation is women-church, "the dialogical community of equals in which critical judgment takes place and public freedom becomes tangible."[42] In direct contrast to patriarchy, which consists of graded subordinations and exploitations, women-church gathers together women and men who are empowered by the Holy Spirit to struggle against patriarchy and to promote a vision of justice and freedom. Schüssler Fiorenza does not intend women-church to be a separatist community. Instead, it is both connected to the universal church and manifests the universal church. A pragmatic, political construct that provides a "hermeneutical space" for feminist interpretation, women-church reads the Bible "against the grain" of patriarchy and is accountable to women in churches. According to the new paradigm for interpretation, the criteria for interpretation arise from the needs of the present community, and in this case the criteria are determined by what is needed for women's salvation. The model of interpretation that arises from these needs will involve suspicion, evaluation and proclamation, remembrance, and creative actualization. Women-church, then, can preserve the Bible as a whole because every text is subject to these hermeneutical methods. Even the most repressive text can be an opportunity for learning about our past and for imagining how to avoid similar repression today. Every text is important for our memory and vision, but not every text is relevant in the same way for the sake of our salvation. Some texts are named for what they are and evaluated as patriarchal and unusable for women. Other texts are remembered as evidence of the struggle for liberation in which biblical women themselves participated. Through these texts the struggle of ancient women encounters and encourages the struggle of modern women. Our empathy with their experience of being inspired by God enables our own inspiration, and the text becomes revelatory for us. Through critical evaluation and creative transformation, the Bible becomes "scripture" (or holy) for the church of women.[43]

Schüssler Fiorenza openly acknowledges that she shifts the location of authority from the Bible itself to the community that interprets it. She argues, though, that others have done the same thing before her, even if not so openly. For her, the "litmus test" for whether the Bible becomes scripture for women-church, for whether it may be invoked as the word of God, is "whether or not biblical texts and traditions seek to end relations of domination and exploitation."[44] She asserts often that the locus of revelation is not (or, as she sometimes says, not simply) the Bible itself. She locates revelation in experience, and, as for Ruether, the experience that she identifies as grace or revelatory event is not some general experience all women have but the particular "experience of women (and all those oppressed) struggling for liberation from patriarchal oppression."[45] What is revelatory is, not the text itself, but the story of the people of God, the story of their process of inspiration. Women-church has the right to decide which texts may be accepted as the word of God and which may not because it uses its fourfold hermeneutical method to uncover the story of women as the people of God.

Once the authority of women-church to interpret the Bible is acknowledged, then it is possible to speak in some sense of the authority of the Bible. Despite her insistence that the Bible itself is not revelation, Schüssler Fiorenza sometimes speaks of the Bible as revelatory. Specific texts and specific histories may transcend and criticize the patriarchy of their own times, and thus they provide a vision for Christian women now. Even in these cases, though, what is revelatory is, not the text itself, but the experience of God in the lives of people that is made available to us through the text. The Bible may not be an archetypal, universal, uniformly authoritative source for truth and revelation, but as prototype, it is a resource that can be revelatory to the extent that it supports women's struggle. Its authority, then, is one, not of control, but of enabling power.

Still, the Bible itself is not normative. What is normative is the struggle that Scripture recounts and authorizes. The criterion for measuring the revelatory character of biblical texts is whether they contribute to the salvation of women, salvation understood here as liberation of the whole person from both sin and oppression. Although she has located authority and criteria for revelation largely outside the Bible itself, Schüssler Fiorenza believes that she is simply doing what others, such as the Roman Catholic Church in its magisterium, have already done. By using the struggle for liberation as the norm, Schüssler Fiorenza reclaims the Bible for women, not on correlation of abstract principles, but on the concrete experience of women, past and present, who have actually used the Bible in that struggle.

Russell's, Reuther's, and Schüssler Fiorenza's attempts to address questions about the Bible's authority from a feminist perspective helped provide direction for subsequent feminist work. Several issues that they raised set the framework for continuing feminist discussion, even though, as we shall see, these issues are often redefined. In this foundational stage of feminist work, basic theological concepts become topics for open and candid discussion. Authority needs to be reconceived in order to distinguish misuse of the Bible from proper use. Similarly, the locus of revelation is reexamined. Revelation is not equated with the Bible, nor is it necessarily contained in the Bible. For Schüssler Fiorenza and Ruether alike, the locus of revelation is experience. Consequently, experience becomes a major theological category for feminist study, and it has remained a topic of crucial importance. Finally, Schüssler Fiorenza's emphasis on the role of women-church has concentrated attention on the importance of studying and understanding interpretive communities. These last two issues, the significance of experience and community, find connection in certain versions of postmodern thought, and several feminist scholars have used postmodern methods and philosophy to advance feminist concerns. In the next section, I will look at the way in which postmodern feminist commitments have shaped further discussion about the Bible's authority.

New Feminist Concerns

Two theologians in particular have combined feminist and postmodern insights in ways that have bearing on the authority of Scripture. Mary McClintock Fulkerson and Kathryn Tanner both take seriously postmodern understandings of text and community, and their work has implications for how feminists conceive of the Bible's authority. Although each of them does make some statements about the issue, neither one offers as complete a treatment of the Bible's authority as found in the work of Ruether, Russell, and Schüssler Fiorenza. Fulkerson and Tanner deal most directly with questions surrounding text, community, and culture, but their answers to these questions suggest a direction for thinking about the sense in which one can (or cannot) affirm that the Bible has authority.

Fulkerson, in *Changing the Subject,* takes up a particular challenge to feminist theology that has emerged in recent years, namely, the challenge made by women in different situations, especially minority women, that white, middle-class, feminist theology does not speak for them. Feminist theologians had made "women's experience" the location for revelation and the test for truth, but minority women declared that their experience of oppression and liberation was different from that of white, middle-class theologians. Fulkerson observes that feminist theology, which denied that male experience is universal experience, had itself fallen into the trap of the "false universal." That is, on the basis of what it understood to be "woman," feminist theology claimed to speak for all women, rather than acknowledge and respect the differences of concrete women.[46] Fulkerson challenges feminist theology to "change the subject" of its study from "woman" to "concrete women." In order to do so, she makes use of poststructural theory, which challenges the notion of the "natural" character of all our categories and which can take multiple identities into account. By moving in this direction, Fulkerson believes that she is taking the feminist insight that all theology is "engaged" rather than neutral, as it either works for or against liberation, to its logical conclusion. In other words, the advocacy stance of feminism requires acknowledging different standpoints and the interests that are embedded in them, even though it has not always succeeded in doing so.

One instance of how concrete women do not always conform to the expectations of feminist theologians is the way that Pentecostal women take passages in the Bible that most feminist theologians would reject outright as patriarchal and use them to resist oppression. Fulkerson uses poststructural discourse theory to acknowledge and to explain this phenomenon. Poststructural theory denies the idea of closed systems, universal truths, and "natural" reality. Human beings come to know reality through language (a word that is extended beyond speech to other kinds of signifying), or we "construct" reality linguistically. That is, we construct the meaning that we attach to the things that are around us. "Reality," then, or at least our understanding of reality, has a certain arbitrariness and indefiniteness to it. Because it focuses on difference instead of unity, poststructuralism draws attention to "gaps" or "fissures" in our patterns of signification. No system of meaning, then, can be closed or complete. The way we understand things is always subject to revision because one pattern can always be destabilized by another pattern of signification. Furthermore, since everything we know is shaped linguistically, human beings are "produced" by the same language with which we have constructed our reality. What we know becomes an intimate part of who we are, so our possibilities and expectations are shaped by the sign systems in which we participate. And if selves are shaped by sign systems, selves are also unstable, because here, too, one pattern of signifying can displace another. In addition, language is always invested with power interests, so each person is produced by power interests and has power interests. Any human is produced in a specific social location, where multiple power interests are at work in multiple discourses, and both oppression and resistance take shape with regard to that social location.

Just as there is no single, universal "woman," there is no single, unitary "text" or a single right interpretation of it. Theories of interpretation commonly assume that a meaning in the text is accessible to those who read it rightly or that there is a universal or ideal reader who approaches the text in a specifiable way. Both these notions have been made problematic by poststructuralism. For Fulkerson, "text" and "interpreter" are unstable concepts, capable of multiple instantiations. We are not usually aware of the vast range of multiplicity for both, though, because both text and interpreter gain some stability through the discursive community in which reading takes place. That is, even though the possible interpretations are endless, a community makes decisions about what to read and how to read. But just as text and reader are never completely fixed and stable, neither is a community a closed system. A community has a dominant discourse, which provides some measure of stability for the community and some direction for interpretation, but that dominant discourse intersects with other discourses and is characterized by "gaps" in the same way that any discourse is. As a result, varieties of readings are always possible.

With this theory in mind, Fulkerson explains how Pentecostal women are able to make use of the Bible to serve their resistance to oppression in a very different way than academic feminist theologians do. Biblical passages about submission are highly problematic for academic feminist theologians and are often rejected as irredeemably patriarchal. Pentecostal women use these same passages to resist oppression and destabilize the dominant discourse in their community. The "canonical system," or the organizing social practice that contains rules for reading, of their community understands the Bible to be inerrant and to say that men should have authority over women. But the community's practices also include a leveling of authority in that the Holy Spirit can call anyone to preach. The tension between these two practices creates the "gap" or "fissure" that allows women to destablize the dominant system. Even though they do not have the same status, roles, and opportunities as men, they can appeal to a call by the Holy Spirit to justify preaching, a role that would normally be denied to them. These women use passages about submission to say that they are simply submitting to God's will and call to preach. The very text that academic feminist theologians reject outright becomes for Pentecostal women a source for resisting the oppressive structure around them.[47] Given the possibilities that are open to them in their social location, where even their very selves are produced by the discourse in which they participate, they have found a way to use the Bible to resist oppression. Feminist theologians should neither ignore nor discount this resistance. All struggles for liberation are formed in relation to a canonical system, so they will look different in different social locations. Women's practices, even when they look different from our own, may be characterized as liberationist when they challenge restrictions on women in the canonical system and the dependencies (for instance, economic) that the system creates and when the source of that resistance is their Christian faith.[48]

Sometimes explicitly and sometimes implicitly, Fulkerson has pushed further some of the central concepts in feminist theology that are crucial for understanding the authority of Scripture. Clearly, Fulkerson's project intends to redefine the notion of "women's experience," and she succeeds in multiplying the subject so that the category is more accurately "women's experiences." At the same time, she has opened up the need to reconsider feminist understanding of revelation. Part of her criticism of earlier feminist work is that it described women's experience on the basis of a prelinguistic self. When feminist theologians, such as Ruether, appeal to "women's experience" to provide an account of revelation that can function as a norm and resource for feminist theology, that experience turns out to be some presocial or nonsituated intuition of the divine that confirms the oppressive nature of religious symbols.

A "self" stands apart from those symbols and authenticates some experience of external reality, whether it is the divine reality that calls patriarchy into question or the social reality that is oppressive.[49] So, by calling into question the earlier version of women's experience as universal, Fulkerson has at the same time made problematic the account of revelation that accompanied that concept.

Even as she multiplies the notion of women's experience, Fulkerson also multiplies the notion of interpretive community. Whereas Schüssler Fiorenza calls attention to the need for a gathering of women and men who share a goal of equality and a struggle against patriarchy, Fulkerson calls attention to the communities in which women are already gathered. For Schüssler Fiorenza, women-church was a necessary construct because the Bible is patriarchal through and through. She found it necessary to identify an interpretive community in which the struggle for liberation is the dominant concern and that can provide the criteria for interpretation. For Fulkerson, though, interpretations and resistances are multiple because the communities in which resistance takes place are multiple. In her article "Is There a (Non-Sexist) Bible in This Church?" Fulkerson argues that just as one cannot say that the Bible itself is meaningful, neither can one say that the Bible itself is patriarchal. The patterns that one finds in the Bible are a function of communal conventions for interpretation. One finds patriarchal patterns, then, because of communal conventions. Conversely, women can develop in relation to those conventions a regime for reading, as exemplified above with Pentecostal women, that constructs a "Bible" that supports their well-being in their community. They create space in the dominant conventions for forging their own conventions, and the "text" they construct has authority for them because it is compelling.[50]

What makes the Bible "compelling" is related to the way that Fulkerson talks about truth. In keeping with her concern to avoid universals, Fulkerson denies that there can be any access to truth apart from communal discourse itself, so there can be no objective knowledge of truth with independent standing. Communal discourse sets the boundary for what is thinkable and meaningful, so whatever we know as "true" takes on a particular shape.[51] Fulkerson's point is, not to deny all knowledge of truth, but to deny a "God's-eye view" of the truth. No community has a monopoly on truth, and since communities overlap, knowledge of truth can be shaped in different ways. There can be no final certainty in this situation. Fulkerson borrows an image from David Toole to speak of truth "like the flash of a fish on your line."[52] We get glimpses of it as it surfaces and recedes. It is real and alluring, but we do not possess it. The test for truth, then, is neither correspondence nor coherence, both of which would close semiotic processes; rather, truth is recognized "in that by which we are persuaded."[53] The truth of the "reasons, rules, and values" of a community is tied to "the visions of the good (however temporary) that come from communities, their traditions, and the practices they produce." We can have no certainty, but once we are persuaded of the truth of a vision, our commitment to certain beliefs and actions is worth a wager. Women, then, have been persuaded of a vision of the world in which we may be whole. That vision, while not available for objective confirmation, deserves our commitment, and to the extent that the Bible enables us to see and work for that vision, it is compelling.

Even as she has reconceived certain fundamental feminist ideas, Fulkerson has retained an essential element of earlier feminist thinking as a constant, namely, struggle or resistance to oppression. This constant becomes important for seeing how her approach might affect a discussion of the Bible's authority. Although she says little explicitly about biblical authority, Fulkerson does speak at length about normativity. The obvious problem that one faces when adopting a poststructural approach to reading the Bible is how to assess multiple interpretations. Are all equally valid or useful? To put the question more pointedly, would an interpretation that supports women's oppression have the same status as an interpretation that resists oppression? Given her avoidance of essentialism, that is, selves and texts have an "essence" that make them what they are, Fulkerson does not want to identify a standard that exists apart from the process of signifying. She recognizes, though, that interpretations need to be ordered in some way, and she turns to "stipulations of relevance" to provide that order. Christians have varying convictions that are used, challenged, and held in different ways. Those convictions orient us toward different stipulations of relevance. Feminist stipulations of relevance prioritize the conviction that Christian faith calls us to resist sin and to consider social justice an aspect of being right with God. So, interpretations that promote liberation are more highly valued than those that do not. Fulkerson locates her norm neither in the text itself nor in a standard method for interpretation. Rather, the constant for feminist interpretation is "the irruption of women's resistance," but this norm always functions in relation to a canonical system, to the way that text, reader, and community interact to open up possibilities for women's resistance. Feminist theology remembers Jesus "for the sake of resisting forms of contemporary social sin," so it privileges acts that resist and transform sinful distortions in the lives of women. Women's interests in this matter are constitutive not merely for the appropriation of biblical texts but for the Bible's being "scripture," and therefore authoritative, at all. The authority of Scripture is found or stabilized not in the text itself or even in the canonical form of the text, but in "practices that create spaces for well-being."[54]

Like Fulkerson, Tanner sees the significance of interpretive communities for understanding the Bible's authority. Although her work on Scripture has not explicitly taken up feminist issues, it is important for considering the way that postmodern concerns influence an understanding of biblical authority that feminists might want to use. Early in her career, and near the time that Ruether, Russell, and Schüssler Fiorenza were working on this issue, Tanner explored the authority of the Bible by developing Hans Frei's understanding of the "plain sense" of Scripture. Although her later work builds more on cultural studies, she has continued to develop some of the insights that she elaborated earlier. I will look first at her understanding of the plain sense and then explore some of her more recent work.

In her essay "Theology and the Plain Sense," Tanner studies the Christian community in the way that a social scientist would study any other community; that is, she attempts to describe how Christians read and interpret the Bible instead of making a claim for a particular way of reading and interpreting the Bible. What emerges from that study is an account of the "plain sense" of Scripture and a description of the role of the plain sense under different circumstances. Like Fulkerson, Tanner has been persuaded that one should avoid essentialist thinking when considering the Bible. For Tanner, meaning is found, not in the Bible itself, but in the way the Bible is used in the community that reads it. The plain sense, then, is not a property of the text; rather, it is the way the community uses the text. The text appears to have an obvious meaning to the community because the community has tacitly agreed on what that meaning should be. In other words, the plain sense is a consensus reading; the community has developed an unself-conscious, habitual way of reading the text so that its meaning seems direct and transparent. This meaning has become established and traditional for the community, so it also becomes authoritative. The plain sense is not only established by the community but in turn establishes the community. In other words, one finds one's place in this community by developing the sensibilities it takes to see this meaning, and the community forms its practices around this meaning. As Tanner says, "The plain sense, as the traditional distillate of communal practice, becomes the norm governing the ongoing practice of using such a text to shape, nurture, and reform community life: the product of traditional practice norms its further operation."[55]

Since her task is descriptive rather than normative, Tanner does not attempt to explicate the plain sense for any community, and in fact she does not want to identify the plain sense with any particular reading. Instead, she elaborates the notion of the plain sense by describing various ways in which text and interpretation can be related to one another under different circumstances. To begin, Tanner argues that the distinction between "text" and "interpretation" does not even arise until the text has become fixed. As long as an editing process continues to revise the text, the community's decisions about what the text means get incorporated into the text itself. The process of recombining passages or repositioning them in new contexts indicates that the community has an unself-conscious confidence that the text really means to say this new thing that the community needs to hear. This practice does not appear to be interpretation because text and communal meaning are not differentiated, and the text itself mirrors changes in communal life. When the text becomes fixed, though, so that actual revisions are no longer possible, and when texts are collected in a canon that becomes the rule for the community, "text" and "interpretation" become differentiated. The text does not change, but the text is claimed to have continual relevance for a changing community. As a result, the community must receive the text through a process of interpretation. Trying to imagine how to know what to make of this text with this plain sense in this new situation compels the community to act creatively in some way.

Several outcomes can result once text and interpretation have become differentiated. The text and plain sense may continue to be the norm that acts as a critical force over the community as its circumstances change. Or a community may instead limit the authority of the text and plain sense to cultic practices; that is, the plain sense establishes group identity as a religion but has no impact on the way the members live in the wider world. In contrast, if one understands one's place in this communal life to affect one's life as a whole, then the problem of interpretation becomes pressing. Tanner describes one possible approach to this problem as self-conscious interpretation. When the community begins to engage in active, creative interpretation, it recognizes that the authoritative meaning, or plain sense, of the text is not as obvious as it seems and has to be drawn out. What is "plain" or obvious is the relevance of this interpreted hidden meaning to the community's situation. Interpretation, because it draws out the "plain," authoritative meaning, comes to share the status of the text's authority. Tanner acknowledges that some may see danger in this focus on communal consensus. Traditional meanings can become repressive and hegemonic if they have priority and unrestricted relevance and are not adjusted to new circumstances in the way that Tanner indicates they can be. Still, she argues that she is describing what communities actually do rather than claiming the appropriateness or rightness of any approach. The plain sense need not become repressive. Sometimes Tanner talks about the plain sense in a different way. What is "plain" or "obvious" is not necessarily the meaning itself but what the community has agreed to look for, such as "the sense that the author intended" or "the sense that God intends" or "the sense a text has when included in the canon."[56] In this case, the community has agreed on how to take the text formally, but it has not agreed on how to take the text materially. In these cases, the plain sense might provide a critical force over hegemonic interpretation. For instance, if the community understands the plain sense to be "what the text itself says," then it clearly distinguishes interpretation from text. Because no interpretation can fully explicate what the text says, every interpretation is partial and provisional, subject to revision based on a better understanding of "what the text says." One way of understanding the plain sense that keeps interpretations open-ended is to construe it as narrative. Faithfulness to narrative does not reside in a specific interpretation or form of life because the narrative itself specifies none; rather, faithfulness involves finding one's place in the story. When one allows oneself to be taken into the story, one's life is reshaped by it. The power of the narrative does not close off possibilities but allows diversity as each person finds her or his own place.

From this early account of how to read Scripture, Tanner's work has moved in two directions that have relevance for our topic. The first is a more developed account of cultural studies, which allows further explorations about communities and about Christian identity. The second is an examination of the Bible as a popular text. Each of these becomes important for drawing out implications for the Bible's authority.

In *Theories of Culture,* Tanner examines the concept of culture itself and how that concept has developed into the postmodern understanding that she uses in her work. Like Fulkerson, Tanner accepts the postmodern emphasis on indeterminacy, fragmentation, and interactive process as the best description of how communities really operate. Cultures do not exist as holistic units that stand alone from the rest of the world, nor do cultures exist as homogeneous units. In fact, one often finds a good deal of conflict within a culture. What makes a culture a *particular* culture is that people are bound together by some common engagement. Cultures are fundamentally relational, and the relationships are built on "common stakes," that is, an agreement "on the importance of the cultural items that they struggle to define and connect up with one another."[57] Members of a culture can engage in certain common practices without agreeing on the meaning of those practices. What they agree on is the importance of those practices, and so their disagreements over meaning become extremely significant. One demonstrates one's identity in a particular culture by participating in its "way of life," and even in participating in arguments about what that way of life ought to be.

Tanner argues that Christian practices constitute a culture, and as such, Christianity will share features with other cultures that can be examined to give insight into Christian identity. If one uses the insights of postmodern anthropological understandings of culture, one does not answer the question,

What makes someone Christian? by looking for some kind of sharp boundary between Christians and other people, nor does one look for some essential agreement in attitude, belief, or rules among Christians. Instead, one looks for the way a person participates in a Christian "way of life." Sharing some affirmations, values, and rituals—for instance, belief that Jesus is the Christ, the need to love others, and the practice of Holy Communion—may identify Christians. Although Christians may agree that these things are important, Christians do not agree on how they understand any of these things. These are the materials out of which Christians construct a meaningful Christian life, but the meanings that are constructed may be quite different from one another. Christian identity, then, is formed in engagement and investigation, not in material agreement.[58]

Even though the boundary between Christian culture and wider culture, or other cultures, is not sharp, it is important. In fact, much of Christian identity forms at the boundary. Questions emerge there about what practices from another culture should be included in Christian practice and how they should be included. Tanner claims that Christians continually borrow from other cultures, but they "make odd" the practices that they incorporate.[59] For instance, the church fathers did not simply take over Greek philosophy in the early centuries of the church. They used the language for their own purposes and transformed certain aspects of philosophy in the process. Questions do not arise only about incorporating new practices, though. Certain materials that are central to Christian identity also become problematic because they have relevance for how the boundary is understood. If a particular claim marks Christian identity in such a way that it serves to help Christians distinguish themselves from other cultures, then it is likely to become the focus for conflict and the source for variety within Christianity.[60] In this understanding of what it means to be a culture, Christian identity is not a possession but a task and is formed in the search for what constitutes true discipleship. That search may lead Christians to understand true discipleship in very different ways.

With Tanner's work on Christian culture as background, one can extend her ideas into feminist discussion about the Bible. The Bible is the kind of marker for Christian identity that elicits great disagreement among Christians. The Bible (Old and New Testaments together) is "our" book and so provides us with a way of understanding ourselves as distinct from the world around us or from other religions. Questions about the use and understanding of the Bible will consequently raise acute questions about Christian identity. It should not be surprising, then, that feminist theologians are sometimes accused of being "not Christian." By shifting the understanding of what it means to be Christian, Tanner provides a way of seeing how feminist theologians are engaged in the very enterprise that demarcates membership in a

Christian culture. That is, they engage in investigation about the meaning of Christian practices, in this case, about the practice of taking the Bible as authority for one's life as a Christian. They have in fact taken this Christian material as significant for understanding their lives as Christians, and they are working to understand its relevance in their contexts. Even the incorporation of feminist theory itself involves a "making odd" of those ideas. Many feminists reject the Bible altogether. Those who remain and wrestle with its meaning for their lives connect their feminist commitments in relation to the Bible in some way. The fact that they see the need to do so shows that they are still involved in Christian practice.

In her work on culture, Tanner has developed her early insights about the "plain sense" of Scripture in a particular way. Although she has retained an interest in communal consensus, she has shifted the discussion from agreement on meaning to agreement about where and how to search for meaning. In other words, she has continued to consider how the plain sense acts as a formal norm (or a pattern for identifying what is normative) rather than as a material one (or a specific content to which understanding and practice must conform). In her work on the Bible as popular text, Tanner has pursued yet another insight about the "plain sense," namely, how meaning appears to be obvious to those who read the Bible. In this area of her work, Tanner explicitly brings up issues about the Bible's authority.

In "Scripture as Popular Text," Tanner explores the "odd power" of the Bible to be "ever contemporary in its salvific effects."[61] This theological claim, that through the Bible the Holy Spirit makes Jesus Christ ever present, has sometimes been explained or supported by literary theories that show how literary works can have relevance in ever-changing contexts. Of these theories, Tanner finds most accurate and promising an approach that avoids essentialist thinking about the text and about the reader. In other words, she takes seriously the postmodern objection to ahistorical, timeless meaning, to qualities inherent in the text itself, and to universal human experience. Texts remain ever timely not because of some static, intrinsic property or even because of an inexhaustible "surplus" or "fullness" of meaning. What makes a text flexible enough to move into new contexts is its indeterminacy. Rather than "fullness," it is "emptiness" that is important. The text has "gaps" and is unfinished until the reader participates in reading. The reader, then, finds her own place in the text and supplies the unity that the text itself lacks. The Bible, like other literary works, functions in this way and is continually relevant because it continually allows readers to fill in gaps about characters' backgrounds and unrecorded actions. Although the theory that Tanner uses comes from secular literary studies, she claims that it supports certain important theological understandings of the Bible by reminding us that God speaks *through* the text rather than *in* it. Maintaining the distinction between the text and revelation, the theory affirms that God works through the messy details of text (and life) in a way that is both uncontrollable and indirect.[62]

So far, Tanner has followed literary theory closely, but she parts company with the tendency to work with high classics, or literary masterworks. The Bible, Tanner says, is more like a popular text. This point is important theologically because it speaks to the accessibility of the Bible to ordinary Christians. To treat the Bible as a high classic is to obscure what theologians such as Augustine have seen all along: that the Bible speaks to everyone, not just educated readers. It speaks with seriousness about mundane matters because no aspect of life is irrelevant to salvation, so even persons of humble circumstances can see their lives addressed here. This classic text is at the same time a popular text in its ability to speak to anyone, and both its attention to the mundane and its "gaps" contribute to its accessibility. Readers participate in meaning making unself-consciously because the text's indeterminacy does not call attention to itself in the way that postmodern literary works do. And the meaning that the readers make extends beyond the text itself into the readers' lives, as they try to live in accordance with what they take the text to say. Again, Tanner finds important theological meaning in this literary approach to the Bible. It encourages us to think about God as working with all, as persuading rather than forcing understanding, and as influencing our lives far beyond the act of reading itself.[63]

This way of understanding the Bible might appear to undercut its authority because so much is in the hands of the reader. The text itself does not seem to direct interpretation, nor is the text clearly of more importance than interpretation. Tanner argues, though, that this approach does not eliminate the Bible's authority; instead, it forces us to rethink what that authority is. It promotes, as she says, "a deeper investigation into the nature of respect and disrespect."[64] One shows respect for the Bible by expecting it to be useful and by acknowledging what it is. It is more disrespectful to try to make it what it is not, namely, a work with a unitary meaning. In fact, closing off meaning is an act of disrespect. In doing so, one fails to acknowledge the provisional nature of one's own interpretation, and one does not allow the text to shatter one's own expectations and conventions. To approach the text instead as unfinished, to repeat and replay it from various angles, allows for the kind of engagement and imitation that enables the text to affect one's life, perhaps in an unsettling way. It is far more respectful to question the adequacy of one's own reading and to attempt to place oneself in the story than to insist on the rightness of one's own reading. The Bible exercises its authority, then, not by giving clear directions, but by disturbing "Christian self-satisfaction and complacency."[65]

Both Tanner and Fulkerson have found postmodern insights to be useful in reflecting on how Christians make use of the Bible in our time. Their work serves to push feminist thinking about the authority of Scripture to another level of questions. Even if women's experience, revelation, and authority need to be redefined in ways that take account of postmodern insights, it is clear that they remain categories with relevance for feminist thinking about the Bible. It is not clear, however, that postmodern thought can provide *all* the resources necessary for addressing feminist concerns about the Bible. Even though our discussion has to take these insights into account, we have to address questions about a strictly postmodern approach to the Bible. Phyllis Bird, for instance, expresses discomfort with the tendency of biblical scholars to focus on varieties of "readings" of the Bible, a tendency that is fueled in part by postmodern emphasis on the construction of meaning by the reader. She is reluctant to give up on the idea that the authors of biblical texts do want to communicate something, and that we have an obligation to try to hear them on their own terms. Although Bird acknowledges the "interpenetration" of production and reception, she finds value in the model of dialogue for feminist purposes. This approach allows for a broader use of biblical texts in that one may find a message that serves feminist purposes even though it has no explicitly feminist agenda, and one is still free to uncover and criticize those messages that communicate ideas harmful to women. She argues that historical criticism, then, still has its place in feminist work.[66] Schüssler Fiorenza also expresses concern about certain uses of postmodern theory, and she urges that any theory, postmodern or otherwise, should be examined critically before use to determine suitability for advancing feminist concerns.[67]

Critical appropriation of postmodernism involves in part the recognition that justice claims require more than postmodern theory alone has so far been able to offer. While uncovering the ways in which reader and community function in interpretation has been crucial for showing how women's voices can and must be heard, locating authority simply in the reader or the community or even in the relevance that a text has for a situation also presents a danger. To locate normativity, for instance, in stipulations of relevance does not indicate what should be stipulated as relevant, and it is quite possible, perhaps likely, that the reader or community may simply see as relevant that which supports its prejudices. Fulkerson attempts to deal with this problem by showing that multiple discourses always exist in a community, and while the dominant discourse sets the limits for the interpretation, there are always subordinate discourses that destabilize the dominant reading. No reading, then, will ever remain unquestioned, so no prejudice remains unquestioned.

Feminism, though, has never been content to remain subordinate. Women who have recognized the harmful effects of oppression want a transformation of the social order, not just a periodic questioning of the status quo. But in order to accomplish that transformation, feminists need to be able to appeal to something that goes beyond what others already take to be relevant. Fulkerson denies access to truth outside of communal discourse and talks about our knowledge of truth in terms of persuasion. The problem with this approach is that people may be persuaded of many things, not all of which are good. Realizing a vision of well-being for women requires making claims on people who are not themselves feminist. At least part of what is required for liberation is the recognition of sin by those who are not already persuaded by the feminist vision. They must *be* persuaded, so there has to be some way to appeal to something beyond the discourse that has already shaped their version of truth. To do that, though, one has to be able to say why one version of the truth is better than another version. Why should a feminist stipulation of relevance be superior to a patriarchal stipulation of relevance, when each is equally persuasive to the parties involved in the discussion?

The problem of persuasion presses questions about the notion of truth itself that I cannot pursue in this book, and I will be unable to discuss grounds for persuasion regarding feminist concerns outside Christianity. Within Christianity, though, the topic of this book has great bearing on this problem. Finding a way to affirm the authority of Scripture aids the task of persuasion within Christian discourse because that affirmation allows us to appeal to others on the basis of a shared commitment. Highlighting the role of readers or specific communities for interpreting the Bible shows the importance of listening to many voices, but this point has been emphasized almost to the exclusion of the Bible's own role. What we need is a way to talk about the Bible's role without giving up the insights that we have gained about the role of readers and communities. Tanner has identified one avenue for addressing this problem, a reconception of authority itself. It is one of the tasks of this book to examine the concept of authority in order to see its proper function. When we understand the complexity of authority relations, the authority of the Bible and the authority of women to interpret the Bible need not be in direct conflict. Without losing the ability to criticize the words of the Bible, feminist Christians can appeal to the word of God as the orientation for our lives and the ground for a vision of women's well-being. To do this, we must also explore the concept of revelation, which will touch on the issues of communication and dialogue that Bird has identified. As we consider the way that knowledge of God is offered and received through narrative, we can see how each side of this complex relation between the Bible and women has its own important role.

Before I undertake those examinations, though, I want to set the stage for the discussion. Current assumptions about the Bible's authority, whether one seeks to uphold it or to challenge it, are shaped by a doctrine of Scripture that was developed in the period after the Reformation, called "Protestant orthodoxy." This understanding of Scripture addresses many levels of questions that were of concern during that time but are not necessarily pressing today. Some of the issues, however, still deserve attention. The carefully worked-out understanding of Scripture during that period is not well known in its entirety. Instead, certain elements of it shape our assumptions, but those elements have been passed down after having been lifted out of the context in which they are rightly understood. In order to combat the assumptions that are harmful, feminists need to understand how they arose. Only then can we engage in appropriate criticism. In the next chapter, I will undertake a historical explanation of this doctrine of Scripture so that we know more clearly how to address concerns that remain and see what we can learn from the theologians who sought in their own time to affirm the authority of Scripture.

NOTES

1. See, e.g., Emily Cheney, *She Can Read: Feminist Reading Strategies for Biblical Narrative* (Valley Forge, Pa.: Trinity Press International, 1996); Athalya Brenner and Carole Fontaine, eds., *A Feminist Companion to Reading the Bible: Approaches, Methods, and Strategies* (Sheffield: Sheffield Academic Press, 1997); Luise Schottroff, Silvia Schroer, and Marie-Theres Wacker, eds., *Feminist Interpretation: The Bible in Women's Perspective* (trans. Martin Rumscheidt and Barbara Rumscheidt; Minneapolis: Fortress, 1998); and Kwok Pui-lan, *Discovering the Bible in the Non-Biblical World* (Maryknoll, N.Y.: Orbis, 1995).

2. See, e.g., Harold C. Washington, Susan Lochrie Graham, and Pamela Thimmes, eds., *Escaping Eden: New Feminist Perspectives on the Bible* (Sheffield: Sheffield Academic Press, 1998); and Kwok Pui-lan and Elisabeth Schüssler Fiorenza, eds., *Women's Sacred Scriptures* (Maryknoll, N.Y.: Orbis, 1998).

3. For an account of how current feminism often forgets the "mothers" and tends to periodize feminist theory in terms of "progress," see Elisabeth Schüssler Fiorenza, *Sharing Her Word: Feminist Biblical Interpretation in Context* (Boston: Beacon, 1998).

4. Feminism has been characterized in stages, often called "waves." Different disciplines sometimes identify these waves differently, but in general, the first wave refers roughly to the period from 1850 to 1920, during which women's struggle for equality was marked by the suffrage movement. In theology, the second wave usually refers to the work of feminist theologians influenced by the women's movement in the second half of the twentieth century. Younger women who were born in the twentieth century but who are coming of age (both personally and professionally) in the twenty-first century often think of their generation as constituting the third wave.

5. Schüssler Fiorenza, *Sharing Her Word*, 5–6.

6. For an example of how these different approaches were brought to bear on feminist scholarship, see Carol P. Christ and Judith Plaskow, eds., *Womanspirit Rising: A Feminist Reader in Religion* (San Francisco: Harper & Row, 1979).

7. The goal is not always stated in this way. Schüssler Fiorenza says she does not seek full humanity for women because males have defined "humanity." Instead she seeks "women's (religious) self-affirmation, power, and liberation from all patriarchal alienation, marginalization, and exploitation." See *Bread Not Stone: The Challenge of Feminist Biblical Interpretation* (Boston: Beacon, 1984), xiv–xv. Still, she indicates elsewhere that her "preferred definition of feminism is expressed by a well-known bumper sticker from the wo/men's movement: 'Feminism is the radical notion that women are people.'" See *Sharing Her Word*, 3.

8. Mary Ann Tolbert, "Protestant Feminists and the Bible: On the Horns of a Dilemma," *Union Seminary Quarterly Review* 43 (1989): 1–17.

9. Rosemary Radford Ruether, "Feminist Interpretation: A Method of Correlation," in *Feminist Interpretation of the Bible* (ed. Letty M. Russell; Philadelphia: Westminster, 1985), 111–24.

10. Ibid., 113.

11. Ibid., 114, 115.

12. Elisabeth Schüssler Fiorenza, "The Will to Choose or to Reject: Continuing Our Critical Work," in Russell, *Feminist Interpretation of the Bible*, 127.

13. Ibid., 128.

14. Letty M. Russell, introduction to *Feminist Interpretation of the Bible*, 14.

15. Barbara Brown Zikmund, "Feminist Consciousness in Historical Perspective," in Russell, *Feminist Interpretation of the Bible*, 21.

16. Margaret A. Farley, "Feminist Consciousness and the Interpretation of Scripture," in Russell, *Feminist Interpretation of the Bible*, 44.

17. Ibid., 42–44.

18. Ibid., 48.

19. Rosemary Radford Ruether, "Feminism and Patriarchal Religion: Principles of Ideological Critique of the Bible," *Journal for the Study of the Old Testament* 22 (1982): 54–56.

20. Rosemary Radford Ruether, *Sexism and God-Talk: Toward a Feminist Theology* (Boston: Beacon, 1993), 33–34, 22–23.

21. Ruether, "Feminism and Patriarchal Religion," 64–65.

22. Ruether, "Feminist Interpretation," 112.

23. Rosemary Radford Ruether, "Is Feminism the End of Christianity? A Critique of Daphne Hampson's *Theology and Feminism*," *Scottish Journal of Theology* 43 (1990): 399.

24. Ruether, "Feminist Interpretation," 115.

25. Ruether, *Sexism and God-Talk*, 23.

26. Rosemary Radford Ruether, *Womanguides: Readings toward a Feminist Theology* (Boston: Beacon, 1985), ix.

27. Letty M. Russell, *Household of Freedom: Authority in Feminist Theology* (Philadelphia: Westminster, 1987), 71.

28. See Maggie Humm, "Authority," in *The Dictionary of Feminist Theory* (Columbus: Ohio State University Press, 1990).

29. Russell, *Household of Freedom*, 21–25.

30. Letty M. Russell, "Authority and the Challenge of Feminist Interpretation," in Russell, *Feminist Interpretation of the Bible*, 143–44.

31. Russell, *Household of Freedom*, 30–32.

32. Ibid., 33–36.

33. Ibid., 138, 139, 145.

34. Elisabeth Schüssler Fiorenza, *In Memory of Her: A Feminist Theological Reconstruction of Christian Origins* (New York: Crossroad, 1984), 17.

35. Schüssler Fiorenza, *Bread Not Stone*, xiii.

36. Schüssler Fiorenza, "Will to Choose or to Reject," 131, 136.

37. Schüssler Fiorenza, *In Memory of Her,* 33.

38. For this example, I am indebted to Charles M. Wood.

39. Schüssler Fiorenza, *Bread Not Stone,* 32–36; *In Memory of Her,* 34.

40. Schüssler Fiorenza, *Bread Not Stone,* x.

41. Ibid., 36–37, 40.

42. Ibid., xiv.

43. Ibid., xvii.

44. Ibid., xiii.

45. Schüssler Fiorenza, "Will to Choose or to Reject," 128.

46. Mary McClintock Fulkerson, *Changing the Subject: Women's Discourses and Feminist Theology* (Minneapolis: Fortress, 1994), 63, 7.

47. See ibid., 239ff.

48. See ibid., 175ff.

49. Ibid., 54–56.

50. Mary McClintock Fulkerson, "'Is There a (Non-Sexist) Bible in This Church?' A Feminist Case for the Priority of Interpretive Communities," *Modern Theology* 14, no. 2 (April 1998): 225–42.

51. Fulkerson, *Changing the Subject,* 303.

52. Ibid., 375.

53. Ibid., 377.

54. Ibid., 164, 378, 369–70.

55. Kathryn E. Tanner, "Theology and the Plain Sense," in *Scriptural Authority and Narrative Interpretation* (ed. Garrett Green; Philadelphia: Fortress, 1987), 63.

56. Ibid., 65.

57. Kathryn E. Tanner, *Theories of Culture: A New Agenda for Theology* (Guides to Theological Inquiry; Minneapolis: Augsburg Fortress, 1997), 57.

58. Ibid., 124–25.

59. Ibid., 113.

60. Ibid., 121.

61. Kathryn E. Tanner, "Scripture as Popular Text," in *Modern Theology* 14, no. 2 (April 1998): 279–98.

62. Ibid., 286–90.

63. Ibid., 290–93.

64. Ibid., 294.

65. Ibid., 295.

66. Phyllis A. Bird, "What Makes a Feminist Reading Feminist? A Qualified Answer," in *Escaping Eden: New Feminist Perspectives on the Bible* (ed. Harold C. Washington, Susan Lochrie Graham, and Pamela Thimmes; Sheffield: Sheffield Academic Press, 1998), 124–31.

67. Schüssler Fiorenza, *Sharing Her Word,* 19.

CHAPTER TWO

⤜✕⤝

The Protestant Orthodox Doctrine of Scripture

The doctrine of Scripture that gave us the terms and concepts that shape so many of the assumptions in current discussions about the authority of Scripture was itself developed in a time of crisis about authority. In the sixteenth century, the Reformers had turned to Scripture in order to find a leverage point for reform in the church. In contrast to the Roman Catholic appeal to tradition as the guarantor of the truth of the Christian faith, Martin Luther and John Calvin both appealed to Scripture alone. Since in their view the tradition of the church had become corrupt, the Reformers needed something external to tradition in order to criticize it. Scripture, as the word of God, provided the norm that was needed in order to correct the abuses of the church. In order for Scripture to function in this way, though, it had to be clear and reliable itself. The Reformers believed Scripture to be clear and reliable because the Holy Spirit wrote it. Scripture was also clearly and reliably interpreted under the guidance of the Holy Spirit. The principle of *sola scriptura* (scripture alone) became the bedrock of Protestant thought. This principle, along with other distinctive Protestant views, was elaborated and systematized during a period sometimes called "Protestant orthodoxy."

THE PRESSURES THAT PRODUCED THE DOCTRINE

In a time of polemic, *sola scriptura* had to be defended against multiple objections. Protestant orthodox theologians, sometimes called the "Protestant scholastics" because their method drew on and resembled the method used by the medieval scholastics, developed their doctrine of Scripture in the years leading up to and during the "crisis of authority" of the seventeenth century.[1] By using the Scripture principle to question the authority of the church, the Reformers had opened the doors to all kinds of questioning, and the unintended consequence of that move was to put at risk the authority of Scripture as they understood it. Among Protestants themselves arose the problem of competing and quite different interpretations of a supposedly "clear and reliable" Scripture. In particular, groups came into being, such as the Anabaptists, that freely interpreted Scripture under the guidance of the Holy Spirit in a way that the original Reformers themselves found unsettling and wrong. On another front, Roman Catholics responded to the Protestant move with their own pattern of reform that undergirded the authority of the church. In part, Catholicism worked to undermine the certainty about inner illumination that Protestants invoked as a criterion for reading Scripture and to emphasize the need for the church's guidance.[2] Protestants and Catholics argued with each other, and Protestants argued among themselves, about who had the authority to interpret the Bible. Multiple "authorities" claimed different things, each saying that the others were wrong. In that polemic, all of the various "authorities" were undermined. Confusion about how to choose among authorities increased, and by the seventeenth century, the appeal to "authority" itself began to break down.

In the midst of this confusion, some turned, neither to the church nor to the Holy Spirit, but to reason as the most credible arbiter of disputes and the most certain guarantee of truth. Socinians, for instance, held that individuals, rather than the church, interpret the Bible and relied on reason rather than the Holy Spirit for right interpretation. Their appeal to reason led them to question even such basic tenets of the Christian faith as the doctrine of the Trinity, which the Reformers themselves never dreamed of challenging. Even more critical was René Descartes's turn to the inner certainty of the reasoning subject for the surest philosophical foundations. His approach rejected any appeal to authority to secure certainty of knowledge and began the quest for certainty in the self.

Reason's position as arbiter of disputes became increasingly credible as discoveries in the scientific world gained a hearing. Copernicus and later Galileo offered a view of the universe that was a clear alternative to the one presented in the Bible. The Bible said that the sun "rose" or "set," but astronomy was finding that the earth revolved around the sun. As evidence mounted for the Copernican view, the biblical picture of the world, regardless of which authority might support it, became less and less credible. Many felt that authorities could, and often did, mislead. By the end of the seventeenth century, reason had gained such prominence that, Jeffrey Stout explains, the "crisis of authority" began to be resolved in the direction of reliance on "sound human judgment," which weighs evidence and calculates probabilities.[3] Our own judgment, then, not the force of authority, becomes decisive.

In this context, Protestant orthodox theologians were pressed to account for more and more difficulties. The theologians of the time devoted much of their creative energy to the task of showing how Scripture could be a reliable norm for Christian faith. Protestant orthodox theologians writing from the latter half of the sixteenth century into the eighteenth century worked out a sophisticated doctrine of Scripture that relies heavily on the notion of verbal inspiration that feminists find so objectionable.[4] Because this notion lingers through assumptions about and approaches to reading Scripture in much current theological thinking, it is useful for feminists to examine this concept in its proper context in order to know how to address properly the problems that it raises. Interestingly, despite great differences that exist between Protestant orthodoxy and feminism, there are some similar impulses. Protestantism was itself a reform movement, and the orthodox theologians who elaborated Reformation ideas into formal doctrines stood in great continuity with those ideas.[5] It is instructive for feminists to see how the impulses behind the Reformation played themselves out in order to see the points at which those impulses bore both promise and problems. An examination of the Protestant orthodox doctrine of Scripture reveals what the doctrine was trying to safeguard as well as how it ultimately fails.[6] In this chapter, I will outline the main themes of the Protestant orthodox defense of Scripture in order to show how this understanding of Scripture was meant to preserve important insights of the Reformation. When the whole argument is seen together, the role of the various elements becomes clearer.

THE PROTESTANT ORTHODOX DOCTRINE OF SCRIPTURE

Despite the enormous pressures on the concept of authority after the Reformation, Protestants in the sixteenth and seventeenth centuries did not give up on the authority of Scripture. The Protestant scholastics worked to safeguard the insight of the original Reformers that Scripture is indeed the clear and reliable work of the Holy Spirit, is clearly and reliably interpreted by the Holy Spirit, and is therefore the rightful authority by which Christian faith and practice must be guided and judged. What lay behind the Reformers' protests against the church in the first place and the Protestant scholastics' systematic doctrine of Scripture in the second place was the need for certainty about salvation. The Reformers felt that the church could not be trusted, for it had become filled with abuses and was not reliable with regard to what we must do to be saved. Scripture provided a standard by which tradition could be judged, but the turn to Scripture alone proved to be equally problematic. How was it possible to know that Scripture was indeed a firm place to stand, the reliable source and measure for matters pertaining to salvation? The Protestant scholastics had to answer that question in their doctrine.

Identifying the Canon

Among the matters that had to be considered in order to say that Scripture was the reliable source and measure for matters pertaining to salvation was the question of what books were to be included in the authoritative canon. The Reformers themselves had challenged the traditional collection, and their Protestant successors had to justify the Protestant orthodox collection in the face of alternative views. On the one hand, Anabaptists and Socinians both saw a substantive difference between the Old and New Testaments, so the status of the Old Testament in the canon was in question.[7] On the other hand, Catholics accepted books as canonical that Protestants considered to be apocryphal. It became necessary for Protestant scholastics to identify which books were canonical and to give reasons for the inclusion and exclusion of certain books. Their reasons reflect the use of the Scripture principle even in this preliminary kind of decision. The selection process itself is a theological issue.

Francis Turretin, a seventeenth-century Reformed theologian, exemplifies the way Protestant scholastics argued for the canon that they used. To answer the question about whether the Old Testament and the New Testament were substantially different, Turretin argues that despite whatever differences there may be, the Old Testament should be regarded as scripture. His reasons include the connection between Old Testament prophecy and New Testament fulfillment, the way Paul regarded the Old Testament, and the similarity of the substance in both Testaments.[8] Regarding the issue raised by the Catholics, Protestant scholastics accepted as scripture only those books that had been considered "from early times" to be of prophetic or apostolic origin, and the books they considered apocryphal could not meet that requirement. In either case, though, the ultimate test for inclusion in the canon was, not how Paul or the early church had regarded the books, but whether or not these books bore in themselves signs of having been inspired by God. In contrast to what he takes to be the Catholic position, Turretin says that the church does not establish the canon or make it authoritative. Rather, the church merely recognizes and proclaims the canon of Scripture by its own internal marks (such as its majesty of style and content, and the consensus and harmony among all the different writers). In discerning which books are canonical, the church is like a goldsmith who distinguishes gold from dross but does not make the gold what it is.[9] For the Protestant scholastics, the internal marks of Scripture provide both justification for including the Old Testament and a leverage point for lifting the apocryphal books from the canon, despite their long-standing use by the church. In this way, Scripture, by displaying its own criteria in its internal marks, has authority over the church even in establishing its own "table of contents."

Having thus delineated the requirements for a book's inclusion in the canon, Protestant scholastics were faced with a further problem. Just as not all Old Testament books had been agreed upon "from early times," not all New Testament books had unanimous acceptance from the beginning. Some books, namely, 2 Peter, 2 and 3 John, Jude, Hebrews, and Revelation were called the "New Testament apocrypha" because some in the early church had doubted their authenticity. Even the early Reformers had felt "less bound" to them than to the other books of the New Testament.[10] Protestant scholastics nonetheless included these books in the canon by arguing for their authorship by the Holy Spirit, as distinct from their human authorship. Any doubt concerning these books, they said, had to do with the human, secondary authors, not with the divine, primary author. Furthermore, they pointed out that only some in the beginning doubted the secondary authorship and that the whole church eventually came to accept the secondary authorship as genuine.[11] This authenticity was finally recognized because, ultimately and again according to the Protestant principle, Scripture proves itself.[12]

Because Protestant scholastics held Scripture to be sufficient for salvation, the question of whether any canonical book had ever disappeared from the canon became important. According to Turretin, some Roman Catholics claimed that books had disappeared. By this claim, he says, they intended to show the imperfection of Scripture and make room for the necessity of unwritten traditions. Turretin, though, argues that not every book written of old was divinely inspired. However, all books necessary for our salvation have been preserved both by God's providence and by the church's faithful fulfillment of its duty to preserve them.[13] We need not worry, then, whether Scripture is lacking anything that we need for our salvation. The canon as delineated by the Protestant scholastics had all that was necessary, and no more.

Revelation, Reason, and Scripture

In contrast to the rationalism of the Socinians, Protestant scholastics consistently placed reason in a position subordinate to revelation, which is not to say that Protestant orthodoxy completely devalued reason. Both Lutheran and Reformed scholastics saw the usefulness of reason even in its corrupted form. Reason could be used to refute heresy and to illustrate or explain matters that have been revealed by Scripture.[14] Reason could even provide some knowledge of God, for instance, knowledge of God's existence, though that knowledge was imperfect and could never be saving knowledge. Because they both came from God, reason and revelation in principle could never come into conflict, as long as reason keeps within its proper limits. Reason has its place, and revelation supplies that which is "above reason" in order to bring us to eternal blessedness. Of course, the fall makes these positive uses of reason problematic. Corrupted reason may overreach itself and try to decide matters that properly fall within the sphere of faith. In that case, reason comes into conflict with revelation. In such conflict, reason could never serve as the rule for correction but can only stand in need of correction itself by revelation, which exposes that reason has overreached itself.[15] The idea that reason, whether in its corrupted or uncorrupted state, is subordinate to revelation ran counter to the rationalism that was represented by Socinianism and Cartesian philosophy and that grew in influence in the larger culture as the centuries progressed. The commitment to knowledge of divine rather than human origin was to have far-reaching consequences for the Protestant orthodox position.

For Protestant scholastics, special revelation was verbal communication, that is, God's revealing Godself by means of the word. Special revelation could be immediate or mediate, the former having to do with God's direct communication to the prophets and apostles and the latter having to do with knowledge of God that has been committed to writing, namely, in Scripture.[16] It was not always necessary, says Turretin, for revelation to take written form, because for a time God communicated by the spoken word. During the time of the apostles, though, God wanted the church to have "the most perfect form of revelation, that is, the written light." Both the content (the teaching) being transmitted and the form (the writing) of transmission were necessary for the church at that time because God's word could be more easily preserved and defended in a fixed, written form.[17] The argument for written scripture highlights the conflict with Catholics. Martin Chemnitz, a sixteenth-century Lutheran theologian, explains that Scripture was written because tradition alone could not preserve pure doctrine. As the church followed tradition more, or rather, than Scripture, it was, in fact, filled with abuses.[18] Returning to the written word was for Protestants the defense against those abuses. The fixed, written form secured the proper transmission of revelation and provided a means to correct its corruption in human hands. This theological point, therefore, was made for very practical reasons and was intended to have very practical consequences.

Because it contains revelation, Scripture contains the truths necessary for our salvation that cannot be known any other way. Hence, we have the Protestant principle of *sola scriptura*. Scripture is the only source and norm for theology.[19] Reason cannot question Scripture any more than reason can question revelation. In case of conflict, the matter is decided in favor of Scripture, although often in such a way as to show that the conflict was only apparent.

For instance, reason may say, against Scripture, that it is impossible for a virgin to bear a child. However, this apparent conflict dissolves when we consider the proper spheres of reason and revelation. According to Protestant orthodoxy, it is not possible for a virgin to bear a child *naturally,* but Scripture shows us that Mary bore a child *supernaturally.* Reason and Scripture each has its own axioms, which need to be left in their own spheres and not confused. When they are confused, the problem, and thus the need for correction, lies with reason.

Inspiration of Scripture

In order for it to be the source and norm of truth about God, Scripture must be of divine origin. Protestant scholastics dealt with this issue through their doctrine of inspiration. Revelation and inspiration are closely related, but Protestant orthodox theologians distinguished them in the following way.[20] Revelation is the manifestation of something that is otherwise unknown, and it can take place in a variety of ways, such as speech, dreams, or visions. Inspiration refers to the manner by which certain concepts are conveyed by the Holy Spirit to an author so that God communicates, not only the concepts, but also the words in which those concepts are expressed.[21] Although both concepts and words are communicated by inspiration, these theologians retained the distinction between the sense of Scripture (*verbum internum*) and its actual expression (*verbum externum*), and one advantage of this distinction will become apparent in the discussion below about Scripture's authority. Concepts that were inspired in this way need not be revelation but could be mundane matters. The point of inspiration is not to claim unique content but a unique process by which any content may be communicated. Distinguishing the two terms in this way enables Protestant scholastics to allow a broader range of revelatory acts than Scripture alone. Conversely, it restricts inspiration to written scripture alone, a move that undergirds the unique status of Scripture. Furthermore, Protestant scholastics could speak of information in Scripture that could be known independently of Scripture, for example, that David was the king of Israel, as inspired even though it was not revelatory. Everything in the Bible was immediately communicated by the Holy Spirit.

Inspiration has to do with supernatural agency, but how does this supernatural agency relate to the human agents who actually set the words down on paper? God's inspiration of the writers of Scripture is unique and is not to be confused with any other instance in which God's action and human action concur. Through the process sometimes called "oral dictation," God both infused concepts into the authors' intellects and also instigated the authors' wills to write.[22] The human agents are considered the instruments of God, sometimes described as "hands," "secretaries," or even "pens."[23] However, Protestant scholastics do not want God's dictation to be understood mechanistically. According to Robert D. Preus, the point of such language is not to describe a psychology of inspiration, nor should the language be taken to indicate a violation of the human authors' personalities. Rather, the point is to stress that God is the author of Scripture. Divine authorship is in no way limited or made questionable by the agency of human authors. Scripture is not a composite of the divine word and human words. It is God's word spoken through human words, but nevertheless spoken by God.[24]

If God is the author of all Scripture, how do Protestant scholastics account for the diversity of styles among the various books? They speak of the Holy Spirit's accommodation to the style and mode of speaking of the human authors.[25] If God's dictation does not violate the human authors' style, neither does it violate their situation. Turretin speaks of how circumstances influenced and even compelled the authors to write, but they were at the same time writing under the command of God.[26] Though the impulse for the will to write comes from God, this impulse seems to coincide with what is also compelling about the author's particular situation. It seems that Protestant scholastics wanted to acknowledge the human agents, but they did not want to rely on them. Human agency is fallible, and without this idea of verbal inspiration, reliable transmission of divine knowledge could not be certain. In the matter of writing Scripture, then, God's agency is decisive.

God's dictation of Scripture was the guarantee that the prophets and apostles had gotten things right. The human writers were as fallible as any other humans in many areas of their lives; but when they recorded Scripture, they did not make mistakes. By the supernatural act of inspiration, God infused both correct conceptions of content and the terms by which that content was conveyed. There were, for the Protestant scholastics, no errors in Scripture, not even about mundane matters. The idea that everything in the Bible was inspired by God, sometimes known as "plenary inspiration," gave a very high status even to the commonplace. Various matters might be considered of relatively higher or lower importance, but because the Holy Spirit had seen fit to put them there, nothing in Scripture could be considered trivial, and none of it could be wrong.[27] To see why this matter was of such importance for them, one must consider the consequence for their position of an error in Scripture. Turretin says:

> Unless unimpaired integrity is attributed to Scripture, it cannot be regarded as the sole rule of faith and practice, and a wide door is opened to atheists, libertines, enthusiasts, and others of that sort of profane people to undermine its authority and overthrow the foundation

of salvation. Since error cannot be part of the faith, how can a Scripture which is weakened by contradictions and corruptions be regarded as authentic and divine? Nor should it be said that these corruptions are only in matters of little significance, which do not affect the fundamentals of the faith. For as soon as the authenticity of Scripture has been found wanting, even if it be a single corruption [of the text] that cannot be corrected, how can our faith any longer be sustained? If corruption is conceded in matters of little importance, why not also in others of more significance?[28]

Having made Scripture the sole source and norm for theology and the sufficient rule for faith and practice, Protestant scholastics had to be sure that Scripture could in fact bear all that weight. The doctrine of inspiration guaranteed that Scripture could be trusted but also forced Protestant scholastics to deny error of any sort. This position bore serious consequences later as Protestant scholastics struggled to account both for internal and external challenges to the truth of Scripture.

The Protestant scholastics' understanding of the verbal inspiration of Scripture was their way of showing that the source of Scripture's authority is God, not anything human. God, not the human writers, is the author who matters because God's own knowledge of Godself is the only reliable source for this saving knowledge. The doctrine of inspiration shows a direct and unfailing relation between God's own knowledge and the knowledge conveyed in the Bible. God's knowledge of Godself is worthy of belief. The human writers' knowledge of God is worthy of belief also because it is inspired by God. Since God inspired both the content and the form of what they wrote, the writings that they produced are also worthy of belief. The knowledge that Scripture provides about God is reliable and worthy of belief because it is knowledge that is ultimately grounded in God's own knowledge of Godself.

Authority of Scripture

Protestant scholastics distinguished two kinds of authority that Scripture has. Though sometimes identified by different names, the two are recognizable in both Reformed and Lutheran theology. First, Scripture has *causative authority* because the inspired sense of Scripture (*the verbum internum*) coupled with the illuminating power of the Holy Spirit actually produce in us the faith by which we believe what Scripture has to say.[29] Because causative authority is connected with the inspired sense, or the conceptions conveyed through the words, not only the original manuscripts but also translations of Scripture bear this authority. Scripture's own truthfulness is ingredient to convincing us of its truth. Because it is self-authenticating, we have no need of any human authority (including, against Roman Catholics, the authority of the church) to convince us of its authority. It bears witness to itself, but the Holy Spirit also bears witness to it. The testimony of the Holy Spirit in the believer's heart convinces the believer "efficaciously." Together, Scripture's own credibility and the Holy Spirit's witness to that credibility bestow divine and unshakable faith. When this faith is produced in us, we are not only illumined but also converted, regenerated, and renewed.[30] Protestant scholastics recognized that assent to propositions alone was not what truly mattered for faith. Though these categories were discussed in different ways in the Lutheran and Reformed traditions, theologians of both distinguished three aspects of faith: knowledge (*notitia*), assent (*assensus*), and confidence (*fiducia*).[31] Knowledge and assent alone do not constitute saving faith because even the devils believe that what God says is true. Many people may believe what the Bible says, but only those who have confidence, along with knowledge and assent, that God's promises apply to them are regenerated. Assent coupled with confidence is produced in us when Scripture exercises causative authority. We are convinced that what Scripture tells us is true, not because we have seen some other evidence that confirms it and not because any other authority has told us so, but because Scripture's own truth is evidence enough and because we have been given illumination by the Holy Spirit to see it. In the sea of uncertainty that marked their time, Protestant scholastics found their anchor, not in something external, as they believed Catholics did, but in internal conviction. That internal conviction, though, was not the same as Descartes's. It was conviction born first, not in knowledge about oneself, but in knowledge about God.[32]

The second kind of authority that Scripture exercises is *canonical*, or *normative*, authority. Because only the original manuscripts were actually dictated by God in such a way as to be without mistake, only the original Hebrew and Greek manuscripts bear this authority. In this way, the originals are the norm for any copy or translation, and any appeal to settle disputes about translations or interpretations had to be made to the original. Scripture as the rule for faith and life exercises *normative authority* in two ways. As a "rule of knowledge," Hollaz, a Lutheran scholastic, says, Scripture is both directive and corrective. Positively, it directs human thoughts so that they "abide within the bounds of truth," and negatively, it corrects errors when human thinking has gone astray.[33] Scripture, then, as canon acts both as guide and judge. Perhaps because of the tenor of the times, what occupied the attention of Protestant scholastics more was the authority of Scripture to settle controversies. According to Turretin, Catholics and Protestants agreed that Scripture was the rule and norm to settle controversy, but he says that Catholics saw Scripture only as "a partial and inadequate one to which unwritten tradition must be added" and which must be supplemented by the decision of some judge, whether the councils, the church fathers, or the pope.[34] Protestant scholastics, though, were wary of the fallibility of human judges. Philip Melanchthon cites numerous examples in which the church fathers had taken positions that were either contrary to Scripture or to each other. If even those admirable persons need to be corrected by the word of God, how much more do we need to be watchful when an "ungodly crowd has control of the church" and "establishes many false and ungodly things in the name of the church."[35] Scripture alone makes a proper rule because it is "certain, fixed, invariable, fundamental, suited to meet every case, always self-consistent."[36]

Even Protestant scholastics, though, had to admit that Scripture needed to be interpreted and that cases of controversy may necessitate human judgment. Every believer has the responsibility to judge privately about matters necessary to salvation and of the clergy to make those judgments publicly.[37] Turretin points out, though, that any human judge is only secondary. The Holy Spirit alone is the supreme and infallible judge, the reliable interpreter of Scripture.[38] The human judge's responsibility is to interpret Scripture according to the Holy Spirit. If any particular controversy cannot be settled, the fault lies, not in Scripture, but either in our not having interpreted Scripture properly, according to the Holy Spirit, or in our not having adopted the proper interpretation.[39]

Scripture's corrective authority was not limited to church controversies. To understand the extent of the authority, one must remember how closely the matter of authority was tied to the doctrine of inspiration. Scripture is worthy of being believed and obeyed because God inspired it. Because it is inspired by God, Scripture is authentic and infallible. Because it is authentic and infallible, it is the only fitting measure for deciding controversy. Its corrective authority mattered most regarding mysteries of the faith, but in order for the Protestant scholastic position to work, this claim had to be extended beyond matters of doctrine. Because authentic and infallible inspiration of Scripture extends to all its parts, Scripture has authority over everything about which it speaks, including matters of science and history.[40] The insistence on the a priori acceptance of the truth of all scriptural statements was a clear alternative to the Socinian view, which held that accommodation to the writer's situations included accommodation to the prevailing, but incorrect, notions about science, geography, and chronology.[41] Furthermore, the accuracy of those notions could be tested by external evidence. If, as the Socinians held, even Scripture's authority could be verified by human investigation and what it said could be tested and corrected in matters of science, and so forth, then its authority in those matters was no more than probable. If Scripture was some-times fallible and its authority was probable, then it could not be considered entirely trustworthy with regard to matters of faith and salvation. If, on the other hand, Scripture is completely infallible, as the Protestant scholastics held, then its authority must be upheld even in matters of science, and so forth, regardless of apparent contradiction with that which can be known by reason. Scripture's contradiction with science and history did not deal the orthodox doctrine a fatal blow at first. Orthodoxy had recourse, as demon-strated with regard to the virgin birth, to distinguishing between the spheres of reason and revelation. Even when the conflict arose between biblical and scientific cosmologies, many Protestant scholastics were able to say that when Scripture says that Joshua made the sun stand still, it was speaking figura-tively, not scientifically.[42] Still, the a priori acceptance of Scripture's truth about everything on which it speaks became increasingly difficult to maintain as science gained greater force with the passing centuries and as the Protestant scholastics' own keen attention to Scripture itself paved the way for source criticism, which raised historical questions about the human authorship of Scripture.

Perfection or Sufficiency of Scripture

In order for Scripture to be the sole source and norm for the production, direction, and correction of the Christian faith, Scripture must teach perfectly everything that we need for our salvation. It does so when it is taken as a whole, not when its parts are taken separately.[43] Some of the discussion about the perfection of Scripture has to do with the perfect formation of the canon. It was crucial for the Protestant scholastics to affirm that we have every book that God ever intended for us to have and that the books we have contain all that we need to know for our faith and life. Scripture does not have to contain all that there is to know about God; God knows more about Godself than has been revealed to us.[44] Nor does Scripture have to contain every detail about Christ and the saints.[45] In fact, some important understandings of God and Jesus Christ have to be drawn out by implication in the doctrines of the Trin-ity and the Incarnation. Protestant theologians considered the substance of these doctrines to be present in Scripture, but the full expression of their meaning, and even the terms in which they are expressed, came later. Neither the things that are missing nor the later elaborations of its sense detract from Scripture's perfection in what truly matters. Scripture is perfect only with regard to its end, which is our salvation. The written word—the actual written expression—provides us with the unwritten word—the content—which gives us Christ, the knowledge of whom saves us. Scripture is perfect in the sense that it contains all that is necessary for us to know for our faith and life.[46]

Perspicuity of Scripture

In order for Scripture to function as the sufficient source, and the only source, for all we need to know to be saved, it must be clear enough to be comprehended by everyone, even the unlearned, which is not to say that everyone will understand Scripture. In the view of Protestant scholastics, Scripture would naturally be obscure to the unregenerate and to unbelievers. Scripture must, though, be understand*able*. While it may be obscure to some, Scripture cannot be obscure in itself, or it will be unable to provide what it must for our salvation.[47] To deny that Scripture is obscure in itself is not to say that no parts of it are obscure. Nor is it to say that Scripture is without mystery. "Scripture," says Turretin, "has its own secrets," which are there "to awaken the zeal of the faithful, to increase their effort, to control human pride, and to purge the contempt that easily could have arisen from too much ease [of understanding]."[48] Just as Scripture does not contain all things about God, it does not make clear all things about God. Still, it must make clear what is necessary for us to know. Because what Scripture can and should make known to us is not always apparent on the surface—there are indeed passages that are difficult to understand—the question of how to interpret Scripture becomes important.

The Holy Spirit is the only infallible interpreter of Scripture because the Holy Spirit is the author. In practice, to say that the author is the only infallible interpreter of what is written means first that the human reader should use Scripture to interpret Scripture. That is, if one passage inspired by the Holy Spirit is obscure, the human interpreter should turn to another parallel passage also inspired by the Holy Spirit to make the first one clear.[49] Second, this understanding implies a correlate principle, namely, that all interpretation should be done according to the analogy of faith. Since all Scripture comes from the same Holy Spirit, all of it is harmonious and perfectly consistent when properly understood. The Apostles' Creed contains a summary of the "rule of faith," and no interpretation should be in conflict with this rule.[50] The human interpreter's task is to find the proper interpretation with the guidance of the Holy Spirit.

Protestants of this period insisted that Scripture had only one sense or meaning, and they did so to counter the Roman Catholic practice of identifying four separate senses of Scripture: literal, allegorical, tropological, and anagogical.[51] The issue for Protestant scholastics was that words or passages of Scripture do not contain multiple meanings, which is important because, according to Turretin, Catholics used the presence of multiple meanings in the text to argue that Scripture is ambiguous and doubtful rather than perspicuous.[52] For Protestant scholastics, the Holy Spirit intends Scripture to have one proper and true sense, called its literal sense, but their understanding of "literal" needs careful attention.[53] By insisting on the literal sense of Scripture as the proper sense, Protestant scholastics did not intend to deny the use of figurative language in the Bible. All passages have a literal meaning, but not all are to be taken literally. The literal meaning is the meaning that the Holy Spirit intends, but sometimes that literal meaning is arrived at by the use of figurative speech, hence the ability to finesse the problem posed by the story of Joshua mentioned earlier. The literal sense, then, is not always simple (i.e., strictly literal, or the natural signification of the words); sometimes it is compound, or composite, so that "mixed meaning" can be found.[54] Mixed meaning, unlike multiple meanings, allows flexibility within a single expression of truth. A historical narrative, such as the narrative about Jonah, may be used as allegory, trope, or analogy, such as when Jonah's stay in the belly of the whale is applied to Christ's stay in the tomb, but when it is used in those ways, the narrative does not lose its strictly literal meaning. Rather, the strictly literal meaning is the basis for the symbolic application. That is, there are not two meanings, but rather one strictly literal meaning is applied to another situation to express something about the second situation in a figurative way.[55] The composite of the strictly literal meaning and its figurative application together constitute the one literal sense, or the sense intended by the Holy Spirit. Even though the one meaning yields several ideas, these ideas are mutually dependent so that the meaning itself remains single.[56] The Protestant scholastics, then, found a way of reintroducing the various readings of Scripture that Catholics used, but they did so in a way that they thought undergirded Scripture's authority rather than threatened it.

As if the problem of interpreting passages within Scripture were not enough, Protestant scholastics also faced the challenge of variant readings of the same text. How could Scripture have a single meaning if even the words of the text were problematic? To answer this question, Protestant scholastics had to determine the norm for making judgments about the correct reading of the text. In contrast to Catholics, who accepted the Vulgate as the authentic, normative version, Protestant scholastics turned to texts written in the original languages, Hebrew and Greek. These were the languages in which the Holy Spirit inspired the prophets and apostles to write. Turretin says that the original texts are authoritative for all copies and translations, but by "original texts" he does not mean original autographs, for those are lost to us. Rather, he means those extant copies that have been passed down to us that "record for us that word of God in the same words into which the sacred writers committed it under the immediate inspiration of the Holy Spirit" and that may be called authentic writings because of their faithfulness to the original.[57] Into these texts, no error has crept, because they have been preserved by God's providence and the copyists' faithfulness. Some copyists, of course, did make mistakes, but the point is that not all did. The text has not been corrupted beyond recovery of the original. Variant readings do not diminish our faith in having access to the authentic text, because they are recognizable and correctable, partly by context and partly by collation of the better manuscripts.[58]

Since the authenticity of the text relates not only to content but also to the form in which the content is expressed, the Protestant scholastics eventually had to deal with the question of the relative newness of the vowel points in the Hebrew text. Those vowel points were not included in the text at the time of its original dictation (when only the consonants of each word were recorded) and were added to manuscripts much later, but Turretin argues that their newness does not mean they are a human invention and subject to fallibility. The vowels, he says, were part of the "sound and value, or power" of the words that were originally written. The vowels were the "souls of consonants" even if they were not committed to writing. When the Masoretes added the vowel points, they merely recorded explicitly what had been implicitly understood from the beginning.[59] The issue of vowel points became important enough to be addressed in the Helvetic Consensus Formula (1675). To uphold its position about the authenticity, clarity, truthfulness, and authority of Scripture, Protestant orthodoxy had to defend the inerrancy of Scripture even to this degree.

Efficacy of Scripture

Perspicuity is closely connected to efficacy because understanding Scripture relates not only to guidance and correction but also to salvation. If the end of Scripture is salvation, and if salvation depends on knowing God, then Scripture must be able to make God known to us in an understandable way. Saving understanding, though, requires more than just clarity of the words; it also requires the illuminating power of the Holy Spirit. The unregenerate can grasp the meaning of the words and even accept the truth of historical or legal statements, but they do not perceive and receive the good that Scripture offers.[60] The efficacy of Scripture relates to its causative authority, that is, to its authority to effect faith and, in consequence, all that follows from faith. Efficacy properly belongs to the word of God that is contained in Scripture, the *verbum internum,* not to "the bare external letters of the written Bible." Still, the written words of Scripture are not dead letters but are truly living and efficacious because of the word they contain.[61] Because of its divine origin, Scripture is never uninspired and is never without the divine word, whether it is in use or not; it possesses divine power *ante usum* (before use) because it can be called the word of God *ante usum.*[62] Furthermore, efficacy is a property not only of the original texts, which are the written word as it was dictated, but also of the translations of those texts. Both contain the inspired sense, which, coupled with the illuminating power of the Holy Spirit, is a means of grace for effecting faith.[63] Not limited to Scripture, the efficacy of the word extends to preaching as well. In both cases, the word is effective because it actually saves souls.

MERITS AND PROBLEMS

The Protestant scholastic doctrine of Scripture was an amazing accomplishment. In a time of great uncertainty, these theologians refused to look for certainty anywhere other than in that which was truly ultimate, namely, in God. Nothing of human origin, whether it be a human institution such as the church or the human self, was grand enough, secure enough, or infallible enough to mark what theologians sometimes refer to as the "really real." In this, Protestant scholastics remained true to the impulse of Christianity to look beyond the creation to the Creator for salvation, worship, and guidance for living a faithful life. They remind us of the problem of human fallibility, and they insist that the norm for correction and direction can come only from God. They also had a sensitivity to the difficulty of making use of that norm. Their insistence on the reliability of the fixed, written form of Scripture was an attempt to ensure that we had dependable access to the truth by which we must live. Whether that attempt succeeds, though, is another matter.

The Protestant scholastic doctrine of Scripture was skillfully elaborated but put the written word in the position of having to bear a great deal of weight. Scripture could not contain a single error, had to be the only rule for all controversies in the church, had to be clear and harmonious, and had to provide all that was necessary for salvation. Scripture's ability to meet all these criteria, however, was challenged from both inside and outside the Protestant tradition. Though its end was salvation and it need be perfect only with respect to that end, Protestant orthodox theologians deemed Scripture reliable about matters necessary for salvation only if it was also reliable about the less important matters that it contained as well. Its authority had to extend beyond matters specific for salvation to the scientific and historical matters about which it spoke. Developments in science, in philosophy, and in biblical interpretation itself chipped away at the reliability of scriptural descriptions of the universe, miracles, and even history.

In addition to problems of reliability were internal pressures on the Protestant scholastic doctrine of Scripture itself. In order to be authoritative for settling controversies and to be a sufficient guide for faith and life, Scripture had to be clear and harmonious. However, Scripture still had to be interpreted both because it contained obscure passages and because manuscripts had variant readings. Problems arise, though, with either of the methods of interpretation that the Protestant scholastics proposed. First, the principle of interpreting Scripture by Scripture involves several problems: how to decide which passages are clear enough to function as the norm, what to do when no parallel passages exist, and what to do when two or more clear passages are in contradiction. Second, when it is not possible to interpret Scripture by Scripture, the final court of appeal is actually the rule of faith that is summarized in the Apostles' Creed and whose implications are drawn out in the foundational doctrines of the early church. No interpretation can be in conflict with this rule. One has to ask, then, whether Protestant scholastics have not located their norm in tradition after all. Finally, part of the impulse for locating the norm for Christian faith in Scripture rather than tradition was to avoid the problem of human fallibility. Protestant scholastics placed confidence in one, right, divinely intended interpretation of Scripture, but controversies over interpretation have persisted. The doctrine of inspiration could guarantee that the prophets and apostles got the matter right, but no corresponding doctrine guaranteed that subsequent interpreters would do the same. The observation of poststructuralism—that the fixed, written form of a text does not guarantee fixed readings of it—has bearing here. As carefully formulated as their system was, Protestant scholastics could not eliminate the problems presented by Scripture.

Some points of connection exist between the concerns and approaches of the Reformers and Protestant scholastics and those of feminists today. Motivated by a concern for salvation, Protestant scholastics of that time saw a corrupt tradition that put the ultimate well-being of Christians at stake and sought to correct it by finding a leverage point that could stand independently of that corrupt system. Instead of submitting to a dominating church authority, they turned to nothing less than the word of God, which they recognized and to which they consented because of an inner experience of the Holy Spirit. Feminists also often appeal to an inner experience of God in order to find a point outside of a corrupt tradition for criticizing that tradition, and they will consent to nothing other than what is confirmed by this experience.

Of course, Protestant orthodoxy and feminism also diverge. The orthodox theologians never imagined appealing to inner experience to criticize Scripture itself. Feminists, on the other hand, see Scripture as part of the tradition that needs to be challenged in light of their experience of God. Feminists extend the traditional concern for salvation by adding women's well-being in the world to concern for our ultimate end and then charge that Scripture itself is corrupt insofar as it is androcentric and limits possibilities of salvation in the fuller sense for women. Whereas Protestant scholastics found no error in Scripture, feminists find problems in numerous texts. Whereas Protestant scholastics turned to divine authorship to help solve apparent contradictions through a single, harmonious interpretation, feminists expose the problems of human authorship, and some even look to multiple interpretations as the way to be faithful to what the Holy Spirit is doing in women's lives. Feminists are quick to notice the differences between the orthodox approach to Scripture and the feminist approach. For one, the doctrine of verbal inspiration is incompatible with the feminist concern to criticize the language of the Bible itself. For another, the feminist emphasis on subjective experience over the objective text more closely resembles developments after the orthodox period, such as the Pietist emphasis on individual experience of the spirit or Deist use of reason, than that period itself. Despite these differences, the similarities indicate sufficient reason to pay attention to the kinds of concerns the Protestant scholastics had about Scripture. I will be trying to find a new way to address many of their concerns as I proceed.

In the chapters that follow, two key issues regarding this doctrine of Scripture require especially careful reexamination as I attempt a constructive alternative in light of feminist concerns. The first issue, which I examine in chapter 3, is the problem of revelation itself. Knowledge of God is central to salvation, and if that knowledge of God is not given directly in the words of the Bible themselves, some other mode of revelation has to be explained. For feminists, experience will have to be basic to any idea of revelation. The second issue, which I examine in chapter 6, is the concept of authority. A reexamination of this idea is central to feminist affirmation of the authority of Scripture.

Notes

1. Richard A. Muller, in *Holy Scripture: The Cognitive Foundation of Theology* (vol. 2 of *Post-Reformation Reformed Dogmatics;* Grand Rapids: Baker, 1993), suggests that the connection between the medieval scholastics and Protestant scholastics may be even more pronounced. He cites numerous substantive connections between the ways that medieval scholastics and Protestant scholastics think about Scripture, including matters concerning authority and inspiration.

2. See Richard H. Popkin, *The History of Scepticism from Erasmus to Spinoza* (Berkeley: University of California Press, 1979). Popkin notes that the crisis begun with Luther's questioning of the church coincided in large part with renewed interest in Greek philosophy. Knowledge of and interest in Pyrrhonic and academic skepticism influenced the manner in which Catholics and Protestants debated each other. Michel de Montaigne, for instance, supplied a "defense" against the Reformation, which Popkin calls "Catholic Pyrrhonism." All must be doubted, and Christianity had to be accepted by faith, but a Pyrrhonist could follow Catholicism as the tradition that guided and governed the community.

3. Jeffrey Stout, *Flight from Authority: Religion, Morality, and the Quest for Autonomy* (Notre Dame, Ind.: University of Notre Dame Press, 1981), 55, 57.

4. Richard A. Muller, in *Prolegomena to Theology* (vol. 1 of *Post-Reformation Reformed Dogmatics;* Grand Rapids: Baker, 1987), identifies three periods of Protestant orthodoxy: early orthodoxy, which extends roughly from 1565 to around 1640; high orthodoxy, which begins around 1640 and extends through the remainder of the seventeenth century; and late orthodoxy, which begins around 1700 and lasts until around 1790. For the purposes of this chapter, I will deal primarily with the doctrine of Scripture as it was formulated during the early and high

periods, before orthodoxy felt keenly the impact of rationalism and, in Muller's words, became "less certain of its grasp of the biblical standard" (14–15).

5. It is common to contrast the first Reformers with their Protestant orthodox successors, usually with the intent to show how far Protestantism fell in the seventeenth and eighteenth centuries from its original promise. See, however, Muller's argument in *Prolegomena to Theology*. His basic contention, which receives careful elaboration in his book, is that the Reformers and their successors shared great doctrinal continuity (23) despite clear methodological discontinuity.

6. In this examination, I will look both at Lutheran and at Reformed traditions. My concern is not to identify what is specifically Lutheran or what is specifically Reformed. Differences between the two traditions, as well as differences among the many theologians within either tradition, may well exist and may be important in some contexts. For the purpose of this book, I want to highlight the position that was shared by both these Protestant traditions over against the other positions of the time and that has come to provide the terminology and assumptions for much Protestant thinking about Scripture long after the orthodox period was over.

7. Heinrich Heppe, *Reformed Dogmatics: Set Out and Illustrated from the Sources* (foreword by Karl Barth; ed. Ernst Bizer; trans. G. T. Thomson; London: George Allen & Unwin, 1950), 13.

8. Francis Turretin, *The Doctrine of Scripture* (ed. and trans. John W. Beardslee III; Grand Rapids: Baker, 1981), 98–101.

9. Ibid., 83.

10. Heppe, *Reformed Dogmatics,* 14. Also Heinrich Schmid, *The Doctrinal Theology of the Evangelical Lutheran Church Exhibited and Verified from the Original Sources* (trans. Charles A. Hay and Henry E. Jacobs; 3d ed; Minneapolis: Augsburg, 1961), 81.

11. Schmid, *Doctrinal Theology,* 90–91.

12. Turretin, *Doctrine of Scripture,* 112, 82.

13. Ibid., 89–92.

14. Schmid, *Doctrinal Theology,* 36.

15. Ibid., 30–31, 34; Heppe, *Reformed Dogmatics,* 2–5; Robert D. Preus, *The Theology of Post-Reformation Lutheranism: A Study of Theological Prolegomena* (St. Louis: Concordia, 1970), 130–40.

16. Schmid, *Doctrinal Theology,* 17.

17. Turretin, *Doctrine of Scripture,* 27–30.

18. Schmid, *Doctrinal Theology,* 39.

19. Ibid., 26–27.

20. Muller argues in *Holy Scripture* that Heppe's exposition of the orthodox theologians misleads one to think that the word as *revelatio* is not connected with the concepts of *verbum agraphon* (the unwritten word) and *verbum engraphon* (the written word), which are associated with verbal inspiration. Heppe also gives the mistaken impression, he says, that the orthodox theologians did not maintain the distinction between written and unwritten word that the Reformers before them had done (185, 199, 204–5).

21. Ibid., 39.

22. Ibid., 47.

23. Ibid., 47; Preus, *Theology of Post-Reformation Lutheranism,* 286.

24. Preus, *Theology of Post-Reformation Lutheranism,* 286–87.

25. Schmid, *Doctrinal Theology,* 48.

26. Turretin, *Doctrine of Scripture,* 36.

27. Preus, *Theology of Post-Reformation Lutheranism,* 278–79.

28. Turretin, *Doctrine of Scripture,* 60.

29. See Schmid, *Doctrinal Theology,* 54, 63. Hollaz says that Holy Scriptures "are employed in every language for producing faith in the mind of an unbelieving man, and for confirming it in the mind of a believer; in which respect this authority is called causative or promotive of faith" (54). He also says, "The *causative* authority of the faith differs from the canonical authority of Scripture, because the Scriptures beget divine faith, through the inspired sense, which sense of Scripture remains one and the same, whether expressed in the original idiom of Scripture, or in a translation conformed to the original text" (63, emphasis his).

In his study of Reformed theologians, Muller also notes a twofold distinction with regard to Scripture's authority, but he describes it differently than I have done. He distinguishes between the "divine" and the "regulatory" authority of Scripture, by which he means the divinity and thus validity of Scripture (its authority in itself, or its essential genuineness and power) and its regulatory function in Christian faith and life (its authority *quoad nos,* "as far as us"). To say that Scripture is divine or genuine, though, is a way of saying that its authority is valid but does not describe the kind of authority that it exercises. Muller, then, has not distinguished two types of authority but has only shown that Scripture's normative (or canonical or regulatory) authority is valid because it is divine.

30. Schmid, *Doctrinal Theology,* 51, 55, 56.

31. Heppe, *Reformed Dogmatics,* 530; Schmid, *Doctrinal Theology,* 414.

32. Klaus Scholder, *The Birth of Modern Critical Theology: Origins and Problems of Biblical Criticism in the Seventeenth Century* (trans. John Bowden; Philadelphia: Trinity Press International, 1990), 117.

33. Schmid, *Doctrinal Theology,* 52, 60.

34. Ibid., 210.

35. Philip Melanchthon, *Commentary on Romans* (trans. Fred Kramer; St. Louis: Concordia, 1992), 245.

36. Schmid, *Doctrinal Theology,* 60.

37. Ibid., 62.

38. Turretin, *Doctrine of Scripture,* 211–13.

39. Schmid, *Doctrinal Theology,* 63.

40. Preus, *Theology of Post-Reformation Lutheranism,* 296–97.

41. Ibid., 299.

42. Muller, *Holy Scripture,* 126.

43. Preus, *Theology of Post-Reformation Lutheranism,* 310.

44. Ibid., 309.

45. Turretin, *Doctrine of Scripture,* 167.

46. Schmid, *Doctrinal Theology,* 64–65.

47. Turretin, *Doctrine of Scripture,* 185.

48. Ibid., 186.

49. Preus, *Theology of Post-Reformation Lutheranism,* 312.

50. Schmid, *Doctrinal Theology,* 76–77.

51. Heppe, *Reformed Dogmatics,* 37.

52. Turretin, *Doctrine of Scripture,* 199.

53. Schmid, *Doctrinal Theology,* 78.

54. Turretin, *Doctrine of Scripture,* 200.

55. Schmid, *Doctrinal Theology,* 78–79.

56. Turretin, *Doctrine of Scripture,* 201.

57. Ibid., 113, 126.

58. Ibid., 130.

59. Ibid., 131–32.
60. Muller, *Holy Scripture,* 353.
61. Schmid, *Doctrinal Theology,* 503.
62. Preus, *Theology of Post-Reformation Lutheranism,* 368.
63. Schmid, *Doctrinal Theology,* 63.

CHAPTER THREE

The Experience of Revelation

Feminist theology has often spoken of its insights into the condition of women and men as revelatory. Along with this revelatory awareness have frequently come claims for new interpretations of the Bible, a new attitude toward the Bible, perhaps even a new canon itself, and new understandings of God. The "newness" of feminist thinking, coupled with the claim that these insights are revelatory, presses the question of the relation of feminist theology to the historic Christian faith. Feminist concern to use different language for God is sometimes taken to be a break with some essential, revelatory element of Christianity. Donald Bloesch, for instance, takes "Father" to be an unsubstitutable name for God because he understands it to be central to understanding revelation in Jesus Christ. Since Jesus is the full, final, and definitive revelation of God, then the denial of this understanding of God constitutes a denial of revelation itself.[1] In some cases, feminist theology is taken not only to deny the definitive revelation of Jesus Christ but to promote a "new revelation."[2] The issue of "new revelation" is not confined to feminism, but clearly feminists are concerned to promote a new understanding of and a new situation for women. How does this new understanding and this new way of living together with men relate to the faith that has been passed down for centuries?

At the heart of this discussion is the concept of revelation itself, which we must explore before taking up the question of newness. Even before the emergence of a vital feminist movement, Christians disagreed about central issues regarding revelation, and to this date we share no consensus on how to resolve certain key problems. Among the disputed points are the relationship between reason and revelation, the distinction between general and special revelation, the mode of revelation, and even what God intends to communicate. Feminist theology, then, has not disquieted an already settled state of affairs, nor should it be expected to resolve questions that have not been successfully resolved through centuries of debate. Feminist theology, though, can add to the ongoing theological conversation certain insights into the way that various understandings of revelation affect women. Although the traditional points of dispute still have importance in larger theological discussion, women have a perspective that needs to be shared so that the theological work on this concept does not ignore the needs of women.

A comprehensive treatment of the concept of revelation and all of the epistemological issues that any claim about revelation raises is beyond the purview of this book, but some orientation to the issue of revelation as it has bearing on the feminist questions I am pursuing is necessary. Although various models of revelation exist, two have particular relevance for feminist theology: propositional revelation, which has been the basis of numerous problems for women, and existential revelation, which intersects in important ways with feminist concerns. Also relevant to the discussion is a proposal made by feminist biblical scholar Sandra Schneiders. She has considered the issue of revelation not only in light of feminist concerns but also in light of current methods of biblical interpretation.

The Concept of Revelation

Despite the lack of consensus on any particular way of understanding revelation, certain elements persist through various treatments of revelation and serve as orienting points for our task here. The central idea in any understanding of revelation is that through some means, we are given knowledge of God that we would not have had simply on our own. The Greek word translated as "revelation" in the New Testament is *apokalypsis*, and it indicates an "uncovering" or "unveiling." Where once something was hidden, now it is revealed. It is visible, and therefore knowable, in a way that it was not before. This idea of uncovering something hidden is especially clear in the case of special revelation, which is often construed as communication of special, supernatural truths that could not be known by us otherwise. In this case, the giftlike nature of revelation is apparent. Even for general revelation, though, one can affirm the idea that God is granting some kind of knowledge of God's self. The claim that such knowledge is generally available does not subtract from its character as *revelation*. Regardless of human use of reason in grasping this knowledge, the knowledge itself would not be there for the having if not for God's gracious desire to make something known. As the idea of general experience has become more problematic and the contextual nature of human knowledge has become more apparent, it has become more difficult to draw a clear line between general and special revelation. Although questions regarding the possibility of general revelation or the possibility of revelation outside Christian faith are important, they are beyond the scope of this book. My focus here is on the Bible's role in what has usually been called "special revelation."

Christians have stressed the importance of special revelation because of its role in salvation. Christian faith presupposes a problem in the human condition that needs to be overcome, and revelation is key to setting us straight about our situation and about God's activity to offer us a way to be whole, as we were created to be. Through revelation, God provides for us what we need to know in order for us to see clearly and respond to God's offer of salvation. Because so much hangs on revelation, its truth and reliability become extremely important. Of course, the ultimate ground for the truth of God's revelation is God, whose goodness and infallibility ensure that we will be presented salvific knowledge without fault or deception. God does not grant us all knowledge through revelation, but God provides for us what we need to know in order to be saved, and God does so in a trustworthy manner.

Revelation's giftlike character indicates something very important about its very nature. Because gifts are both given and received, revelation is fundamentally two-sided. Knowledge is not successfully communicated unless it is both presented and grasped, and human reception is an indispensable component of revelation.[3] Whether that human reception is relatively passive, in the case of a "dictation" theory, or relatively active, so that human distortion may creep in, is of course a disputed point. What is clear, though, is that God's effort to be known is not complete without some human receiving. Furthermore, the situation of the human receiver plays some role in the way that revelation takes shape. Even the dictation model depicts God as accommodating God's own understanding to the understanding of the writers. When one allows for more human involvement in reception, one also allows for more interpretive activity on the part of the authors. The chances for misinterpretation also increase. The more one acknowledges human activity, the more one also has to acknowledge that even if God always, without fault or deception, attempts to communicate saving truth, we do not always grasp that truth perfectly.

The matter of human reception can be viewed from a number of angles, and these various elements often contribute to disagreement about the "locus" of revelation, that is, where and when revelation actually takes place. For instance, one can speculate about the way in which an individual or community received knowledge of God in the past, such as through mystical experiences, resurrection appearances, or direct conversations with God. Whatever knowledge may be received through any means, though, remains entrapped in a particular place and time and thus becomes ineffective unless it is passed on in some way. So, testimony or witness becomes an essential way in which others receive knowledge about God, and recording and handing down the knowledge of previous generations has become an essential role of tradition in the church. In Protestant theology, though, receiving past information, while important, has never been sufficient by itself as saving knowledge of God. Only when this knowledge has been appropriated personally through faith does knowledge of God become truly salvific. Revelation, then, only becomes effective in the life of the Christian when she or he appropriates it existentially. Events or experiences in the past, the records of those events or experiences, and the present experience of comprehension all involve receiving knowledge in some way, and all at some time have been called revelation. In dispute is the relative importance of each of these aspects of reception; in fact, sometimes they are pitted against each other. In part, the current controversy surrounding feminist theology involves the question of whether present experience and knowledge of God should be more highly valued than past experience and knowledge of God.

How one negotiates the problems of identifying the locus of revelation depends in part on what one takes revelation to be. To say that revelation is "disclosure" of something that could not be known otherwise does not by itself determine what is disclosed. Two of the important options that have bearing on feminist theology are the disclosure of verbal communication and the disclosure of God's self, or the disclosure of conceptual information and the disclosure of relationship.

DISCLOSURE OF VERBAL COMMUNICATION

The understanding of revelation in the Protestant orthodox doctrine of Scripture may be called "propositional." In this view, revelation is verbal communication by which the authors of Scripture recorded exactly what God wanted to say to us, so Scripture reveals knowledge of God through propositions, or statements that claim to make true assertions. On our own, we are unable to know that which is necessary for our salvation, so God reveals in the Bible supernatural truths to which we have no other access. This understanding of revelation relates to an understanding of Scripture that emerged because of a particular polemic with the Roman Catholic Church at a particular time in the church's history, which is not to say that prior to the Reformation Christians never believed that the Bible contained true propositions. They did. Indeed, pre-Reformation Christians understood many assertions in the Bible as statements of fact and did not question their truth.[4] After all, these Christians considered the Bible to be a faithful record of God's actions in the world, especially of God's involvement with the people of Israel and of the life, death, and resurrection of the Lord Jesus Christ. Still, even though Christians assumed that the Bible recorded certain important events in history, they had no developed doctrine that claimed inerrancy for every word in the Bible until after the Reformation. Prior to that time, theologians were quite willing to read the Bible for a spiritual meaning beyond the literal meaning of a text, particularly when that text proved problematic on the literal level.[5] The reliability of God's revelation in Scripture did not stand or fall with the truth of every biblical assertion taken at face value. Only when Protestants needed to assert the authority of Scripture over the church did the truth of every proposition become a central commitment that they had to defend.

The Protestant version of propositional revelation, though, is not the only one. In its Roman Catholic form, doctrinal assertions can also take on the status of propositional revelation. As in Protestant orthodoxy, this approach acknowledges the need for supernatural truth to be revealed to us, but that revelation is not strictly contained in the Bible. The Bible needs to be interpreted, and the magisterium in its teaching office bears responsibility for that interpretation. We have reliable knowledge of God through the official dogmas of the church, which have made clear the proper understanding of Scripture. For instance, the Bible itself does not present a fully developed doctrine of the Trinity, but God has supplied us with a proper understanding of the nature of God's self through the divinely guided conciliar decisions of the church. The Roman Catholic version of propositional revelation relies on a two-source theory of divine revelation, which has its roots in the Council of Trent but was developed fully over time. According to this view, Scripture and tradition constitute parallel and equal sources of revelation. In the neo-Scholasticism that prevailed between 1850 and 1950, Roman Catholics shared the Protestant concern for verbal communication by God but extended it to dogma. Revelation is conceptual knowledge that is transmitted by words (or speech), and the assertions that present this conceptual knowledge to us require our assent. Since the deposit of faith is found not only in the Bible but also in those dogmas that clarify the biblical message, doctrinal propositions were key to providing us with saving knowledge of God.[6]

In either form, propositional revelation emphasizes two forms of human reception: the way that humans received knowledge of God in the past (whether through dictated biblical texts or divinely guided conciliar decisions) and the faithful transmission of that knowledge in the passing down of the Bible or doctrine in the church. Propositional revelation in both forms presents enormous problems for women. Intense focus on assertions, which are true as they are stated and to which the only proper response is assent, leaves no room for the kinds of challenges and questions that feminists raise about those very assertions, whether they be biblical or doctrinal. If proscriptions against women's participation in certain activities or descriptions of God as Father or portrayals of women's virtues have been delivered verbally and directly by God, then it is impossible to challenge those assertions without at the same time challenging God's truthfulness and authority. This emphasis on assent to propositions leads to a dichotomous choice: either these words are in fact revelation to which one must assent, or they are not. If they are, then the very act of questioning is out of order. If they are not, then they should be rejected or replaced with a more adequate expression of God's truth. Such polarized options lead easily to fierce and acrimonious debate.

Quite apart from feminist concerns, though, propositional revelation has come under serious questioning with the rise of historical criticism. Although it is defended by some scholars (and largely assumed by many ordinary Christians), the understanding of Scripture that lies behind a commitment to propositional revelation has largely changed in the academic world.[7] Biblical scholars have learned to read the Bible as a document shaped by its historical situation. Rather than explaining differences, contradictions, omissions, and even factual errors by an appeal to God's accommodation to the understanding of the authors, scholars have come to acknowledge the authors' active involvement in the selection, editing, and writing of biblical texts. Feminist scholars have made good use of historical critical insights for understanding, challenging, and relativizing patriarchal understandings of women in the Bible. Once verbal descriptions, proscriptions, and prescriptions are seen as historically conditioned statements rather than God's direct communication, these assertions are all open to questioning and do not require unquestioning assent.

But feminists have also recognized that words, even if understood in historical context, cannot be taken for granted. Efforts to promote inclusive language in biblical translations, worship, official documents, and our conversations with each other find their basis in the recognition that words can hurt. Not only may they be offensive and inaccurate, but they may negatively shape our understanding of ourselves and others. In contrast, words can also shape our understandings in positive, important ways. The point of inclusive language, after all, is to broaden our understandings. Feminists who remain in the church do so in part because we recognize that somehow the words of the Bible have managed to convey to us an understanding of ourselves and of God that transcends patriarchy. In any case, feminists cannot afford to ignore language, and one of the important developments in feminist theology is an attention to language about God that has been informed by philosophical accounts of metaphor. To say that language about God is metaphorical,[8] in the ways that will be explained below, is to acknowledge the revelatory power that words have to disclose something to us but at the same time to recognize the distinction between the words themselves and what they disclose. The latter point allows a critical stance toward these metaphors that propositional revelation itself does not allow.

Both Sallie McFague and Janet Martin Soskice have examined theories about how metaphors work in order to understand better the way in which we use language about God. Soskice's work is especially helpful in understanding the revelatory power that words have, and McFague's work represents typical feminist use of insights about metaphor to make critical judgments about certain biblical images for God. According to Soskice, "metaphor is that figure of speech whereby we speak about one thing in terms which are seen to be suggestive of another."[9] Stating positively what metaphor is, even in this most general way, involves certain negations (e.g., metaphor is *not* a physical object, *not* a mental act). In fact, saying what metaphor is not becomes as important as saying what it is. Various theories have treated metaphor as ornamental speech or as fairly simple comparison, but both McFague and Soskice argue that metaphor is much more. Although McFague and Soskice finally rely on different philosophical accounts of metaphor to make their points, both agree that metaphor adds to our understanding by producing new and unique meaning. Metaphor, then, is not simply descriptive or emotive but cognitive.[10] It discloses conceptual understanding, and when used for things divine, it has important implications for understanding revelation.

Soskice builds her argument for the conceptual nature of metaphor by showing the way in which it discloses new understandings of things in our ordinary world. To begin, Soskice points out that metaphor as a speech act gains its meaning at the level of the complete utterance, not at the level of the individual words that make it up. Some theories about metaphor attempt to explain meaning by concentrating on its component parts. Comparison theories, for instance, try to show how one word in the metaphor illumines another word in the metaphor (e.g., "This house is a beehive"). The comparison works for us because we know something about houses and something about beehives so that we can see the similarities between them. Even more sophisticated interaction theories, which seek to go beyond simple comparison, focus on how the individual words in the metaphor transform our understanding of each. For instance, the metaphor "Children are the sunshine of the world" may leave us with a different understanding of "children" and "sunshine" when we begin to draw out the similarities. Children may seem more bright and warm, and at the same time sunshine may seem more innocent and playful.[11] Soskice points out, though, that sometimes metaphors bring together thoughts rather than words. In the metaphor "A stubborn and unconquerable flame/Crept in his vein and drinks the streams of life," the two thoughts brought together are about fever and flame; however, fever is not mentioned explicitly.[12] Furthermore, the subject of the metaphor is neither fever nor flame but the physical state of the sick person. Together, the idea of fever and the idea of flame provide us with insight into the person's condition that we would not have had otherwise. Neither a clinical description of fever nor a comparison with the heat of a flame alone could produce the conceptual and emotional awareness of his debilitating condition. Soskice claims that we understand something new through the metaphor, so it functions cognitively for us.

Metaphors, Soskice says, depend on models for the associations they bring about in our minds. Unlike metaphors, models need not be linguistic. A model is an object or state of affairs in terms of which another object or state of affairs is viewed. For instance, a toy train is a model (homeomorphic) of a full-size locomotive, or a computer is a model (paramorphic) for the brain. In the latter case, the model provides a frame by which our understanding of the brain can be developed through metaphor, as when one speaks of "neural programming."[13] Although they are not themselves linguistic, models provide the associations that give rise to such linguistic developments. From "neural programming," one can go on to consider if the brain gives "feedback" or has "data banks." As they build on the associations provided by models, metaphors enlarge our lexicons and actually expand "the conceptual apparatus with which we work."[14] Thus, metaphor becomes part of the way we interpret our world. It allows us to say something we could not say otherwise and opens up conceptual avenues for our understanding.

Here, Soskice begins to link metaphors from daily life with language about God. She does not make the claim that all language for God is metaphorical. Although she recognizes the need to indicate that human language does have to be stretched in some way to apply to God, she argues that analogy is the better category to explain much of our language about God. Soskice reserves the category of metaphor for language that produces an imaginative strain that generates new perspectives beyond our ordinary understanding.[15] This specific attention to metaphor, then, bears a close relationship to revelation, which is a way of knowing God that provides us with understanding we can have in no other way. Soskice's predominant concern is to show how metaphorical language for God can refer to something real, so her efforts center on examining questions of meaning, reference, and reality depiction. One aspect of her careful argument relates to the purview of this book: how her understanding of metaphor connects with the theological idea of revelation.

Referential language has its basis in experience of some sort, and metaphorical language for God is rooted in religious experience. By "experience,"

Soskice means both specific, dramatic experiences (e.g., mystical or conversion experiences) and more diffuse, ordinary experiences of daily life that prompt religious reflection (e.g., the experience of finitude that leads us to wonder about the infinite). In addition, referential language takes shape in a particular communal context, which has shared assumptions, interests, and vocabulary, and again, metaphorical language for God is no different. When religious experience comes to expression, it does so in the vocabulary that the community has available to it. Whether attempting to give an account of mystical experience or trying to put into words some experience shared in common with others, religious teachers draw from models that are familiar in order to speak metaphorically. To speak of God as "spirit," for instance, might use wind as a model for God's presence so that one may begin to understand God's activity according to the associations that one has with wind. It is not necessary to believe that this metaphor was given in some cosmic disclosure to see its relevance and appropriateness for helping us understand God. Soskice believes it is more likely that religious teachers through the centuries have been seeking to express experiences of God in halting approximations, making use of the models available to them. Their metaphorical speech helps others to perceive God more clearly, and so it has cognitive power. Over time, some models and metaphors become preferred to others, but a rich assortment in the tradition of the community always exists. This accretion of images, all approximations rather than precise descriptions, but confirmed as enlightening by generations of believers, makes up a large part of what we consider revelation.[16]

Revelation, then, involves communication, and words are crucial to that communication, but revelation is not "verbal communication" in the sense that propositional views have claimed. The words are not themselves identified as revelation. Instead, revelation is the insight that one gains about God through the words as the metaphors prompt and shape one's understanding. One's tacit awareness may be heightened. One may gain a fuller appreciation for the experience of God. One may begin to draw out the implications of that experience. In various ways, the metaphors "communicate," but not by way of assertions. The proper response to this kind of revelation is, not assent, but imaginative grasp of the associations created by the metaphor.

Words, then, are crucial to revelation, but they must also be qualified. Soskice points out that religious people generally recognize that these metaphors do not capture fully what they want to say about God. She also remarks that any metaphor can be pushed to the point of absurdity. For example, using billiard balls as a model for gas molecules does not mean that the molecules are made of plastic. Similarly, using "father" as a metaphor for God does not mean that God has a wife. There is a certain "failure," then, in any metaphorical

language about God. Soskice and McFague understand the extent of that failure, and thus the possibility for a critical stance toward certain metaphors,
somewhat differently. Although every metaphor is revisable in principle, Soskice believes that some metaphors have worked so well in communicating an
understanding of God that they have become more than simple metaphors
and are "almost emblematic."[17] Not only do they interpret God to us, but they
provide the descriptive language with which our experiences of God may be
interpreted. Although she seems to share many feminist concerns, Soskice is
cautious about questioning the use of certain metaphors for God, such as
"father," that have become fundamental to Christian tradition, and she seems
to prefer a revitalized, nonpatriarchal understanding of what those metaphors
mean.[18] In that sense, she does exercise a qualified critical interpretation of
the dominant metaphors in Christianity. McFague's criticisms, though, run
deeper.

McFague presses the point that metaphors depend on imaginative strain in
order to produce new understanding. Many metaphors for God have lost that
imaginative strain, and we need to search for new metaphors that can enliven
our understanding of God. McFague uses the word "model" differently than
Soskice does, meaning instead a metaphor with "staying power."[19] She takes
the metaphor of God the Father, for instance, to be a model in that it has provided a pattern for understanding God that has been relatively comprehensive
and long lasting. This model, while useful in the past, has become stale. So
familiar that it no longer disorients us from our conventional ways of thinking, this model no longer shocks us into seeing the God-world relationship in
a new way. Furthermore, and more important for McFague's concerns, it
tends to be co-opted by conventional thinking so that it supports, rather than
dismantles, the hierarchical understanding of the God-world relation that
threatens to lead us to nuclear and environmental disaster. When placed next
to metaphors of God as king or lord, the metaphor of father communicates
less about the nearness of God than it does about distance. In order to recap-
ture the imaginative strain a good metaphor needs, and to find ways of talking
about God that suit the new sensibility of our age, McFague suggests experi-
menting with new metaphors, such as God as mother, lover, and friend.

Although McFague clearly wants to move beyond the dominance of certain biblical metaphors for God, she is not leaving the Bible behind. In two
ways, Scripture serves as a source for the criteria that determine which
metaphors to use. First, the rich, varied, patchwork collection of images in the
Bible, each emerging in a particular time and place to communicate God's
offer of salvation, shows us we should also seek images that communicate
God's offer of salvation in our own time and place. Second, the story of Jesus
serves as the paradigm for every new image. This story reveals God's relation

to the world. Since his story shows a destabilizing, inclusive, nonhierarchical vision for creation, we should look for metaphors that correspond to that vision.[20]

For McFague as for Soskice, metaphors disclose an understanding of God. "King" discloses a different understanding than "friend," so the choice of metaphor becomes crucial. Whereas propositional revelation insists on retaining the images of God that are presented in the Bible, McFague argues that images for God do not need to come straight from the Bible in order to convey the crucial biblical understanding of God, which one finds, not in the metaphors themselves, but in the story of Jesus. In fact, in our time, many central biblical images do quite the opposite. We need new sets of associations in order to evoke the God-world relation that Jesus demonstrated. In one sense, the content of our understanding will be new as we imaginatively draw out the implications of the new metaphors, but in another sense, the content of our understanding will be quite old because these new associations are bringing us to perceive God's relationship to us according to the insights that Jesus himself displayed.

Relationship is, after all, the point of using metaphors for God. As important as it may be to demonstrate the cognitive nature of metaphor, intellectual knowing is not finally the point of revelation. As Protestants have stressed from the beginning, the crucial point of human reception is the point at which this conceptual knowledge "hits home" so that one's relationship to God and to those around takes on a new character. The understanding of propositional revelation that early Protestants developed had not initially been intended to substitute for that experience. Instead, it was a way of explaining how Scripture reliably bears the witness needed to bring about this relationship. Through words, one may come to an experience of God and realize a salvific relationship. What is communicated through them is not simply information but God's very self.

DISCLOSURE OF GOD'S SELF

As it became more and more difficult to defend a propositional understanding of revelation in light of developments in many branches of scholarship (both secular and religious), many scholars sought for another way of understanding revelation. Even if it had been born to serve other concerns, propositional revelation itself soon came to be the focal point of much theological discussion. Commitment to verbal communication could be worked out in a variety of ways, some more capable of development in the modern world than others, but those who championed Enlightenment concerns largely took propositional revelation to be untenable in light of modern knowledge.

Liberal theology in the nineteenth century, for instance, tried to offer an alternative to belief in propositions by grounding the truth of Christianity in the subjective awareness of God that belongs to human experience. In the early twentieth century, many theologians saw that propositional revelation stood as a barrier to maintaining the truth of Christianity, but they were also dissatisfied with the liberal alternative, which seemed to reduce revelation to a vague, romantic idea of experience itself. Instead, they began to develop the idea of revelation as an event that disclosed, not propositions, but God's very self.

Understanding revelation as God's self-disclosure became the dominant assumption of a large number of theologians of the time, including Karl Barth, Rudolf Bultmann, H. Richard Niebuhr, John Baillie, and Emil Brunner. Despite this generally shared starting point, these theologians developed their understanding of revelation in different ways because of other commitments that they held, and it is not possible to generalize about shared conclusions.[21] Their debates are well known, and they indicate the complexity involved in moving from a simple definition of revelation to any developed theological point. For the purposes of this book, I want to examine two of these theologians as examples of how this understanding of God's self-disclosure was developed: Bultmann and Niebuhr. Both of these theologians provide a description of the kind of experience that was revelatory, both allow for critical distance from propositional views of revelation, and both have ideas that have become important in further theological development in feminist studies. They can help, then, in identifying some of the key issues for thinking about revelation now.

In his lectures on "Theological Encyclopedia," delivered from 1926 to 1936, Bultmann deals directly with the problem of revelation, and the basic position that he worked out there continues to appear more indirectly in his later work. Bultmann's concern for the knowability of God is connected to the particular problem of his time regarding the adequacy of theology to be an intellectual discipline at all. Theology has its own object of study, he says, but this object has to be specified carefully because it is constantly in danger of being misconstrued. Its object is not doctrine (against Protestant orthodoxy's emphasis on the *fides quae creditur,* or "the faith which is believed"), nor is it the human spirit or faith itself (against liberalism's emphasis on the *fides qua creditur,* or "the faith by which something is believed"), nor is it humanity's thinking about God (against positivism's emphasis on empirical study of the world). Instead, the proper object of study for theology is God as God is accessible to us through faith, or God together with faith.[22] In other words, Bultmann brings the *fides quae creditur* and the *fides qua creditur* together, and he also redefines the *fides quae creditur* as God rather than doctrine. Bultmann grounds his view of revelation in this understanding of faith's relation to God.

Even after defining theology's object of study, Bultmann still has to defend this object as something that can be known. Positivism held that the only real knowledge anyone could have is empirical knowledge, but Bultmann called reducing knowledge simply to empiricism a mistake. Genuine knowledge, Bultmann says, is defined by its object, and the object gives with itself its own criterion of truth. Just as mathematics and art require different criteria for assessing their objects of study, so too does theology. In one sense, God is an "object" of study; that is, God is that which is studied in theology. In another sense, however, God is not an object at all. God is not, as Bultmann says, at our disposal, to be controlled or mastered. In fact, God is the supreme subject, who addresses us in every moment and summons us to authentic existence. Bultmann understands "existence" as much more than simply "being there." Humans, unlike bumblebees and frogs, have our lives as tasks; in other words, we have our lives before us in such a way that we are constantly deciding how to actualize ourselves as humans. We express the most profound aspect of our humanity through those decisions. As the Lord of all things, God claims us in every moment and summons us to live in love in every concrete situation. Moment by moment, then, we choose the character of our existence, either authentic or inauthentic, as we respond to this claim. Because God is a subject who addresses us, and because this address presents us with a decision, God's "objectivity" is of a special kind, unlike other objects in the world. Because God is the ultimate subject, God is never simply available to be studied in the way that ordinary items in the world are. The *idea* of God, Bultmann says, is present to human existence itself in that we can conceive of the question of God apart from faith and we know implicitly that in our decisions we do or do not live authentically. However, *God* as the subject who actually encounters us in such a way that our situation is clarified, so that we know the answer to the question of God and we know whether our decisions have in fact realized authentic existence, is seen only in faith, and this seeing constitutes revelation. The encounter with God's own self is the disclosure that demonstrates that God can be truly known.[23]

To say that God can be truly known does not mean that God can be completely known. Even in disclosing Godself, God remains subject and thus is never simply laid bare as knowledge for us to "possess" in toto. As Bultmann describes it, revelation is both a mediating of knowledge and an event. Something unknown is made known, but for Bultmann this knowledge is decidedly not propositional and is never fully accomplished. Propositions are static communications, but revelation never stays still. As an eschatological event, revelation has the character of "already" and "not yet." Revelation takes place *in actu*, that is, in the present moment as one perceives God by faith.[24] It happens, then, but it has never simply happened. What is "known" is, not information, but God as the subject who is being encountered. God remains subject and never becomes simply the object of our knowledge. Furthermore, God's revelation is never finished because God always stands before us to be encountered again. Fixed texts and doctrines lose the "not yet" side of this tension. Still, once one has recognized that revelation is not propositional, in the sense that Protestant orthodoxy understood it to be, it does not follow that one can say nothing about the meaning of revelation. Bultmann himself describes the nature of this encounter with God in terms of sin and forgiveness, and he presents an understanding of Jesus Christ as central to understanding God's act of love. These descriptions, though, even in the form of assertions, do not themselves constitute revelation.

To recognize this point does not deny the significance of past experiences of God. The encounter with God that our forebears had leads them to witness to that encounter through preaching, and in that sense something is "handed on." Yet preaching is more than a report, more than passing on propositional knowledge. I will borrow Bultmann's own example of friendship to show the distinction he wants to make.[25] I do not make a friend by studying friendship. It is possible to describe and analyze friendship, and I may learn a great deal about friendship that way, but I do not simply by this objective knowledge come to have friends. In order to have and to be a friend, I must enter into an existential relationship with someone, a relationship that involves trust and decisions. The character of my friendship, whether authentic or inauthentic, will be determined by the way I actually choose over and over again to relate to my friend, not by any intellectual study. In fact, one of the fastest ways to kill a friendship is to overanalyze it. Similarly, the point of preaching is not simply to tell about God but to proclaim afresh the possibility of a new encounter with God, a present disclosure to this person in this time and place. Each of us, then, has the same original relation to revelation that our forebears have had, so in this sense revelation is "ongoing."[26] What is new about revelation from this point of view is not its content, because it is always the same God who is disclosed regardless of the time and place, but its character as happening now.

For Bultmann, the Bible must be interpreted properly in order for its proclamation to be heard as an invitation to receive this disclosure of God's self in faith. Since revelation consists of encounter rather than propositions, biblical texts should be understood as bearing witness to the possibility of authentic life before God rather than as giving empirical descriptions of historical occurrences. Bultmann's argument for demythologizing aims to show that the truth of the Bible depends, not on its accuracy as historiography, or as a record of empirical history, but rather on its ability to present us with the eschatological event of God's address to us in our personal, or existential, history.[27] Biblical texts are mythological because they use the language of one kind of history (empirical) to speak about how God meets us in another kind of history (existential).[28] Demythologizing does not eliminate myth; rather, it interprets biblical language so as to bring out its own intention.[29] Gaining critical distance from the text, then, actually enables it to function as a medium for revelation. To take biblical texts as empirical descriptions is to miss their point. One puts oneself in a position to hear their witness only when one recognizes that the witness presents, not facts, but a call to live in authentic relationship with God.

For Bultmann, then, revelation is clearly located in one's present reception. The content of revelation is God, not assertions, so disclosure is existential rather than informational. In this sense, the newness of revelation is not informational either. Revelation is ongoing in the sense that God encounters us again and again, not in the sense that we have communication of new facts. The Bible serves as a medium for the encounter with God, which is revelatory, but the Bible is not itself revelation. Furthermore, the Bible must be interpreted carefully in order for it to serve as this kind of medium. The distinction between empirical history and existential history forms the basis for appropriate interpretation because it allows us to recognize inaccuracies and contradictions in the Bible's description of events without calling into question its ability to proclaim God to us. Faith perception, not sense perception, is at the heart of revelation.

H. Richard Niebuhr also distinguishes between aspects of history when he talks about revelation to show its relevance to modern theology. Just as Bultmann understands revelation to be grounded in God and faith taken together, Niebuhr understands revelation to be grounded in God and history taken together, but his claim can only be understood in light of his careful argument of the way history is involved in revelation.[30] In *The Meaning of Revelation*, Niebuhr seeks a critical reappraisal of revelation in light of our awareness of historical relativism. He openly acknowledges that Christians often appeal to revelation in order to support authoritative structures, but he argues that revelation does not have to be tied to reactionary conservatism.[31] To speak of revelation now, one must come to terms with the insight of our time that "all knowledge is conditioned by the standpoint of the knower."[32] Revelation is an encounter with God, but it takes place from within a point of view. His distinction between internal history and external history allows him to explain the way that encounter is shaped by a Christian standpoint.

The problem of relativism has arisen, Niebuhr says, in many areas of learning, but the area with which he is most concerned is history. Every human being occupies a spatiotemporal point of view, and Niebuhr calls history the "medium" in which we live. It is just as impossible for us to step outside history as it is for a fish to live out of water.[33] One cannot seek, then, any kind of understanding that is completely general because all one's knowledge will be conditioned by one's historical experience. Our ideas are shaped by the words we use to express them, and language is always particular and historical. There is no escaping the particularity of human thinking, and thus no escaping relativism, but Niebuhr does not push this idea to the point of utter skepticism or subjectivism. He says instead, "Without a universal language there can be no universal thought, though every particular language expresses ideas about universals."[34] He wants to walk a path between totalitarianism and solipsism by acknowledging the impact of our point of view on our ideas while also recognizing the need and possibility of reflecting critically on our perspectival knowledge. He applies this task to understanding revelation by examining the standpoint that Christians have when they make universal claims about God. Christian faith is, he says, "objectively relativistic," by which he means that it has confidence in an independent reality at the same time that it knows its assertions about that reality will be meaningful only to those who share this standpoint.[35] Revelation, then, involves understanding God from a point of view, and Niebuhr's task is to explain what that point of view means for Christians.

The point of view that Christian faith occupies can be understood only when one recognizes that revelation takes place in the history of selves, or internal history.[36] Events, Niebuhr observes, may be seen historically from the "outside" or from the "inside." By "outside," he clearly cannot mean getting outside history altogether since it is the medium in which we live. I do not think that Niebuhr is committed here to a notion of complete objectivity or some "God's eye" view of the world. Rather, he is indicating the kind of perspective we have on certain events within history, a perspective that involves an existential distance from that which is being studied. One can observe events with a certain detachment, as when one studies the development of a movement or idea impersonally, that is, without regard for the significance it might have for one's own life. Even human beings may be studied in such a way by abstracting from their hopes, fears, and motivations and seeking only data that may be described apart from such existential involvement. Niebuhr describes this kind of history as external because one treats these items as outside of and apart from oneself. Internal history, on the other hand, does not simply deal in succession of events or data. Rather than abstracting from

events in history, it is involved with them. Rather than simply looking for
cause and effect, it seeks to understand the relevance of an event for one's own
destiny. Rather than seeing events in a series that recede into the past, it
understands that we remain connected to those events in an organic and
social way. Those who have gone before us make up our community as surely
as those who are alive now do. We share in their aspirations and failures, and
the consequences of their actions continue to unfold in our lives. Although
internal history is in one sense the history of a "self," in another sense it is
strikingly communal. One "self" is associated with other "selves" in such an
intimate way that who others are shapes who one becomes. One belongs to a
community that shares a past, present, and future. The human association
that constitutes internal history is marked, not by abstraction, but by participation, and we become who we are by our involvement in it.

Niebuhr claims that when the first evangelists and their successors pointed
to the connection between faith and history, it was connection with this kind
of history that mattered.[37] Christian faith is confessional, not detached. Niebuhr imagines that when pressed to explain what all their parables and
prophecies and remembrances were about, the early preachers would have to
say, "What we mean is this event which happened among us and to us."[38] Fundamentally, they would have to tell the story of their lives because the event
that they wanted to explain took place in their lives, namely, that they had
come into relationship with God through Jesus Christ. They were not trying
to relate an impersonal event that could be studied with detachment. They
were trying to relate something that had taken place in their own personal,
internal histories. The sphere in which revelation takes place is internal history because that is the aspect of history in which the relevance of events is
understood. A chain of events does not constitute revelation, though it is
often misunderstood in this way, but rather the meaning that an event or
events have for us is what constitutes it.[39] However, Niebuhr explains that if
revelation cannot be equated with external history, neither can it be equated
with all of internal history. While many events have meaning for us, not every
meaningful event is revelatory. "Revelation," he says, "means for us that part of
our inner history which illuminates the rest of it and which is itself intelligible." It is like coming across in a book a "luminous sentence" that suddenly
clarifies the whole argument.[40] With this insight, we are able to see a pattern
that makes sense, that clarifies obscurities, and that supersedes any other patterns we may have vainly attempted to make before. Because it makes things
intelligible, revelation is not, as many have claimed, opposed to reason. Revelation is intimately connected to reason, but this connection is better
described as "reason of the heart," as Niebuhr says, than of the head because it

is personal rather than impersonal.[41] "Head" and "heart" are not in conflict here. Niebuhr is simply indicating, as he did with external and internal history, that the kind of intelligibility revelation brings is practical and participatory, not detached and observing. Revelation depends less on logic than it does on imagination, although it is not thereby illogical. It does bring intelligibility, but in a way that involves us as whole selves and not merely as thinkers.

The pattern that revelation provides involves value and belief. Any internal history depends on believing and valuing because beliefs and values supply the framework for the way we understand the relevance to our own lives of the things that are happening around us. Because we seek this relevance, human beings must believe in something; we must value and live our lives toward something. That aspect of human existence is inescapable, and it is the essence of what it means to "have faith." Recalling Luther's statement that whatever our hearts cling to becomes our god, Niebuhr argues that in our internal histories we inevitably direct ourselves toward gods or toward God, toward "evil imaginations of the heart" or toward the right kind of imaginations provided by revelation.[42] Because it is inevitable that we will employ patterns for understanding our lives, we come to develop understandings of ourselves and of others whether we have revelation or not. Those patterns, though, that we develop without revelation are inadequate and even "evil" in the sense that they lead to destruction because of their inadequacy. Such patterns might arrange human lives according to who is "superior" or "inferior" or might cause one to see oneself as the center of meaning for every action. Revelation enlarges the adequacy of our patterns. As it unifies and uncovers more of our remembered past, it brings more people into the pattern and provides us with a vision toward which we can live our futures. While we never gain through revelation the view that God has on the world, we gain more of God's perspective on ourselves and others so that we may live with patterns of meaning that more adequately employ the values and beliefs God would have us hold.

But revelation is more than simply gaining a pattern of beliefs and values. That pattern itself is grounded fundamentally in a relationship, namely, in God's self-disclosure as the one who knows, authors, judges, and saves us.[43] Our present values are overturned, not simply because we are presented with another option, but because we experience ourselves in a relationship that calls our former values into question. We know ourselves to be known by God so that all our failures and achievements are brought to light. We find ourselves to be valued, not simply by another finite individual, but by the universal God, who values others as deeply as ourselves. In this recognition lies both love and judgment, for we find that we have not valued either others or ourselves as God values us. What we discover about ourselves and about God in this encounter is not radically discontinuous with what we have known before. For instance, Niebuhr acknowledges with Immanuel Kant that we seem to know our moral duty prior to any religious articulation of that duty as God's will. What we have in revelation is, not the deliverance of moral law (or right beliefs), but an encounter with the lawgiver. This encounter "reconstructs" the moral law (or beliefs) to give us a new understanding of them and how they should be applied. In other words, what we receive is, not new information, but a new understanding of the information we already have because we have met with the source itself.[44] For instance, with revelation, Kant's moral imperative is grounded in an indicative, namely, the assertion of God's love for all. Furthermore, we see that we have applied the moral imperative only partially and self-interestedly. Revelation illumines the limits in which we have exercised our moral duty and calls us, then, to a more extensive and intensive application of it.[45] In the presence of the source itself, we see more clearly the requirement. God's self-disclosure illumines us and our situation so that God's intention for us cannot be ignored.

Although the illuminating encounter that Niebuhr describes is with the universal God and presses us toward more universal understanding and action, the acknowledgment of "point of view" remains important for several reasons. First, since this encounter takes place in one's own internal history, others cannot observe it. The same event may seem illuminating to one person and ordinary to another. For instance, to a detached observer, Jesus' death may seem nothing more than an execution of a political criminal, but to the involved believer, it is the atoning work of God. Second, the community within which this encounter takes place also has a point of view and in that sense an "inner history." The Christian community has a pattern of values that centers on Jesus Christ and a history in which its members participate. Revelation is never strictly individual, even though it is personal, because religious experience takes on a particular character in a particular social setting. One recognizes an experience of the "Christ within" because the community has a history of worship centered on Jesus Christ. Apart from that social history, the experience would be identified in a different way. Furthermore, the community becomes very important for discernment of what counts as a genuine experience of the "Christ within." Niebuhr observes, for instance, that some "numinous experience" may accompany human sacrifice to pagan deities but that the Christian community would not identify that feeling with Christ.[46] Third, because the Christian community has a point of view, it is distinct from other religious communities. Christians see their own history internally and the history of other communities externally. Conversely, other communities view Christian history externally and their own histories internally. Recognizing the double-sidedness of history allows Christians to affirm the reality of their own participation with God without denying the reality of another participation in another community. We cannot know those other histories "from the inside" without becoming a part of those communities themselves. Furthermore, Christians must pay attention to the perspective that other communities have on us. Because they see us externally, they are able to point out important things to us, particularly our failures to live out what we claim to know of God through revelation. When we listen attentively, those external observations can become a part of our internal history as we reflect upon the meaning of our actions in light of the values we say we hold. Our understanding of ourselves may be increased as we learn through outsiders to see ourselves more and more as God sees us.[47]

With the complex relationship between individual and community, and between internal and external history, it is not surprising that the relationship between past and present is equally complex. Niebuhr takes up the question of "newness" by exploring "progressive revelation." Niebuhr conceives of revelation, not as the delivery of new truths, but rather as the grasping of some knowledge in a new way. If anything is "delivered," it is a new pattern of meaning in which the information we have makes new sense, not information itself.

In keeping with this understanding, Niebuhr speaks of how revelation is progressive in two senses. First, a revelatory event is the starting point for a pattern by which past, present, and future history may be interpreted. Because they knew God to have acted in history to bring Israel out of bondage, the prophets saw God acting in the history of the nations in their own time. Revelation is "progressive" in the sense that new events may be brought into the revelatory pattern and understood in its light. It is not progressive in the sense that a new revelatory event can be substituted for a previous one. For the church, the unsubstitutable event is Jesus Christ, by which every other moment of history is interpreted. Although he does not say so explicitly, Niebuhr seems to indicate that the adoption of a new event as revelatory constitutes a fundamental shift away from a former pattern and toward the formation of a new community around a new illuminating pattern. For instance, the Christian community sees Jesus Christ, not simply the deliverance of Israel, as the center of its pattern. The history of Israel is not left behind in the formation of a Christian community, but it is itself reinterpreted in light of Jesus Christ. And just as the past is brought under the new pattern, so too are present events. Christians continually bring their sufferings, joys, and frustrations under the light of this revelatory event, and its ability to clarify those other events demonstrates its validity anew. With every progressive validation, the revelation is repeated and continued so that it is brought forward into our histories. Although it rests on an event in the past, revelation is

> a moving thing in so far as its meaning is realized only by being brought to bear upon the interpretation and reconstruction of ever new human situations in an enduring movement, a single drama of divine and human action. So the God who revealed himself continues to reveal himself—the one God of all times and places.[48]

Second, revelation is progressive in the sense that our understanding is continually enriched as we move back and forth between our experience and the pattern. We understand more deeply not only the meaning of our experiences but also the meaning of the revelatory moment itself. We see more clearly how the pattern applies with every new event that has to be brought into its light. Not only do individuals grow in this understanding, but also each generation has to participate in this dialectic. Niebuhr's metaphor for this kind of progressive understanding is a journey up "a well-known peak we never wholly know, which must be climbed again in every generation, on every new day."[49] So, the newness of revelation consists in its progressive validation and interpretation and in the progress we make toward understanding its meaning in our lives and times.

As they reconceive revelation as God's self-disclosure, both Bultmann and Niebuhr open up avenues for thinking about revelation that are promising for feminists. They each acknowledge the role of present human reception in different but equally vital ways. By doing so, they contribute to the recognition that experience is a critical category for understanding revelation. Neither, though, forgets the link to the past. For Bultmann, although our own relation to revelation is fundamentally as "original" as that of the first disciples, proclamation is critical to bringing one to that revelatory moment. Our own experience is in some way dependent on the testimony of others, including the first disciples, even though our encounter with God is in itself immediate. For Niebuhr, the formative event for the community begins a history in which we participate. Our personal insight takes particular shape within our shared history. Although present human reception is critical, neither Bultmann nor Niebuhr takes that reception to occur in isolation from others or completely apart from some kind of "handing on." While tradition does not amount to passing on information, the past does play a role that we should not ignore.

Similarly, both Bultmann and Niebuhr acknowledge the role of some perspective in revelation. To understand revelation as God's self-disclosure does not mean that God is fully and objectively available. Whether it is by faith or within a particular history, we come to see God from a point of view that is not necessarily shared by others, and our perspective is never to be equated with God's own perspective. In this way, Bultmann and Niebuhr anticipate some of the discussion about social location that has become important in recent feminist studies. Niebuhr acknowledges more than Bultmann does the fact of historical relativism and the role of formation in community, and Bultmann acknowledges more than Neibuhr does the importance of one's decisions and openness to the encounter itself, but both recognize that revelatory knowledge of God is not detached, objective, and complete. What one sees depends in part on where one stands, and it requires personal involvement.

Finally, for both Bultmann and Niebuhr, revelation is dynamic because it is fundamentally relationship with a living God. Bultmann sees revelation as ongoing in the sense that our encounter with God takes place in every moment. Authentic relationship with God can never simply stand still because it must be actualized continually. Niebuhr's understanding of revelation includes cognitive growth, but he is not talking about new information. Our understanding is enlarged when new experiences are seen in light of the revelatory event and when our appreciation for the significance of the revelatory event becomes more profound. For both theologians, the "ongoing" character of revelation matters in order for it to continue to have relevance for our lives. These theologians, then, present a way of talking about "newness" in revelation without indicating that the initial, crucial content, namely, an encounter with God, has been superseded by some other content. This way of thinking about newness may help feminists out of the bind we face when propositional revelation is the only model. With propositional revelation, newness is a threat because the need to assent to concepts leaves two fundamental options: either one sees a new idea to be an attack upon God's unassailable word in the old idea that is being superseded (and defense often takes the form of denying the right to question the Bible at all), or one questions the reliability of the words in the Bible to such an extent that one calls for them to be replaced on the basis of a new and improved communication. When one understands revelation to be God's disclosure of self, though, a certain kind of newness, far from being a threat to God's reliability, is in fact necessary. Encounter with the living God must be experienced and conceived in relation to the new events that take place in one's life, but this kind of newness does not mean a break with the past or the founding of a new religion. This way of talking about newness may enable feminists to speak of dynamic revelation, which enables us to see ourselves and our world differently without severing our relation to the historic Christian faith or rejecting the central revelatory event of

Christianity. An encounter with the living God in a new situation calls for new understandings and behavior, even if the God whom we encounter is the same God who has been present and active in former situations.

Understanding revelation as the disclosure of God's self holds promise for feminist theology, but feminists cannot afford to ignore the role of words either. As feminists have come to understand, language mediates reality to us. The Bible, as written language, plays a central and irreplaceable role in revelation for Christians. How can it be understood in such a way that feminists can affirm its role? One feminist scholar who has wrestled with this question is Sandra M. Schneiders.

THE REVELATORY TEXT

In *The Revelatory Text*, Schneiders uses hermeneutical theory to explore how the Bible, and especially the New Testament, may function as "locus and mediation of revelatory encounter with God" for those who read it. Historical critical interpretation has ignored the lived experience of those who find the Bible not simply historically interesting but also spiritually transforming. Schneiders is interested in showing how text and reader interact in order to bring to light the way the Bible may be involved in such transformation. Key to her exploration is an understanding of what it means to call the Bible "the word of God."

For Schneiders, the phrase "word of God" is a root metaphor that provides a rich and complex image of how the Bible reveals God to the reader. A root metaphor is capable of evoking imaginative response over and over again, unlike a "dead metaphor" that eventually becomes so fixed in meaning that we no longer see its metaphoric character. Although some Christians mistakenly treat this metaphor as dead, in that they take it to refer directly to the words in the Bible, Schneiders argues that in recognizing "word of God" as a root metaphor, we may become aware of a far more complex reality. The metaphor "word of God" refers ultimately, not to the Bible itself as God's actual words, but to revelation, which Schneiders understands as "God's accepted self-gift to human beings."[50] This brief definition contains many elements, and the metaphor "word of God" works well to evoke multiple dimensions of the nature of revelation.

Although revelation involves a kind of "knowing," the knowledge most fundamental to revelation is not informational. Revelation is primarily a sharing of self, a disclosure of one's interiority to another; so such disclosure can never be one-sided. The invitation to understand oneself must be met with acceptance by another self, and it ought to result in a reciprocal disclosure. Schneiders describes revelation, then, as "mutual self-gift expressive of and terminating in love."[51] The primary way in which we give ourselves in this way to one another is through language. Schneiders describes language as symbolic activity; it mediates an encounter with the real by making something present. As such, language does not function as much to inform as it does to communicate. Primarily, language communicates one person's experiences to another person so that the two interact more deeply than they could simply through seeing one another's bodies. They can begin to share a world, or a common life, because language has made their interior experiences present to one another. As symbolic activity, language has the capacity to reveal. It can make present something that is otherwise imperceptible, and by making that reality present, it calls for response in the one who now perceives the linguistic symbol. As a mode of presence, language participates in that which it makes present so that language and the reality it expresses are intimately bound together. However, language never fully expresses the reality it represents, so even as it "says" much, it also leaves much "unsaid." Interpretation attempts to draw out the inexhaustible content of what has been said, but it can never completely bring forward the fullness of the represented reality. Through language, we reveal ourselves to one another, never fully and completely, but in such a way as to make possible an encounter that creates intimate relationship.

When one understands how language works to reveal human selves to one another, one can begin to see how the metaphor "word of God" refers to divine revelation. In order to be accessible to us, an otherwise imperceptible God has to communicate with us symbolically, that is, through perceptible reality that can mediate God's presence to us. Throughout time, God has disclosed Godself symbolically in a variety of ways, for instance, through nature and history. The ancient Israelites knew God in these ways, but they began to express their experience of God in terms of language, for instance, in the way that prophets were understood to give voice to God. As they committed their experience of God to writing, images that draw from our use of language gained importance for expressing God's presence in the history of Israel. Written records were not an exclusive locus of God's revelation, but they did become a central way in which God's relationship to Israel could be called to mind and interpreted. The group of Jews who became known as Christians saw in Jesus Christ the presence of God, so he was for them the ultimate symbolic expression of God. As they recorded their experience and proclamation of Jesus Christ in the writing that became the New Testament, images based in our linguistic life gained importance for articulating their experience. Jesus Christ was understood to be the Word of God, the very expression of God's disclosure, and the New Testament was understood to be the word of God, the privileged witness to the divine self-gift in Jesus Christ.[52] These metaphors, which express God's self-disclosure in terms of language, are apt images of revelation because the gift of self takes place most fully in language. God's revelation is not limited to verbal activity, and the metaphor "word of God" refers fundamentally to revelation itself and not simply to Scripture, but the image of "conversing" conveys God's effort in all revelation to communicate with us. In revelation, God is making God's own self known to us in such a way that we may be involved in intimate relationship. What language does for us in human relationships, the word of God, or revelation in all its complexity, does for us in divine-human relationship.

Although the "word of God" refers properly to revelation itself and not simply Scripture, using this metaphor for the Bible does bring to light the way that it mediates encounter with God. Schneiders explains how the Bible may be at the same time human words and the word of God, in the sense described above, and her explanation involves the way that physical object and meaning are associated in sacrament and art. The Bible is a physical object, a collection of written texts that becomes meaningful for us when it is read and interpreted. As sacrament, the Bible mediates grace (not exclusively but in a particularly clear and powerful way) because the symbolic material is appropriate to the divine-human encounter it mediates and because the church has identified this material as a privileged symbol for that encounter. Although no symbol can ever be completely unambiguous, the Bible as sacrament has a particular clarity for believers when it is read and interpreted in the context of communal liturgy. Public proclamation focuses attention on divine-human encounter, and it may even make us more aware of possibilities for that encounter in other places. Similarly, the Bible may be described as an art object (the physical book) and a work of art (the meaning it has for readers as it is read and interpreted). As an object, the Bible endures through time, but it becomes a work of art only intermittently as its potential to speak to us is actualized through our contemplation of it. Whether considered as sacrament or art, the physical object has a special place because it mediates and stabilizes the meaning that we gain in our reading.

The Bible as physical object is a human artifact, and as such, its origin has a human explanation, even if such explanation is in fact difficult to achieve. When this object, though, discloses the divine, faith perceives it as being more than simply a human artifact. It may be called "inspired," not in the sense that it has a unique, divine origin (such as being dictated by God), but in the sense that it has been divinely influenced. Empirical study of the Bible will not discover that influence, just as empirical study of the universe will not prove that God is Creator. Schneiders argues that this influence becomes apparent only to the eyes of faith, so the affirmation that the Bible is inspired follows from an experience of disclosure, that is, revelation. Once one encounters God through reading or hearing the Bible, then one understands the Bible to be inspired. Inspiration and revelation are mutually illuminating concepts, but they are not identical. As Schneiders says, "Inspiration focuses our attention on the divine influence at work in the text and reader while revelation focuses our attention on the disclosive potential of the text as it comes to actualization."[53] Inspiration refers to the divine influence at the time of writing and at the time of reading/hearing, while revelation refers to the disclosive encounter itself.

Schneiders does not restrict the possibility of revelation to the Bible alone, but it does enjoy a privileged position among Christians. The New Testament is written witness to the primordial disclosure of God in Jesus Christ, so it serves as a touchstone of authenticity to that foundational revelation. Schneiders acknowledges the critical role of tradition in selecting what the church "hands on," including the Bible itself, and in the ongoing, conscious appropriation of revelation in the Christian community.[54] Still, the Bible has a unique place in the church. Since revelation is realized most fully in language, the written witness to Jesus Christ provides the church with its fullest opportunity for encounter with the Word of God. The Bible has a privileged potential to mediate revelation to the present community through the living interaction between text and reader/hearer. Because of its special role, it "grounds and governs the ongoing revelatory experience of Christians in succeeding ages."[55] Not only is its written character crucial for revelation; the fixed written form also provides stability for ongoing interpretation of that revelation. Schneiders draws from Paul Ricoeur to say that it "captures" the event of spoken witness in an "ideal meaning" so that the event may be reactualized at a later time. She describes the stability that the written text provides as continuity rather than as restrictive repetition; insight may deepen, new understandings may emerge, and corrections may even take place. What remains stable through this development is appeal to the revelation that took place in Jesus Christ. No other revelation may be substituted for this foundational disclosure; in a real sense, then, the Bible is normative and authoritative for Christian faith.

Schneiders describes the Bible's authority as "dialogical" or "disclosive" rather than absolute and coercive. That is, by providing us with the opportunity to encounter God, the Bible invites us to share in God's life. The proper response to this invitation is, not assent to doctrines, but an openness to the encounter and a willingness to commit oneself to the compelling vision of the reign of God that one finds in the Bible. Because revelation takes place at the intersection between invitation and response, between text and reader/hearer, the revelatory character of the Bible is actualized most fully when the Christian community interprets it with explicit attention to continuity with the foundational experience of Jesus Christ. Although the Holy Spirit works in every Christian to help bear, interpret, and pass on this witness, no one does these tasks in isolation. Furthermore, not all believers have equal gifts for or interest in these tasks, so others need to develop expertise in interpretation in order to ensure the necessary continuity with the foundational witness. Toward this end, Schneiders affirms the need for authoritative interpretation, a task she sees carried out by the magisterium. Still, the need for teaching authority in the church does not diminish the Bible's privileged place. It remains the norm for interpretation even as it is itself interpreted, and it remains the primary way in which God's presence is mediated to all members of the Christian community.

Schneiders, then, has worked out a way of understanding God's self-disclosure as not exclusively but critically tied to the Bible as written text. Since revelation takes place most fully through language and since the written language in the Bible preserves and makes available foundational witness to God in Jesus Christ, the Bible has a unique mediatorial role in God's self-disclosure for the Christian community. The Bible itself is not revelation, but it is revelatory because it makes possible an encounter with God. The Bible not only mediates God to us; it also mediates past witness to God to us so that we may test our own experience and understanding against that which has been found by the community to be authentic. Schneiders allows for "correction" of past understandings as we encounter God in new situations, but the core witness to Jesus Christ as the primordial disclosure of God is never replaced. Past and present, then, depend on each other even though they are not identical. Without the past witness, present reception of God's revelation through Jesus Christ could not occur. Without the present reception, past witness to God's revelation through Jesus Christ would become ineffective. Revelation is ongoing, dynamic, and new as each encounter with God unfolds, but it is never severed from revelation that has taken place before.

The words of the Bible, then, are neither the word of God (revelation) nor the Word of God (Christ), but they mediate both. Schneiders affirms the importance of the words of the Bible for Christian faith without elevating them to a status that defies criticism. The language of the Bible as symbol both reveals and conceals that which it makes present, so at the same time that it makes possible an encounter with God, it also calls forth further interpretation of that encounter. Continual interpretation leads to continual revelation; it is ongoing and new in the sense that riches continue to unfold in a living relationship with God.

REVELATION AND FEMINIST CONCERNS

Objections to the Bible often assume an understanding of propositional revelation as a starting point, a model of revelation that is indeed enormously problematic for women. Rejecting a straightforward notion of propositional revelation, though, does not mean rejecting all of the insights that notion has tried to retain. Propositional revelation has attempted to safeguard the reliability of God's communication of saving knowledge to us in the Bible. The Protestant orthodox understanding of Scripture, despite its attempts to remove problems that would threaten reliability, only managed to shift the questions to another level. Human reception could still go wrong in interpretation, even with God's own infallible dictation of the words being interpreted. While it is important to affirm that God reliably offers us saving knowledge in revelation, the problem of human reception is not prevented by an account of revelation as propositional. Furthermore, the words themselves were never the point, no matter how hard Protestant orthodox theologians argued for their accuracy. Salvific knowledge of God finally consists in relationship. If reliability and relationship are the critical elements in the understanding of Scripture that was formulated by Protestant orthodoxy, can these elements be retained in feminist understanding without the framework of propositional revelation?

Soskice and McFague both show that verbal communication about God can take place in ways other than literal assertions. Metaphors do communicate concepts, but understanding those concepts involves an imaginative grasp of what the words convey rather than simple belief in what the words say explicitly. Because metaphors communicate in complex ways, the question about reliability becomes equally complex. The adequacy of those metaphors to convey concepts of God cannot be judged by a simple test of "right" and "wrong," or "true" and "false." Reliability depends not only on the appropriateness of the metaphor to its subject matter but also on whether the associations are in fact perceived. Successful communication relies not only on "getting" the associations but also on identifying where the limits to the metaphor's associations lie. Both the connections and the limits may change over time as the associations that we have with the object of comparison in our daily world change. According to Soskice, putting an experience of God into speech takes place in "halting approximations" using language available at the time, and McFague clearly indicates that some metaphors lose their ability to evoke the very concepts they ought to be conveying. New expressions in new times may be needed to communicate the same, or at least a similar, idea.

Metaphors communicate concepts, but concepts are themselves secondary matters. As even the Protestant orthodox understanding of propositional revelation recognized, revelation is fundamentally about salvation, and salvation is fundamentally about relationship. We must always distinguish God from our concepts about God. The living God whom we encounter is never identical to the way we think about that God, so our conceptions are always open to revision. God is always "more" than what we say about God. This recognition allows us to continue to monitor what we say even as we recognize the power of words to shape our understanding. Concepts of God play a role in bringing us into relationship with God, and they can do so in better and worse ways. What we understand about God will influence the kind of relationship that we have (e.g., conceiving God as wrathful leads a person to respond in fear), so what we communicate through concepts, while secondary, is still vital. Feminists bring out precisely this concern when criticizing patriarchal images of God. Women have pointed out that some ways of understanding God and talking about God do not promote a beneficial relationship and may, in fact, promote a destructive relationship. The reason that we question certain metaphors is, not to deny revelation, but to allow it to do its work, namely, to provide saving knowledge of God. Even as we reject propositional revelation insofar as it entails reading the Bible for true literal assertions, feminists do in a very real way engage the notion of verbal communication. The conceptual knowledge that we gain through the words of the Bible matters, and it matters precisely because the purpose of such knowledge is relationship with the living God whom we struggle to conceive.

Schneiders argues that the Bible provides language through which God gives God's self; and in making this point, she holds together the importance of verbal communication with existential encounter. Concentrating on relationship as the fundamental goal of revelation opens up possibilities for feminists to use some of the insights about existential revelation for addressing concerns that have been raised regarding feminist theology. Questions about the relation of new to old have been with Christianity as far back as controversies over whether the Hebrew Scriptures should be included in the Christian canon. Feminists have not raised this problem for the first time, although we have presented a side to the problem that had not been addressed until a critical mass of women began formally and openly engaging in theological discourse. For Bultmann and Niebuhr, historical questions prompted a revised understanding about Christianity's relation to its past, and their insights into that issue may be instructive here. If what is revealed is not information but God's self, then a living relationship with God requires a certain kind of newness. We must constantly bring our relationship with God to bear on how we understand the circumstances of our lives, and we must always bring the circumstances of our lives to bear on how we understand our relationship with God. Far from threatening revelation, this kind of newness is absolutely essential.

Furthermore, far from breaking with the past, this kind of newness depends significantly on the past. The witness that others can give to their relationship with God enables me to open myself to relationship with God. Their circumstances, though, are not identical to my circumstances, so my relationship to God will include some different insights and questions. To say that revelation is "ongoing," then, does not mean that it replaces the foundational event. It is ongoing in the sense that God is alive and relevant to life as it is now, which is quite different in many respects from life as it was before. The role of witness is to mediate encounter with God, not to dictate the details of the way this relationship with God should be lived out now. To recognize the mediatory status of witness is not to devalue it; the long tradition of Christian faith provides the critical context for present Christian experience. Its value, then, is clear but not ultimate. It serves an end beyond itself, namely, salvific relationship with God; and where it fails to further this relationship, we may criticize and reinterpret it. Relationship with God does not occur in isolation from relationship with others, whether those others are in our past or our present, and we are called both to listen to what others tell us and to attend carefully to what we ought to say as we formulate our own witness.

The witness in the Bible is fixed in such a way that the authors themselves cannot adjust their proclamation to our circumstances. As Schneiders has pointed out, though, this fixed character does not mean that their witness is strictly uniform or one-dimensional. Any written text must be interpreted in order to become meaningful; the Bible must be interpreted in order to become revelatory. The written character of biblical witness allows a range of possible interpretations that are quite open, but it also provides stability in two senses: it links each generation to the primordial event of revelation, and it captures the meaning of that event as it was understood by early witnesses. For Schneiders, the community has a long tradition of making judgments about whether certain interpretations have attended to the text in ways that are continuous with the insights of those early witnesses. Those communal judgments (particularly for Schneiders, those made by the magisterium) also provide an element of stability. (Of course, communal judgments are also secondary to encounter with God and should be open to revision just as metaphors and concepts are.) With appropriate attention to these factors, revelation that occurs through an interpretation that addresses new circumstances will not be discontinuous with revelation that has occurred through interpretation that addressed past circumstances.

To place so much emphasis on interpretation, though, raises again the question of reliability. Since the point of revelation is salvation, we naturally want to know that our salvation is secure. The more emphasis we place on human reception, the more vulnerable we are to mistaken understanding. The theory of propositional revelation arose in order to show how we may be sure that the Bible delivers faithfully to us the knowledge of God that matters for our salvation, and anyone who denies this theory, whether feminist or not, has to address the issue of reliability in a different way. If revelation is constituted by relationship, the question of reliability also has to be shaped by that insight. Reliability may not be about being "right" as much as it is about walking in faithful relationship. Even if our words to describe an experience of God are "halting approximations," we may yet affirm that God will never fail to be in relationship with us, to seek to enrich that relationship, and to elicit our response. What is in question is not really God's reliability to honor that relationship but our own.

Still, since our relationship is partially shaped by the witness to God that we find in the Bible, we have good reason to keep asking about what that witness tells us. How does the Bible point to God in such a way that an encounter with God becomes possible? I am suggesting that it is not just language but using language to tell a narrative that is central to the way the Bible bears witness. The Bible brings us into a narrative world that helps us see from a particular perspective. As it does so, it also makes possible the gift of God's self that constitutes revelation. As a form of communication, narrative "tells" in a way that is both common and complex, and understanding how it communicates to us in our daily lives will help illumine how the Bible can mediate God's communication to us. In the next chapter, I will concentrate on narrative itself, and then in chapter 5, I will show how reading the Bible as narrative offers us the opportunity to encounter God.

NOTES

1. Donald G. Bloesch, *The Battle for the Trinity: The Debate over Inclusive God-Language* (Ann Arbor: Servant, 1985), 26–27, 29–41; see also David Curry, "Inclusive Language Liturgies: The Renunciation of Revelation," *Churchman* 105 (fall 1991): 54–70.

2. These were often the claims made about those who participated in the Re-Imagining Conference held in Minneapolis, Minnesota, in November 1993. This conference brought together about two thousand women and a few men to mark the midpoint of the Ecumenical Decade for Churches in Solidarity with Women. New images for God and Jesus Christ that were used at the gathering received a great deal of criticism.

3. For an account of how the New Testament depicts human involvement in receiving revelation, see Dan O. Via, *The Revelation of God and/as Human Reception* (Harrisburg, Pa.: Trinity Press International, 1997). For an account of human reception in the history of religion, see Keith Ward, *Religion and Revelation* (Oxford: Oxford University Press, 1994).

4. For an account of the way in which Christians took biblical narrative to be historically accurate, see Hans W. Frei, *The Eclipse of Biblical Narrative: A Study in Eighteenth and Nineteenth Century Hermeneutics* (New Haven: Yale University Press, 1974), chap. 1.

5. See, e.g., Origen, *On First Principles* (ed. and trans. G. W. Butterworth, 1936; repr., New York: Harper & Row, 1966), 4.2.

6. Avery R. Dulles, *Models of Revelation* (Maryknoll, N.Y.: Orbis, 1985), 41–45.

7. For instances of recent defense of propositional revelation, see Jack W. Cottrell, "The Nature of Biblical Authority: A Conservative Perspective," in *Conservative, Moderate, Liberal* (ed. Charles R. Blaisdell; St. Louis: CBP, 1990), 21–40; Carl Henry, "Inerrancy and the Bible in Modern Conservative Evangelical Thought," in *Introduction to Christian Theology: Contemporary North American Perspectives* (ed. Roger A. Badham; Louisville: Westminster John Knox, 1998), 53–65.

8. I am not here taking up the important philosophical question about whether *all* language about God is metaphorical. Such a claim unnecessarily reduces the resources theology needs in order to be able to talk adequately about God, but I cannot argue here a counterclaim. *Much* language about God is clearly metaphorical, and the work I will discuss here is very important for understanding how such language can be revelatory.

9. Janet Martin Soskice, *Metaphor and Religious Language* (Oxford: Clarendon, 1985), 15.

10. McFague's work draws on the interactive theory of Max Black, but Soskice believes that Black's theory finally reduces to comparison. She prefers to use the work of I. A. Richards. Despite drawing on different theories to make their points, Soskice and McFague agree that metaphor produces new understanding. See Sallie McFague, *Metaphorical Theology: Models of God in Religious Language* (Philadelphia: Fortress, 1982), 16, 32–33; and Soskice, *Metaphor and Religious Language*, 31, 44, 89.

11. Soskice, *Metaphor and Religious Language*, 24–26, 40–43.

12. Ibid., 45.

13. Ibid., 55.

14. Ibid., 62.

15. Ibid., 63–66.

16. Ibid., 149–54.

17. Ibid., 158.

18. See Janet Martin Soskice, "Can a Feminist Call God 'Father'?" in *Speaking the Christian God: The Holy Trinity and the Challenge of Feminism* (ed. Alvin F. Kimel Jr.; Grand Rapids: Eerdmans, 1992), 81–94.

19. Sallie McFague, *Models of God: Theology for an Ecological, Nuclear Age* (Philadelphia: Fortress, 1987), 34.

20. Ibid., 44–50.

21. Avery Dulles even takes these theologians to represent different models of revelation. He places Baillie in the historical model and Barth, Bultmann, and Brunner (despite their disagreements over other issues) in the dialectical presence model, and he identifies Niebuhr as a forerunner of the new awareness model. See *Models of Revelation*, 53, 85, and 127.

22. Rudolf Bultmann, *What Is Theology?* (Minneapolis: Fortress, 1997), 1–49 passim. See also "Theology as Science," in *New Testament and Mythology and Other Basic Writings* (sel., ed., and trans. Schubert M. Ogden; Philadelphia: Fortress, 1984), 52–54.

23. Bultmann, *What Is Theology?* 50–75 passim.

24. Bultmann, "Theology as Science," 60.

25. Rudolf Bultmann, "Science and Existence," in Ogden, *New Testament and Mythology and Other Basic Writings*, 139–40; "Wissenschaft und Existenz," in *Glauben und Verstehen* 3 (Tübingen: J. C. B. Mohr, 1965), 116.

26. Bultmann, "Science and Existence," 76–103 passim.

27. Bultmann often indicates the distinction between these two levels of history by using different German words: *Historie* and its cognates for empirical history and *Geschichte* and its cognates for existential history. *Geschichte* has the connotation of "story" rather than simply "historiography." For instance, he explains the significance of certain biblical and doctrinal statements about Jesus in this way:

> It seems clear enough that the point of statements about preexistence or virgin birth is indeed to express the significance of the person of Jesus for faith. What he is for us is not exhausted by, in fact, does not even appear in what he seems to be for ordinary historical observation (*die historisch-feststellende Betrachtung*). We are not to ask about his historical origin (*historische Herkunft*), because his real meaning becomes evident only when this way of asking questions is set aside. We are not to ask for the historical reasons (*die historischen Gründe*) for his story (*Geschichte*), his cross; the significance of his story (*die Bedeutung seiner Geschichte*) lies in what God wants to say to us through it. Thus, his significance as a figure is not to be understood in an innerworldly context; in mythological language he comes from eternity, and his origin is not human or natural.

See Rudolf Bultmann, "New Testament and Mythology," in Ogden, *New Testament and Mythology and Other Basic Writings*, 33; "Neues Testament und Mythologie," in *Kerygma und Mythos* 1 (2d ed.; Hamburg: Herbert Reich-Evangelischer Verlag, 1951), 41.

28. Bultmann, "New Testament and Mythology," 42 n. 2; "Neues Testament und Mythologie," 22 n. 2.

29. Bultmann, "On the Problem of Demythologizing," in Ogden, *New Testament and Mythology and Other Basic Writings*, 99; "Zum Problem der Entmythologisierung," in *Kerygma und Mythos* 2 (1st ed.; Hamburg: Herbert Reich-Evangelischer Verlag, 1952), 184–85.

30. H. Richard Niebuhr, *The Meaning of Revelation* (New York: Macmillan, 1960), 54.

31. Ibid., 1–5 passim.

32. Ibid., 5.

33. Ibid., 5–11 passim.

34. Ibid., 10. For an account of how Niebuhr understands the social nature of knowledge, see H. Richard Niebuhr, *Faith on Earth: An Inquiry into the Structure of Human Faith* (ed. Richard R. Niebuhr; New Haven: Yale University Press, 1989), 31–42 (chap. 3).

35. Niebuhr, *Meaning of Revelation*, 16.

36. Ibid., 44.

37. Ibid., 53.

38. Ibid., 34.

39. Ibid., 55.

40. Ibid., 68.

41. Ibid., 69.

42. Ibid., 17, 69–71.

43. Ibid., 111.

44. Ibid., 125.

45. Ibid., 120–25.

46. Ibid., 37–41.

47. Ibid., 59–66.

48. Ibid., 99.

49. Ibid., 100.

50. Sandra M. Schneiders, *The Revelatory Text: Interpreting the New Testament as Sacred Scripture* (San Franciso: HarperSanFrancisco, 1991), 34.

51. Ibid.

52. Schneiders distinguishes carefully between the two terms "Word of God" and "word of God." "Word of God" (with a capital *W*) denotes the Second Person of the Trinity, Jesus as this Person incarnate, and the mystery of divine self-revelation wherever that takes place. The "word of God" (with a lowercase *W*) is used to speak of Scripture as potentially or actually revelatory. See p. 7.

53. Schneiders, *Revelatory Text*, 51.

54. Schneiders distinguishes between "apostolic tradition," which spans about two centuries, and "ongoing tradition." Apostolic tradition was both unwritten and written, and the New Testament is a portion of that written apostolic tradition. Also unwritten and written, ongoing (postapostolic) tradition is how the foundational witness is expressed and transmitted in a living way. See *Revelatory Text*, esp. 75 and 81.

55. Ibid., 45.

CHAPTER FOUR

✺

Narrative in Human Life

The discussion of revelation that we undertook in chapter 3 hinted at times to the role that narrative plays in our knowledge of God. Sallie McFague claimed that certain metaphors should be tested by the story of Jesus. H. Richard Niebuhr described the only appropriate medium for faith's confession as telling the story of our lives. Beyond these explicit references to story, the involvement of narrative lies in the background of much that was said. History, a central idea for both Rudolf Bultmann and Niebuhr, is a form of narrative. Even our understandings of the terms that are brought together in metaphor have careers of use that are shaped by narratives. The importance of narrative for revelation is even more extensive than these examples indicate. Narrative has a place in features of human life that are involved in the possibility of revelation, such as cognition, communication, and even selfhood. In this chapter, I want to engage in an explicit discussion of narrative in human life in order to bring out those connections. They will become relevant as we explore in chapter 5 the way that the Bible works to mediate an understanding of God that can in turn enable an encounter with God.

WHAT IS NARRATIVE?

Because the term "narrative" may be used in many different ways, I want to distinguish various meanings and identify how the term will be used in this discussion. I will first show some of the many different ways in which the term "narrative" is employed, then I will suggest a definition that attempts to identify what is common among most of these uses and what I think is most significant for my work in this book.

"Narrative" is often used to identify a genre of literature that is distinct from other genres. It is generally recognized that narrative is prose rather than poetry, but beyond that simple description is little consensus about what kind of prose narrative is. Narrative may be identified as "a work with a plot," but epic poems and sometimes other forms of poetry have plots also. Furthermore, not all works with plots (a drama, a film) fall under the category of "narrative" as it is usually conceived in literary studies because they "show" rather than "tell." Robert Scholes and Robert Kellogg, however, treat film as a form of "telling" because the director "narrates" through choices of how to present events. They do not consider drama to be such a telling because members of the audience have the freedom to look at many different things on the stage. As Gérard Genette uses it, the word "narrative" refers, not to a genre, but to one of three levels within a single work. In his usage, "story" refers to events (real or fictitious), "narrative" refers to the oral or written statements that tell about those events, and "narrating" refers to the act of telling itself.[1] Although most often plot is considered an essential ingredient of narrative, the two terms can also be distinguished, so that under one possible view narrative states temporal events ("The king died, and then the queen died") while plot shows the causal relation between those events ("The king died, and then the queen died of grief").[2] Even in the field that studies it the most, "narrative" turns out to be a slippery term. What does seem to be clear in literary studies is that narrative must recount an event or events (real or fictitious); otherwise, the prose is merely description.

Although "narrative" has been conceived in a variety of ways, the role of events provides a starting point for identifying the way that a narrative works. In what follows, I will follow a common, rather than technical, usage so that "narrative" is synonymous with "story" when each refers to a specific "telling." I am here thinking of "event" as a complex interaction of character, action, and setting. In most understandings of narrative, events are emplotted. The concept "plot" is no less complex and problematic than "narrative," and I will not attempt to examine all the technical difficulties regarding plot that literary studies have uncovered.[3] Theological discussion of narrative usually works with a fairly simple understanding of plot that will serve our purposes here. Stanley Hauerwas and David Burrell call plot the "connected unfolding" of the elements that constitute a narrative.[4] That is, plot displays a pattern of relevance among discrete events that unfolds as the narrative is told. Plot, then, provides what is sometimes called "connective tissue" or "followability." Characters and their actions become intelligible as a narrative unfolds: we see who they are, and we understand the reasons for and the consequences of what they do as we follow the narrative, that is, as we come to see those patterns of relevance and where they lead. Because emplotted events unfold, a narrative is dynamic, not static. It moves forward, and as it does so, it moves our understanding forward, toward some goal or point. The outcome of a narrative is not like the conclusion of a logical argument, which reaches a necessary end if one follows the reasoning precisely. The events that plot connects are contingent, and the reader follows a development that is not completely predictable (we will ask as we move through the story, "What happens next?"). Even though developing events are not predictable, they are held together by some purpose that the author has in mind. Narratives, then, are in some way teleological; that is, they move toward an end that is not simply a stopping place. They display some kind of intention or purpose that becomes the organizing center for the pattern of relevance.

One way of speaking of the kind of intelligibility that belongs to a narrative is to speak of it as creating a "world" that characters inhabit and take unselfconsciously as the context for their "lives." Stories create a time and space that resemble, but are not identical to, the time and space in which we live. Time, for instance, normally moves forward in narrative, but it may be compressed by skipping years, drawn out by lengthy descriptions, or repeated as different scenes that took place at the same time are related individually. The story's connection with the real world can range widely, from fantasies, which create highly imaginative worlds that have no exact counterpart in our reality, to historical fiction, which borrows actual settings and sometimes characters from events that did occur. In either case, what makes a story intelligible is, not an accurate portrayal of the time and space within which we live, but its verisimilitude, that is, its ability to seem real because of its own internal coherence. Since the world of every story is unique, it is sometimes spoken of as a "closed universe," but that does not mean closed to the reader. Success in understanding the story requires "entering" that universe. The point of calling it "closed" or "autonomous" is that the reader has to take it for what it is rather than fit it to the reader's own experiences. In order to follow the story, one has to go along with the narrator, attending to the events as they are narrated and recognizing the values and beliefs that inform those events. Only when one is able to do so is one able to make sense of what is narrated.

Literary studies have had an increasing impact on biblical studies, largely because so much of the Bible is composed of narratives. In biblical studies, "narrative" may identify a kind of writing in the Bible that is distinct from other kinds of writing, such as laws, genealogies, and apologetic arguments. It may also be used to speak of a larger unit composed of several kinds of writing, as when Robert C. Tannehill speaks of the "narrative unity" of Luke–Acts. Literary study of biblical narrative attends to various features that are important for telling a story, such as character, setting, plot, and dialogue, and much careful and creative work has been done in current interpretation by examining these features. Thinking of certain biblical writings in terms of "story" has brought many important elements to our attention, but some important differences exist between biblical narratives and some other kinds of stories with which we are familiar. In contrast to novels, for instance, biblical narratives are often the result of a long process of collection and editing rather than the work of a single author. They were told, written, and compiled in different historical contexts, each of which has left some mark on the final product. Textual differences among manuscripts sometimes present a problem for establishing the details of a narrative, and the meaning of several words in their original languages is uncertain. All these characteristics make studying biblical narrative complex and multifaceted, with value in employing various kinds of criticism besides literary criticism. Concepts from literary studies, though, have enabled biblical scholars to put back together stories that other methods often pull apart. Tannehill, for instance, demonstrates unity in Luke–Acts by using the concept "implied author" or "narrator," who weaves the various materials together under a comprehensive purpose in a final redaction.

On the level of the canon as a whole, questions about unity become even more complex than in a single gospel because there are so many more authors and editors. Nor was any one person responsible for collecting the books that constitute the Bible, so it is difficult to argue textually for a single, identifiable narrator. For these reasons, the canon is sometimes called a "library." Furthermore, while a large portion of the written material collected in the Bible may fall under the category of narrative, not all of it does. Because its contents are so varied, speaking of the Bible as narrative cannot mean simply that it is made up of narratives, or stories. Nor can it mean that it develops one straightforward story from beginning to end in the way that one expects a novel or perhaps even a gospel to do. Although there are undoubtedly parallels between the unity of a book in the Bible and the unity of the Bible as a whole, the cases are not identical. For instance, the final form of the canon has more to do with communal usage than with the work of a thoughtful and imaginative editor. To treat the Bible as a whole as a single "text" is difficult, although I do want to argue that on a comprehensive level it does present the outlines of a story. Because of these differences, the technical concepts that belong to the study of a genre of literature will not be as helpful to this project as more general insights about narrative, many of which have already been illuminating for other fields outside of literary and biblical studies.[5]

The writing of history, for instance, can be understood as narrative because it involves telling about events. On a commonsense level, history and story may often be distinguished as "fact" and "fiction" respectively, where history is an objective account of things that really happened while story is an inventive account of things that happen in the imagination; but on closer examination, that distinction begins to break down. The writing of history often involves more than chronicling what happened. That is, it attempts to go beyond mere listing of events to show the connection and significance of those events. When it does so, history takes a form similar to story (an unfolding "plot"). Different interpretations of events tell different "stories" in this sense, so that from one point of view the bombing of Pearl Harbor might be a tale of courage on the part of those attacked, or from another point of view a tale of strategy on the part of the attackers, or from yet another point of view a tale of suffering for those who lost loved ones.

As it has become more and more apparent that history is not simply straightforward representation but involves interpretation, and thus yields multiple stories, an even deeper recognition of the role of narrative has emerged. Even the "facts" under interpretation are themselves couched in narrative.[6] What may seem securely factual about the attack on Pearl Harbor is that it occurred on December 7, 1941; but December 7, 1941 matters to the historian because it is the date on which some crucial event in a larger story (for instance, the unfolding of events in World War II) took place. Other things happened on December 7, 1941, that do not capture the attention of the historian who is telling this particular story. Furthermore, other stories would focus attention on other dates, other events, other individuals, that is, on other "facts." Even what one identifies as an "event" will be affected by the story that one wants to tell. The entire attack could be the "event" in a history of World War II. A history of the attack itself, on the other hand, would divide up "events" into more discrete components, such as the meeting at which the attack was planned and approved, the first bomb dropped, etc. A history that followed the involvement of one individual in this attack might identify events even differently. Events are facts, but facts are "made" (and this meaning may even be derived from the Latin *factum*, which is related to the verb *facere*) in the context of narrative.

Some historians have taken this insight so seriously that they see little if any difference between fact and fiction (another kind of "making" or "shaping," from the Latin *fictio*, which is related to the verb *fingere*). Peter Novick argues that historians' claim to objectivity has become so compromised that they should think of their work more like poetry or painting, and judge their work then by aesthetic and pragmatic criteria. Although he still wants to maintain accuracy about facts (so history cannot completely be reduced to fiction), he believes those facts to have no ability to determine interpretation in any way. In answer to Novick, Judith Lichtenberg argues that appealing to accuracy does more to constrain interpretation than he believes. It is true, she says, that facts underdetermine interpretation, but the plausibility of any interpretation stands or falls on how well it fits the facts. A fact or facts may find a place in many stories, but "some stories will not fly."[7] Lichtenberg's way of thinking on this point has the advantage of acknowledging the importance of narrative in history while also acknowledging that historians are not free just to make up any tale they want to tell. The narrative context highlights which data (the things which are "given," or are simply there because they occurred) are important facts (data selected for their relevance) for this particular study of history. The narrative that the historian has in mind already affects the assumptions and questions that the historian asks when looking at the evidence. The importance of the facts is then displayed in the way that the narrative is told, and it is always possible that the telling the historian first had in mind may have to be adjusted if new data are discovered to be relevant. There is both a "finding" and a "fashioning" in the writing of history.

Since no single definition of "narrative" exists and since it may be used as a category that encompasses more than works of literature, I want to suggest a way of understanding narrative that will be operative in this book. A narrative is a kind of "telling" (spoken or written) that relates a sequence of events in such a manner as to bring out relations of relevance between those events. Narratives have a structure, namely, a beginning, middle, and end. This structure is connected to the temporality of existence in which things happen, but narrative does more than relate events chronologically. Events may appear in the narrative in an order that does not follow strict chronological happening (e.g., as memories or predictions), and not every event that happens (or might happen) in a given time has relevance to the narrative. Narratives move toward a goal (not simply an ending point), and events find their place in the narrative in relation to that goal. Just as they are not simply chronological, neither are narratives simply logical. They do not arrive at their goal in the way that arguments arrive at conclusions, namely, by logical entailment. Their coherence lies in the way that they unfold so that the events "hang together," and the outcome of those events may not be altogether clear until the end. Narratives have a goal because any narrative involves a selection of what to tell. Narratives may, in fact, have multiple goals that influence this selection. Various subplots might require the telling of different events. There may also be a point to the story (a moral) and a point to the telling of the story (to inspire or caution the listeners/readers). In this example, the narrator might have to select *what* events ought to be related to serve the moral and also determine *how* those events ought to be related to serve as inspiration or warning. An event may be relevant to a particular narrative on account of its causal relationship to other events in the narrative, but just as it is not merely a list of happenings, a narrative is not simply a list of causes either. For instance, a breakfast may be relevant to a narrative because an important conversation takes place there, but it is not necessary to relate who cooked the breakfast and which hen laid the eggs unless those events advance the narrative goal or illumine some aspect of the narrative. Many of the interesting discussions that take place today about narrative, particularly for feminists, deal with issues of relevance and the selection that goes along with what is considered important to say.

COGNITION, COMMUNICATION, AND CONSTRUCTION

Although specific stories and manners of storytelling differ, narrative in some form seems to be found universally among human beings. Some scholars have suggested that it is central to human cognition. I want to explore the link between narrative and human thinking because if these arguments are correct, narrative may be a key concept for understanding revelation. It may shed light on how God becomes known in human life.

In 1971, Stephen Crites wrote a seminal article in which he argues for the narrative quality of experience.[8] Narrative, he says, is one of two cultural forms capable of expressing coherence through time (the other being music, which he defines as the "style of action" so that it encompasses much more than instrumental and vocal sounds). Human selves are conscious of being bodies affected by the world and moving through time. Since we are temporal creatures, the events of our lives occur in succession, but we come to understand those events as more than simply successive. Human consciousness perceives not just that things have happened in a certain order; it also understands its own present and anticipates a future. In other words, human consciousness can recollect (i.e., collect again and organize) events that have occurred, understand their meaning now, and project their consequences onto the future. Memories organized and reorganized in this way provide a sense of self, or personal identity, that moves through time with continuity. The temporality of narrative, which links events in more than mere succession, matches the temporal modes of human existence. Furthermore, Crites claims that human consciousness requires narrative form to express and make sense of its temporal unity. Just as we need to know our personal experiences as unified to have personal integrity, we also need an integrated world to provide an intelligible context for our lives. Stories, Crites argues, are central to the unity of both selves and worlds.

Crites distinguishes between stories of two types, which he calls "sacred" and "mundane," although he is not entirely content with either designation because the adjectives carry connotations that do not fit his ideas. "Sacred" does not mean "religious" as opposed to "secular," and it does not simply have to do with a realm of gods, although many sacred stories do involve deities. "Sacred" seems to indicate for Crites a sort of depth or comprehensiveness. A story is sacred if it provides the fundamental understanding of the way things are, in which our sense of self and world takes shape. As Crites describes it, a sacred story is "anonymous and communal," a common sensibility that surrounds and informs those who participate in it but which does not have a particular author or originator. Living in this story involves both awakening to it and formation in it, that is, both seeing that this is the way things are and coming to see the way things are in this way because consciousness has been shaped to remember, experience, and anticipate by means of this story. The effects of sacred stories are profound, although they are rarely recognized.

As Crites describes them, sacred stories are not "stories" in our common use of the word. They are deep understandings rather than specific tellings. What makes them narrative is primarily that they provide contours for our existence that allow us to move through time with continuity. Any attempt to put those contours into words is a mundane story, though hardly ordinary because all our myths, epics, and scriptures fall in this category. They are efforts to articulate that which we know already in our shared understanding about the way things are. While these two types of stories are distinct, they are also integrally related. A sacred story implies mundane stories, and mundane stories are grounded in sacred stories. We come to understand a sacred story through hearing mundane stories, and those mundane stories resonate with us because we recognize in them the sacred story that they are trying to express.

The actual telling of stories is important because it allows us to test various possibilities for our lives. We see from decisive moments in narratives what our own decisions might yield. Some endings are happy, others tragic; and we learn as much from thwarted expectations as we do from fulfillments. Telling stories is vital for orienting ourselves toward our futures; they help us interpret our temporality and find our place in our society. Though they influence us in critical ways, the stories we tell always remain open to revision. Mundane stories may be criticized and retold in order to resonate better with the sacred story they try to express. We try out stories as we try out possibilities through stories, and some will be better than others in clarifying our situations.

When Crites wrote his 1971 article, he took some things as self-evident and acknowledged that he could not support by external evidence the things he understood to be the very conditions for human existence. Not everyone accepts the assumption that experience itself really has a narrative quality. Instead, we may live in a flux of experiences, random and by themselves meaningless, that we make comprehensible through the narratives that we tell.[9] One does not have to claim a direct link to the way experience is to see the centrality of narrative in human understanding. Even for the latter view, narrative still is indispensable to human cognition because it provides the relevant connections that help us make sense out of the raw experiences that we have. Since the 1970s when Crites wrote his essay, numerous studies have brought to light more about the way that humans construct and comprehend narratives. Although we do not yet have a full understanding of the way that narrative functions in human thinking, some recent work suggests that narrative abilities, such as temporal organization and seeing causal connection between events, appear across cultures and come with maturity as a natural part of human development.[10] It takes time to acquire the skills to tell a story, and different cultures tell stories in somewhat different ways, but the ability to understand stories appears quite early in human life.[11] Even if narratives are not fundamental in the sense that they are foundational to all experience and cognition, they surely have a universal and indispensable place in human thinking and can thus provide a crucial vehicle for God's revelation.

In order to lay the groundwork for how God can communicate with us through narrative, I want to explore briefly how communication is connected with human cognition. Anthropologists often study human cognition in light of how we are like and unlike other primates, and their studies point increasingly to the role that language plays in our unique development. Other primates have social interactions, ways of communicating with each other, and even some very broadly defined cultural traditions; under very specialized conditions, some primates learn to communicate to some degree with humans. Still, human children have an enormous advantage over other primates in learning to use linguistic symbols. One way to explain this advantage is to focus on the human ability to enter into a "joint attentional scene," that is, the ability of one human to interact with another human in such a way that both persons are attending to a third thing.[12] In other words, when I talk to you about some item in the world (a thing, event, or even another person), we are both giving our attention to that item at the same time. This ability is so common that it seems unremarkable until one begins to think about how it works and what becomes possible because of it.

Entering into a joint attentional scene requires the ability to recognize that the other human being involved is a mental agent who can have specific intentions, just as we ourselves are mental agents who can have specific intentions. Attention and intention are related to each other because in order to follow an intended path successfully, one must pay attention to one's goal and how to bring it about. Awareness that another is "like me" in these ways provides the foundation for social interaction and usually appears in human infants by the age of nine months. This ability allows for active teaching, a practice that is distinct from simple learning (taking in information on one's own) and seems to be unique to humans.[13] By understanding that adults have intentions, children may imitate those intentions (not simply mimic an action) and thus begin to share a social world. For instance, children learn conventions (socially shared practices) by imitating particular ways of manipulating objects—sipping from a cup, writing with a pencil, hitting a nail with a hammer. That these uses of objects is not mere mimicry is made apparent by the ability of children to manipulate them playfully in other ways for other intentions— wearing a cup for a hat, hammering with a pencil. Both learning the conventions and innovatively changing the conventions depend on understanding intentionality behind the convention. This kind of imitation extends to the use of language. A child understands that a linguistic symbol stands for some item in the world because she or he can recognize that someone else is using that symbol to refer to that item, and then she or he can also use the word in the same way (or use it playfully in another way).[14] Learning language, which allows us to share a social world, depends on this kind of intersubjectivity.

Language use, of course, is much more complex than discovering a simple referent for a single word. As children come to learn a language, they learn multiple meanings for a single word, multiple words for a single referent, and even multiple grammatical structures to express an event. Each of these forms takes a particular perspective on an experiential situation. Consider various ways one might describe a particular dwelling: "a house," "their home," "that eyesore," "the place for sale." Or consider different ways of reporting something that happened: "John hit Bill with a hammer." "The hammer hit Bill." "Bill got hit by a hammer." "It was John who hit Bill with the hammer." "It was a hammer that hit Bill." Each of these ways of speaking calls attention in a different way to the experiential situation under discussion. Each communicates something a little bit different, and the speaker normally chooses which expression to use depending on what aspect of the situation the speaker wants to highlight for the hearer. Socially shared linguistic symbols, then, are not only intersubjective but also perspectival.[15]

The various perspectives available in the language that a child acquires enable her to conceptualize, categorize, and schematize events and things with more complexity and flexibility than would be possible without language. Language does not create these abilities; nonhuman primates and prelinguistic infants also have them.[16] Language does, though, increase our sophistication in using them. Language may shape how we construe (take a perspective on) a certain state of affairs, it may allow us to construe it in more than one way, and it enables us to recognize the differences between our construals and the construals of others. As children mature and become more adept in language use, they also become more aware of differences in perspectives. This awareness leads to disagreements, clarifications, and discussions about why those views are different. Perspectives may be shared, as they must be to create a joint attentional scene, but they also may differ in a variety of ways and some of them may be false. Eventually children learn that it is possible to hold multiple perspectives simultaneously on a single situation, and this ability allows the kind of flexible interaction with others that is required in a social world.

As communicative needs become more complex, language forms also become more complex. Narrative meets a communicative need that simple reference cannot, although it also communicates by being intersubjective and perspectival. A narrative creates a world that we have to enter in order to understand, and the natural human ability to identify with others makes such an engagement with the world of a story possible. A narrative also has a point of view, so entering that world involves coming to see from that point of view. Because narrative has these features, it can become important for cultural transmission, a complex process of communicating such things as attitudes and values from one generation to another. Part of what culture transmits to us is a sense of order, and this sense of order is what is indicated when sociologists and others talk about "constructing a world," a human activity about which an enormous body of literature has been written.[17] "World" here does not mean the planet earth or physical items in their simple concreteness; instead, it refers to a context of meaning for those items. The term borrows much from the idea of "world view" in anthropology, where the phrase highlights the way in which culture provides a people with its most comprehensive ideas of order.[18] Whether any correspondence exists between our constructions of the world and the physical world is a disputed question, but many disciplines from anthropology to philosophy acknowledge that culture has some degree of influence on our understanding of the way things are. Because it has to do with order and meaning, a "world" is fundamentally about intelligibility. Human beings need some structure in which events make sense, and culture helps provide that structure. Because narratives create "worlds," they are apt vehicles for transmitting cultural understandings of "world." Narratives, whether they may be historical, scientific, or mythological, help us identify and elaborate relevant connections among things that happen to us and around us. These kinds of narratives provide intelligibility and followability for our lives just as a narrator does for a story's characters and readers, and most of the time, we take the context of relevant connections that constitutes our world as unself-consciously as characters in a fictional story do theirs.

Cultural transmission, though, does not simply provide order. As important as imitation is to sharing a world, innovation and conflict also take place. We do not simply learn from others, we learn through others by identifying with them and seeing some aspect of the world as they see it. However, the learner is also a mental agent with a perspective, and that perspective will never be in every way identical to the perspective of the teacher. Furthermore, no one learns just one story in a society. Different teachers share different stories, each with a point of view; sometimes those points of view will be in tension or outright conflict with one another. In fact, our very ability to see that it is possible to hold multiple perspectives on a single experiential situation means that new or competing perspectives are always possible. Disagreements, clarifications, and discussions about why we hold our views do not end in childhood. They are an ongoing part of life among mental agents.

As we participate in the world that narratives help us construct, we also construct our sense of self. Selfhood is another complex idea that deserves and has received more discussion than I can include here. Some researchers suggest that our early narrative abilities (e.g., temporal organization and causality) play an important role in gaining a sense of self even as young children. Not only do they help us comprehend narratives that are told to us, but they enable us to take an active role in ordering events for ourselves.[19] Probably, some combination of cultural influence and our own active appropriation make us who we are, and as we become more and more proficient members of culture, it can have more influence on us. Again, what constitutes a self is a disputed question, but to whatever extent culture is involved in our coming to be who we are as thinking, acting, and emotional persons, narratives will play a significant role. We become agents in a context that provides an intelligible way of viewing the world, and in doing so it identifies what is worth acting for, thinking about, and even feeling.[20] Becoming a self surely involves more than narratives alone, but narratives selectively highlight aspects of the world that we ought to attend to, show how our lives connect with other lives, and, as Crites suggests, offer opportunities for us to imagine how the consequences of our actions and attitudes might unfold. Our values, relationships, and imaginations take the shape they do at least partly because of the stories we are told.

As narrative's influence on self-understanding has become clearer, storytelling has become an important component of some approaches to psychotherapy. I want to mention two ways in which narratives may be therapeutic because of the relevance these ideas have for the wholeness that salvation brings. First, the act of constructing a story itself seems to have health benefits. The ability to "make sense" of episodes in one's life by finding relevant connections and seeing their unfolding consequences is a major accomplishment. How narratives help us heal is not exactly clear, but one suggestion is that they help us achieve a changed relationship to our past. A person who begins therapy because of some past trauma already has some perspective on that trauma, even if it is not well understood or articulated. Narrating the event, whether to another person or even to oneself, brings about a reflective distance from it through which one gains a new perspective.[21] Interestingly, having a completed story matters less than movement toward developing a story.[22] Perhaps the ability to construct a story matters more because we are always adding to our stories as new episodes in our lives take place and new dimensions of past episodes become evident.

Second, our stories can change, and sometimes that change brings health benefits. A new story may reflect a new level of assimilation of past problematic experiences in one's life.[23] A person may also try out different perspectives by telling different stories, and thereby discover aspects of one's own self that have been hidden or peripheral.[24] Narrating, then, is an ongoing process in one's life. Emphasis on process has led some to suggest that the act of construction itself is all that matters, in other words, any story will do. Others point out problems with this approach, and the debate in some ways replicates issues in the field of history. While it may be true that more than one story can be "true to the facts" (or better, to the "data") of our lives, it may also be that some stories fit the givens of our past and allow for a flourishing life better than others.[25] Narration may well be a process, but engaging in that process does not mean simply making things up.

Although these insights come from a field that studies the way narrative works in psychotherapy, what happens in therapy to some extent also happens as we engage in storytelling with the people we encounter in daily situations. Narration there will surely be less directed and less concentrated on therapeutic goals, but we surely can use narratives to gain reflective distance and try on new perspectives outside a therapeutic setting. We construct our worlds and our selves, and we sustain relationships by telling stories to each other. Narrative is part of the very fabric of our social lives, both reflecting and shaping what we know.

Since narrative has such a central place in our communication with one another, it should also have a central place in God's communication to us. In chapter 3, we examined the central features of revelatory communication. Revelation discloses God's self so that we may enter into relationship with God, and this revelation often takes place when the words of the Bible mediate God to us. For the Bible to function in this way, several things are at work. Experience is crucial because revelation is fundamentally an encounter with God's self. As the Bible bears witness to God, we are linked to the past, connected to a community of others who have also experienced God. The knowledge that we gain through revelation includes some kind of cognitive growth that brings with it a new perspective on our situation. Because relationships are dynamic, and because the life situation of any human being will change daily, revelation can never be static. Our understanding of God must be related to every circumstance in order for our relationship with God to retain its relevance, so revelation is ongoing in the sense that we are always gaining new insights about God's involvement in our lives. Our understanding of God may be broadened and deepened with each question that life poses. The issue now before us is how understanding the Bible as narrative contributes to this understanding of revelation. It is time to turn to the Bible itself to see what kind of narrative it provides to us, so that we can explore how that narrative enables God to communicate with us.

NOTES

1. Jeremy Hawthorn, "Narrative," in *A Glossary of Contemporary Literary Theory* (New York: Oxford University Press, 1998), 222–23; Robert Scholes and Robert Kellogg, *The Nature of Narrative* (London: Oxford University Press, 1966), 280.

2. Stephen D. Moore, *Literary Criticism and the Gospels: The Theoretical Challenge* (New Haven: Yale University Press, 1989), 14–15.

3. For an introduction to some of the technical problems, see "Story and Plot," in *Glossary of Contemporary Literary Theory*, 330–32.

4. Stanley Hauerwas and David Burrell, "From System to Story: An Alternative Pattern for Rationality in Ethics," in *Why Narrative? Readings in Narrative Theology* (ed. Stanley Hauerwas and L. Gregory Jones; Eugene, Ore.: Wipf & Stock, 1997), 177. Originally published in Stanley Hauerwas's *Truthfulness and Tragedy: Further Investigation in Christian Ethics* (Notre Dame, Ind.: University of Notre Dame Press, 1977), 15–39.

5. Although history is an obvious example, some have argued that even the most logical disciplines are couched in narrative. According to this view, even science and mathematics have narrative traditions of how things are done. Scientific theories tell stories in the sense that they seek to explain facts in a domain of interest; and in making selections, finding relevant connections, and opening possibilities for explaining yet unobserved instances of an empirical phenomenon (a sort of unfolding), science works narratively. Mathematics also involves storytelling in the sense that one has to learn to follow a process within a narrative tradition that organizes items in the world and works in a particular way. That there are options to a base ten numbering system or Euclidean geometry shows that those who use these systems have learned a story to which there are alternative stories. See George S. Howard, "Culture Tales: A Narrative Approach to Thinking, Cross-Cultural Psychology, and Psychotherapy," *American Psychologist* 46, no. 3 (March 1991): 187–97; and Alasdair MacIntyre, "Epistemological Crises, Narrative, and Philosophy of Science," *Monist* 60, no. 4 (October 1977): 453–72; repr. in Hauerwas and Jones, *Why Narrative?* 138–57.

6. For two accounts of how narrative affects selection of what to include in history, see Jerome Bruner, "What Is a Narrative Fact?" in *The Annals of the American Academy of Political and Social Science*, Alan W. Heston, ed., vol. 560, *The Future of Fact*, Jeffrey J. Strange and Elihu Katz, eds. (Thousand Oaks, Calif.: Sage Publications, 1998), 17–27; and Louis Mink, "Narrative Form as a Cognitive Instrument," in *The Writing of History: Literary Form and Historical Understanding* (ed. Robert H. Canary and Henry Kozicki; Madison: The University of Wisconsin Press, 1978), 129–49.

7. Peter Novick, "(The Death of) the Ethics of Historical Practice (and Why I Am Not Mourning)," and Judith Lichtenberg, "The Will to Truth: A Reply to Novick," in *The Annals of The American Academy of Political and Social Science*, vol. 560, *The Future of Fact*, 28–54.

8. Stephen Crites, "The Narrative Quality of Experience," *Journal of the American Academy of Religion* 39, no. 3 (September 1971): 291–311; repr. in Hauerwas and Jones, *Why Narrative?* 65–88.

9. Louis O. Mink represents this position in "Narrative Form as a Cognitive Instrument," in *The Writing of History: Literary Form and Historical Understanding* (ed. Robert H. Canary and Henry Kozicki; Madison: The University of Wisconsin Press, 1978), 129–49.

10. One research team studied how children tell stories to other people by using a book, *Frog, Where Are You?* which consists only of illustrations by Mercer Mayer. These illustrations show a sequence of events following a boy's search for a frog that has escaped from a jar. In extensive data gathering, researchers elicited an articulated story about these illustrations from preschool, school-age, and adult narrators in five languages. Three themes emerge in their study: the "filtering" of experience through language, the "packaging" of event descriptions in narration, and the development of cognitive and psycholinguistic abilities that increased proficiency in "filtering" and "packaging." It will come as no surprise to anyone acquainted with the problems of biblical interpretation that all the participants in this study told their stories in different ways, and some of the differences came from the range of options (such as tense) that was available in the specific language used. But despite differences in language and other perspectives, participants in the study showed similar narrative abilities when compared with others in their age group. See Ruth A. Berman and Dan Isaac Slobin, *Relating Events in Narrative: A Crosslinguistic Developmental Study* (Hillsdale, N.J.: Lawrence Erlbaum, 1994).

11. The ability of young children to make causal connections has not always been clear, and another research team tested that ability in a recent study. They were partly prompted to do so because the prevailing view (based on one of Piaget's studies) held that children younger than seven or eight years of age cannot correctly order events and do not make appropriate use of causal connectors when retelling a story because they could not tell the difference between cause, consequence, and logical justification. These researchers reexamined Piaget's own data and conducted new research of their own. They found even in Piaget's own data that children do order major episodes correctly. They also found that three-year-olds do not have difficulty comprehending causal connections, and in fact they are proficient in understanding simple antecedents and consequences for both physical and psychological states when asked direct questions about them. Although the spontaneous use of causal connectors increases with age, young children who have not yet reached that developmental milestone can still understand cause and effect. When they do use causal connectors, they do so correctly. It is not the ability to understand causal connections that develops but the ability to identify and articulate a sustained plot. Narrative comprehension, then, at least in the basic form of understanding the directionality of a story, can exist quite early, even if proficiency in narrative construction takes time and practice. See Tom Trabasso, Nancy L. Stein, and Lucie R. Johnson, "Children's Knowledge of Events: A Causal Analysis of Story Structure," in *The Psychology of Learning and Motivation: Advances in Research and Theory* (ed. Gordon H. Bower; vol. 15; New York: Academic, 1981), 237–82.

12. Michael Tomasello, *The Cultural Origins of Human Cognition* (Cambridge: Harvard University Press, 1999), 97. In the discussion about language that follows, I will be presenting several ideas from Tomasello's book that I find relevant for helping us see how we understand and interpret the Bible.

13. Ibid., 70–81.

14. Tomasello relates the findings of studies he and others have conducted on how children come to understand the use of a linguistic symbol in the flow of social interaction (*Cultural Origins of Human Cognition*, 108–18). I will summarize some of the important points here. When an adult uses a new word, a child has to figure out what that word intends to communicate. For instance, if an adult picks up a ball and says a word, a child who has never heard that word before has to grasp whether the adult is using the word to name the object (ball), name the motion (picking up), start a game (catch), or something else that may in fact have nothing to do with the ball (for instance, greeting the child). In various studies in which adults use novel words (such as "dax" and "toma") that could potentially refer to multiple things in the situation but have a specific intended referent, Tomasello has observed that children by the age of eighteen to twenty-four months are quite skillful at determining what the adult intends. Children were capable of doing so not only when directly instructed but also in the natural flow of conversation because their ability to recognize intention and attention allows them to sort through otherwise highly ambiguous possibilities. Once the intended referent has been identified, the next step in learning the word is role-reversal imitation, in which a child tries using the word in the same way that she has understood the adult to use it. At this point, child and adult together share a way of understanding the novel word, and they are able to communicate with it. This shared understanding of a symbol Toma-sello calls "intersubjectivity."

15. Tomasello, *Cultural Origins of Human Cognition*, 118–23.

16. Ibid., 150–60, 169.

17. An important source of information about world-building and world-maintenance, and particularly the role of religion in each, is Peter L. Berger, *The Sacred Canopy: Elements of a Sociological Theory of Religion* (New York: Anchor, 1969).

18. In *The Interpretation of Cultures*, Clifford Geertz defines "world view" as a people's "picture of the way things in sheer actuality are," or "the assumed structure of reality." Clifford Geertz, *The Interpretation of Cultures* (New York: Basic, 1973), 127, 129.

19. One collaborative study shows how we are actively involved in constructing a sense of self through narratives from a very early age. The researchers involved in this study used tapes that parents made of their daughter Emily as she was talking to herself before going to sleep. They taped this naptime and nighttime "crib talk" for fifteen months, starting when Emily was twenty-one months old. During this time, Emily worked on temporal ordering and causality, and she sorted out expectable events from unexpectable events. These tasks helped her find order in the things that occurred in her day. Furthermore, she started to indicate her perspective on events by naming how she felt or what she thought about them. The researchers hypothesize that through these soliloquies, Emily was learning to make sense of her world and to develop a sense of self (with agency, coherence, continuity, and affectivity) through her narration. For the full discussion, see Karen Nelson, ed., *Narratives from the Crib* (Cambridge: Harvard University Press, 1989). See esp. Jerome Bruner and Joan Lucariello, "Monologue as Narrative Recreation of the World," 73–97.

20. For a discussion of how emotions are shaped by narrative, see Martha Nussbaum, "Narrative Emotions: Beckett's Genealogy of Love," *Ethics* 98, no. 2 (January 1988): 225–54; repr. in Hauerwas and Jones, *Why Narrative?* 216–48.

21. Aaron L. Mishara, "Narrative and Psychotherapy—The Phenomenology of Healing," *American Journal of Psychotherapy* 49, no. 2 (spring 1995): 180–95.

22. Óscar F. Gonçalves and Paulo P. P. Machado, "Cognitive Narrative Psychotherapy: Research Foundations," *Journal of Clinical Psychology*, 55, no. 10 (1999): 1179–91.

23. William B. Stiles, Lara Honos-Webb, and James A. Lanji, "Some Functions of Narrative in the Assimilation of Problematic Experiences," *Journal of Clinical Psychology* 55, no. 10 (1999): 1213–26.

24. Hubert J. M. Hermans, "Self-Narrative as Meaning Construction: The Dynamics of Self-Investigation," *Journal of Clinical Psychology* 55, no. 10 (1999): 1193–1211.

25. For a discussion and criticism of constructivist models that still defends the importance of narrative, see Charles Guignon, "Narrative Explanation in Psychotherapy," *American Behavioral Scientist* 41, no. 4 (January 1998): 558–77.

CHAPTER FIVE

Reading the Bible as Narrative

Some central features of the Bible affect the way in which one can reasonably consider it as narrative and thus affect reading Scripture as narrative. First, one must acknowledge that the Bible was not written by a single author to be a single narrative with a sustained plot and coherent and consistent characters. The texts that we use are the product of a long process of construction by multiple authors and editors, beginning with oral traditions that were written down over time and then selectively brought together in documents we now call "books." Second, the collection of books that the Bible includes differs among Christian communities because the process of selecting the materials to be included in the canon also took place over a long period of time and was influenced by a variety of factors. Roman Catholics accept apocryphal books as canonical, while Protestants do not. Roman Catholic and Eastern Orthodox churches differ over which apocryphal books they consider canonical.[1] Third, regardless of which collection is under discussion, the materials included in the Bible can be read and used in a variety of ways. They may be studied as literary products, ranging from legal documents to hymns. They may provide a source for certain kinds of historical information. They may be compared to other types of religious writings. In other words, they may be "construed" differently; that is, they may be taken in different ways for different purposes. As we have seen, taking a perspective on any concrete item in the world is a natural and necessary human activity. What this insight means for studying the Bible is that it must always be taken "as" something—as history, as literature, etc. Taking the Bible "as" narrative involves adopting a perspective, a hermeneutical approach, that needs to be justified to the extent that it can be shown to be appropriate to the item itself and to some purpose, but that does not rule out other justifiable perspectives on the material.

One perspective important for this project is construing the Bible as scripture. "Bible" and "scripture" are often used synonymously, but the term "scripture" clearly indicates a kind of perspective held on the Bible, namely, that one takes it to have religious authority. Christians take the Bible "as scripture" in different ways, but David Kelsey has provided a sophisticated analysis of claims that are made by various theologians with quite different points of view about the Bible to show how those perspectives display a similar logic. He points out that construing the Bible as scripture, and particularly using it as authority for theology, yields four implications: (1) using the Bible in certain ways is essential to establishing and maintaining the community's identity; (2) it has, then, authority for the church's common life; (3) a certain kind of "wholeness" can be ascribed to it, despite its complex character; and (4) acknowledging the Bible as scripture commits one to using it as the authority one believes it to be.[2] These four points, Kelsey maintains, cut across theological identities so that they apply as much to conservatives as to liberals or any particular theological point of view. Construing the Bible as scripture is central to the way I will argue for construing the Bible as narrative. In the remainder of this chapter, I will deal with questions of communal identity and the "wholeness" of the Bible. In chapter 7, after having considered the concept of authority itself, I will examine how the Bible may then be used for the common life of the Christian community under this understanding.

The Bible as Narrative

As Frances Young has pointed out, the character of the Bible as "library" would have been more obvious to the ancients than it is to us because they would have been dealing with collections of rolls or codices rather than a bound book.[3] The history of the collection and use of certain codices as scripture for the Jewish and then the early Christian community is well documented elsewhere.[4] Here I will only briefly examine the major outlines of that process. For the earliest Christians, "scripture" was first Hebrew Scripture (what came to be called the "Old Testament"), and only later were new works that documented events and gave guidance to the Christian community written down, circulated, and read along with Hebrew Scripture. That group of new works included more than what we now recognize as the "New Testament," and part of what had to take place in the early centuries of Christianity was a decision about the status of these new manuscripts with respect to Hebrew Scripture and with respect to each other.

That decision process was intimately connected with a process of defining self-understanding among Christians under the pressure of alternative possibilities, especially those that incorporated gnostic ideas in their understanding of Jesus Christ. Two figures especially focused questions about canon:

Marcion, who rejected the God of Hebrew Scripture, and Montanus, who claimed that the Holy Spirit continued to give new dispensations beyond the gospels and epistles that were circulating in his time. Both the relationship of Christianity to its Jewish heritage and the relationship among various groups that worshiped Jesus Christ were at issue during the early centuries, and the effect of these relationships on the formation of the Bible continued to be worked out over a long period of time. The earliest surviving statements about what constitutes scripture appear in the second century, but the list of books considered scripture was somewhat fluid at least until Athanasius specified a list in 367 C.E. that corresponds with what we now consider the Bible. Even then, some questions about peripheral books persisted so that even as late as 692 there was some disagreement over inclusion of the book of Revelation. Over time, a core understanding about canon emerged that was closely connected to the emerging identity of the church. By continuing to recognize the Hebrew canon as scripture, an increasingly Gentile Christianity refused to sever its connection with its Hebrew heritage even as it simultaneously reinterpreted that heritage in light of Jesus Christ. By accepting some new writings as having the status of Scripture along with the Hebrew canon, Christianity became itself a new religion. And by rejecting other new writings as representing heretical ideas, Christianity was making a determination of which understanding of Jesus Christ would be normative for the community. Although "scripture" consisted of a library of materials, decisions about what belonged in that library were based on theological concerns, and they were made in connection with decisions about identity. This collection of codices belonged together because of an emerging understanding of God's work in Jesus Christ that was held by a community that identified itself with that understanding. Canon and identity came into being together. This community accepts these writings as scripture, so these writings define this community. As a result, the Bible can be called "canon" in two senses: as collection and as criterion.

Although I have used the word "decision" above, the process of "deciding" was not exactly formal, and it may often have been tacit rather than explicit. Young describes the process of determining the canon as in some ways "haphazard," but she also sees in it the emergence of a communal consensus.[5] Individuals voiced arguments about which materials should be considered scripture, but those individual arguments would not have been convincing unless much of the community itself already held a similar view. Irenaeus, for instance, in speaking of a "new testament" was likely giving voice to an unarticulated perception of the status of certain Christian literature, so that once articulated the idea caught hold widely and firmly. In practice, an unspoken understanding lay behind the acceptance of particular books as scriptural. Although scholars of the time often appealed to apostolicity to justify the inclusion of some books and the exclusion of others, that criterion itself had less to do with perceived apostolic authorship than with whether the testimony contained therein seemed reliable. In particular, the inclusion of gnostic ideas (which militated against the oneness of God with a mythology that told of the emanation and proliferation of divine beings, or which called into question the historical reality of Jesus' life and death because of a distaste for the material world) made certain books suspect. For instance, some gospels bearing the names of apostles (Thomas, Philip) did not conform to "apostolic" teaching, while other gospels not bearing the names of apostles (Mark, Luke) did. While those former gospels must certainly have seemed reliable in some communities, a growing sense in the church at large determined that they deviated from some basic understanding that was ancient and held largely in common.

Why did gnostic ideas seem so unreliable to so many? According to Young, Gnosticism, with its hierarchical scheme of divine beings and its low regard for the material world, forced the question, Is this God's world or not? This question has two senses. First, is this *God's* world? And second, is *this world* God's? Or to put it another way, does the ultimate divine being have anything to do with the physical, historical reality of things and events in which we live? A negative answer to these questions directly opposed foundational ideas that Christianity had inherited from Judaism, namely, devotion for the one God who created the universe and called it good. Irenaeus's arguments for the reliability of certain apostolic writings were intimately connected with these questions. His identification of what was appropriately called scripture was designed to rule out negative answers to those questions.[6] He conceived of an overarching story in what he understood to be scripture in which the same God created this world, saw it fall, made covenant with Abraham, and spoke through the prophets to foretell Jesus Christ, through whom creation would be restored. Elements of this story appear in other writings, but they use those elements to teach a fundamentally different story. Irenaeus describes the difference in teachings by comparing the "reliable" teaching to a mosaic of a king and the "unreliable" teaching as a mosaic in which the same pieces of stone are rearranged to depict a dog or a fox. While one may recognize the stones, one surely cannot recognize the king any longer. Using another example, Irenaeus describes how one might take lines from Homer and construct them into new poetry. One could recognize the lines, but not the story, as Homer's.[7] Similarly, unreliable writings have taken parables, sayings, and prophetic utterances and rearranged them to mean something altogether different than they should mean.

In the case of competing gospels, how does one recognize the story? One has to have a framework for seeing how the pieces ought to fit together, and Irenaeus argued for a framework passed down from antiquity, namely, the rule of faith that he took to be the genuine apostolic tradition of the church. When Irenaeus actually articulates the rule of faith, the details vary and do not simply summarize "the story of the Bible" by following all the major events (such as the flood or the exodus) from creation onward.[8] Instead, each distinct articulation of the rule of faith provides a perspective on God's activity in the world, namely, a plan of salvation that affirms the unity of God, the unity of Scripture, and God's own action in the Jesus who walked among us. Recognizing "the story," then, involves recognizing this perspective. While Irenaeus appeals to the story to justify the perspective that this is God's world, he also appeals to the perspective that this is God's world to justify what he identifies as the Scripture that tells the story. The two are mutually supportive. Story and perspective belong together.

Today we may have to acknowledge that other frameworks are also ancient and that one finally took precedence over the others. The point here is that the gaining of ascendancy of one framework was not arbitrary and was not simply imposed by individual scholars. For their arguments to have any force at all in the community, there had to be some sense already of what that story was, probably through what was being taught in catechesis and read, preached, and practiced in liturgy in large numbers of churches. To point out the presence of implicit communal agreement about the story does not mean that this agreement was complete. Other possible frameworks did exist, but over time and in the face of competing alternatives, a widespread consensus emerged. Being a part of this community meant sharing a particular perspective that was shaped by a particular canon.

Of course, establishing a canon did not eliminate disagreements among Christians over how to understand salvation through Jesus Christ. For several centuries, the most vigorous arguments took place over how to interpret the collection that the community at least tacitly agreed could rightfully be called "scripture." At stake in the Trinitarian and christological controversies in the fourth and fifth centuries was the proper way to read key passages in Scripture that were thought to provide clues to understanding the nature of God and the relationship of Jesus to God.[9] While they had distinctive emphases, these controversies followed naturally from the controversies over the canon itself. In fact, some key ideas in the later controversies were already expressed during the time of the shaping of the canon (Irenaeus, e.g., laid the groundwork for certain christological ideas that became central in later centuries). Part of what had been at issue in canonical decisions was commitment to one, true

God and this one, true God's activity in the real world. The same God who was at work in the history of Israel was also at work in the history of Jesus Christ. Writings that were thought to undermine this unity or God's salvific involvement in Jesus' real life and death had been rejected. But as Christian thinkers began to work out the way in which God could have been salvifically involved in the history of Jesus, those very commitments came into question once again, albeit in different ways.

As Christians gave affirmative answers to both senses of the question, Is this God's world? they had to work out the salvific implications of those affirmations in light of the history of Jesus. The controversies that eventually produced what we now know as the doctrine of the Trinity and the doctrine of the incarnation took shape in the face of pressures that continued to push the church to make decisions about its understanding of God and how God worked for our salvation. As it became increasingly Gentile, Christianity was more and more influenced by Greek philosophy of the time. Although it had rejected Gnosticism, Christianity still made use of ideas that took shape in a philosophy that regarded the material world as unreliable and sought God by abstracting away from it. The one God whom Christians worshiped was conceived as perfect in the way that Greek philosophers described perfection: utterly simple and unitary, with no parts, no change, and no possibility of division into discrete units. Christian practice, though, worked against this idea in at least two ways. First, from very early times Christian faith suggested some kind of threeness for God. Because baptism involved three statements of belief, one for Father, one for Jesus Christ, and one for Holy Spirit, catechumens must have been instructed in the faith so that they could make this tripartite confession.[10] Already by the second century, theologians were defending worship of all three, and the tension between the above understanding of God's perfection and Christian practice produced various attempts toward resolution. Second, Jesus' birth, life, and death on the cross also presented problems for this way of understanding perfection. These events implied participation in the changing material world that seemed antithetical to the ideal of divinity conceived by the best thinkers of the time. It was not easy to do justice to Christian experience given these prevailing assumptions.

Over time, Christians worked out what they wanted to affirm about God by rejecting attempts that seemed to give up something that seemed central to Christian faith. The history of these controversies is enormously complex, with names and proposals too numerous to mention here. We can see, though, through a few examples how the presence of rejected alternatives shaped what came to be known as orthodox faith. Jesus was not a mere man (against Theodotus), but neither was he simply God the Father in a different "mode" (against Sabellius). Jesus is the Son incarnate, and while the Son is distinct from the Father, the Son is not subordinate to the Father (against Arius). These decisions affirmed that our salvation requires nothing less than God to be present in Jesus Christ, but God must be present in a way that divinity is not compromised either by division or by its involvement with human nature. Furthermore, our salvation also requires that this incarnation involve a complete human nature (against Apollinaris) because all of a human being, not simply the flesh, needs redemption. Human nature and divine nature, however, cannot come together in the incarnation by mere association (against Nestorius), or the healing effects cannot really reach us. But on the other hand, the divine nature and the human nature have to be held together in the incarnation in a way that each retains its integrity (against Eutyches), or we lose our point of contact between our human problem and the divine solution. Through the gradual and painful process of sorting through these options, the church eventually arrived at doctrines that continued to define the identity of the community.

Claiming implicit consensus may be more difficult here than with canonical development. Arianism, for instance, had large numbers of proponents among ordinary Christians as well as political leaders. Similarly, the continued presence and influence of Nestorian and Monophysite Christians led to schismatic churches in several areas of the Mediterranean world. What divided Christians in these cases was not so much the canon itself as it was how to read the canon. Different interpretations of Scripture were possible (e.g., how to read Prov 8:22 was central to the Arian controversies), and given the presuppositions of the time, some made more sense than others. In fact, what is remarkable about the development of these central doctrines is that the church that identified itself with them consistently took the option that was harder to defend logically. The church refused to resolve the tensions between Christian faith and the prevailing understanding of divinity, leaving affirmations that were finally beyond the grasp of finite intellect, and it did so because the unity of God and the historical reality of salvation in Jesus Christ, two commitments that also shaped canonical decisions, continued as convictions that had to be honored despite the clear difficulty in doing so.

At stake, then, through canon formation and doctrinal formulation was a perspective on reality that was shaped by and in turn shaped a perspective on Scripture. The story that Scripture told through an informed reading of it provided a narrative "world" in which God's action in Jesus Christ was intelligible and followable. The Bible may not be a story in the way that a novel is, but its very shape as Christian canon indicates broad narrative features. It is a telling in which God's action in the world unfolds, with a beginning (creation), a middle (which encompasses God's involvement in the history of Israel, the history of Jesus, and even the very early church), and an end (God's rule is firmly established over all things). The establishment and wholeness of the canon is important, even if not in exactly the way that Protestant orthodox theologians thought. The final form of the Bible that Christians use includes texts that were taken to be relevant to this overarching story, and the differences among specific collections used by Roman Catholics, Eastern Orthodox, and Protestant churches do not alter this fundamental shape. While the diverse texts included in the Bible may not be utterly consistent with one another, they cohere (hang together) in that they all contribute in some way to understanding that this world is God's. The canon has these narrative features because the community that collected it read these texts narratively. Text and community are intimately related.

But more than this, Christians claimed that through this narrative the reality in which we live is made intelligible, too; that is, through it we gain a "world," a context of meaning in which all aspects of our lives make sense. In one sense the goal of the story is the vision at the story's end, but the telling of this story has other goals as well. By collecting, transmitting, teaching, and preaching these texts, the Christian community is sharing a perspective about reality itself, the "contours of existence," as Crites says, that allow us to find our place in a world that has order and meaning and to live with integrity in it. Scripture's story was saying, "Attend to the real world (actual things, people, and events) in such a way as to recognize it as God's," and furthermore, "Attend to how God is present and at work in this world in Jesus Christ." The story is not only perspectival but also intersubjective because coming to know it involves sharing this way of understanding the world with others. One cannot read this story straight from any particular text or groups of texts, but reading the texts that have become Scripture for the Christian community in the way that this community has read them can foster certain convictions in us. We learn through the community how to read this story in the Bible, and the story in turn helps us to "read" the world in which we live.

We live at a time when many of the presuppositions shared by Christians in the first century are no longer viable. Good historians often have to adjust their narratives to fit new "facts" that have become relevant. For instance, we know the canon speaks with many voices, and the historical context of individual writings in the canon have to be taken into account in any interpretation of them. We may question the accuracy of many texts, both with regard to history and even with regard to how they depict God's action in the world. We may also have to work out our most basic doctrines in a way that takes account of issues that were not present in the first centuries. Earlier Christians were trying to work out how to articulate their basic convictions in their time with the conceptions that were available to them, and it seems to me that our task remains the same. Honoring the commitments that shaped canon and doctrine does not necessarily mean retaining the exact articulations of those commitments as they were expressed in a former time. Given different presuppositions, the overarching story may find expression in different ways. Just as the story of Pearl Harbor may continue to unfold as new perspectives are considered or as its implications continue to be drawn out, the story of God's presence and work in this world in Jesus Christ admits of expansion and adaptation. It could not have been told with success in other cultures if it were not so. Sharing this story with Christians of the past does not mean conformity to static formulations. Neither does sharing this story eliminate disagreement. Our experiences of reality are complex, as are the texts through which we seek to encounter God. Still, taken together, the various components that make up the Bible have a shape that provides a fundamental orientation to the world: there is one God, who made covenant with Israel and then was disclosed in Jesus Christ, and those who embrace a relationship with this God find wholeness and hope. How that relationship may be fostered through these diverse texts is the topic to which we now turn.

NARRATIVE AS GOD'S COMMUNICATION

While I have argued that the Bible Christians use is shaped to tell an overarching story, one hardly ever hears that story "in a nutshell," as it were. Christians do not generally hear a succinct outline of God's involvement with the world. Nor do they usually come to know the Bible in the first place by reading it from beginning to end. Even if they eventually do so, most Christians come to know the Bible through hearing or reading bits of it in liturgical activities, preaching, Sunday school, and Bible study. They gradually gain a perspective on God's presence in the world through hearing or reading diverse, individual texts from the Bible, usually in the context of a community that interprets those texts. For instance, having readings in worship from both the Old Testament and the New Testament indicates some connection between God's involvement with Israel and with the church. Similarly, the liturgical year moves through the story of Jesus' life, death, and resurrection so that the diverse texts read in worship find some place in that overall framework. Through practices such as these, people implicitly come to recognize the presuppositions that lie behind individual texts and connect them. Still, particular passages and not the whole story itself are usually at the forefront of people's encounter with the Bible. How acquaintance with those individual texts enables God to communicate to us remains to be explored.

The Bible is made up of texts that have been passed on and preserved because they have been thought to tell something of importance for knowing God. These are human documents, and perhaps not all of them had their origin in specifically religious contexts, but they have been collected together in a book that now does have a religious purpose. Just how that purpose ought to matter for our use of them is a topic that has been given considerable discussion by Charles M. Wood. One way that he approaches that question is by distinguishing between the Bible as source and as canon (which here indicates its function as criterion rather than as a collection).[11] As human documents that preserve something of the past, these writings can be used as a source of information about the periods of history from which they come and, more specifically, can be used by the church as a source of information about its heritage. Texts taken individually can provide evidence for ancient lifestyles, concepts that arose in particular situations and worship practices. Taken together, they can give an indication of the sweep of historical, theological, and sociological developments among the people who regarded these texts as scripture. In both cases, the Bible is an irreplaceable source of information about the traditions that are included there. Interest in such information could be strictly historical, that is, seeking a better understanding of what has happened in the past in this particular stream of human events. In this case, extracanonical writings may be as important as canonical ones because they, too, provide access to the past. Canonical writings cannot be presumed to be more helpful for reconstruction than other writings of the same period. All of them have to be examined with the careful analysis that any good historian brings to bear upon any human record of the past.

The Bible informs us about our past in another way that is quite different. Not only does it serve as a source for historical information; it also serves as a resource for thinking about Christian witness. In this case, it does have a different standing than extracanonical material would because the documents in the Bible have been regarded as documents for that very purpose. The materials in the Bible inform us about our past in order to help form us as Christians. When the interest in the material is Christian formation, the Bible does have a status that rejected materials do not. As a resource for Christian witness, the Bible presents to us a wide array of concepts, practices, metaphors, and moral injunctions upon which to reflect. In some way, each of these items has had a place in our past, and we will have to come to terms with them as Christians who live in a new situation. Knowing how to make use of them in current practice will lead us to thinking about the Bible as canon, but first I want to examine Christian understanding itself.

Understanding, according to Wood, is ability; that is, one understands something when one is able to make appropriate use of it. To understand a map, he says, is to be able to find one's way around with it. To understand algebra is to be able to perform certain mathematical operations, including knowing when those operations are called for. To understand the Bible, then, will also involve making use of it. The Bible may be construed and therefore used in a variety of ways, but here we will look specifically at making use of it to form Christian understanding. Christian understanding of Christian texts, Wood suggests, has as its primary aim knowing God, so appropriate use of the Bible in this case will be governed by this aim. This "knowing" is not simply a distanced knowledge *about* God but is rather knowledge *of* God that involves personal awareness and existential apprehension. In other words, it is knowledge gained by the kind of encounter with God of which we spoke in chapter 3. A person who comes to know God as a self with whom she has a relation will also come to know herself and those around her in light of this knowledge of God; that is, it will illumine her life situation. As H. Richard Niebuhr says, she gains a perspective, a pattern of relevance in which all things can be understood and find their value. How is it that the Bible can lead to this understanding?

The very diversity of the Bible turns out to be an aid in forming the kind of understanding that Christians seek through it. Wood explains how conceptual growth is aided by examples, of which the Bible abounds.[12] Because examples relate particular situations in which some concept is employed, they allow one to enter that situation and follow its use. We come to see through examples when and where a certain concept pertains, or perhaps when and where another concept is better suited. Take, for instance, the tension in Christian faith between mercy and judgment. It is one thing to explicate the meaning of these terms (a complex, difficult, and necessary process in itself); it is quite another thing to know how and when to apply mercy and judgment in concrete situations involving real people. In between lies the need for seeing how mercy and judgment are employed in particular cases in order to test that employment and learn (perhaps both positively and negatively) from those cases. Stories are particularly useful as examples because they create a world and invite the hearer or reader to enter it and follow the action, and Jesus' practice of teaching through parables underscores the importance of stories for coming to Christian understanding. While stories provide the best example of how a reader can enter a world and follow it, the Bible, of course, includes many other kinds of texts. Laws, moral injunctions, and poetry also represent some aspect of human life and provide opportunity for identification and insight. The reminder that these texts, too, are embedded in narratives greatly helps such identification. Even a dry, boring, seemingly unimportant genealogy may become illuminating when one is reminded of the narrative in which it belongs, that is, reminded of who these people were and how God worked in their lives. Understanding of anything, whether maps, algebra, or the Bible, does not come to us fully formed in an instant. It takes time to develop as we consider diverse conditions under which its use pertains and as we build on understanding that we have already gained under other circumstances. Just so, the diverse texts in the Bible offer us the opportunity to grow in understanding of God as we consider how God has engaged others with whom God has sought relationship.

Such understanding of God does not come automatically. I hinted above that explication is also necessary to understanding, and learning about the usage of words, utterances, and genres in the Bible takes considerable effort and discipline. Biblical texts have been shaped by conventions or practices that were widely used in their time but that we do not always share, and coming to understand them well requires an effort. To this end, biblical specialists are invaluable. Involvement in a Christian community is also invaluable because specifically Christian understanding of Christian texts has its own conventions. Such a community often reminds its members to approach the text in a way that seeks after God, to recognize the overarching story in which these texts find their place and the need to put to use what they are learning. Formation is not passive, then; Christians are not simply "formed" by something outside of us. Instead, formation requires some effort on our part to engage the text and to engage each other so that our understanding will in fact grow instead of stagnate. But in yet another sense, such understanding does not come automatically. While we must make some effort to make good use of these texts, we can at best dispose ourselves to understand God through them. "Dispose" here indicates our willingness and receptivity to acquire knowledge of God, not any certainty about attaining it through our own efforts. God must also "make use" of the texts in order to encounter us. The Bible is instrumental to this encounter, both for us and for God, so Christian understanding is formed through the Bible rather than by it. Without disposing ourselves to this possibility, though, we seriously reduce our ability to gain the knowledge of God that we seek.

Young's work allows us to consider further how texts help us grow in understanding. Entering a textual situation and following its use require that in some way we are able to read ourselves into that text, and Young draws on ancient discussions about art in order to explain how we can do so.[13] Texts communicate through mimesis, that is, through representing some aspect of human life in a way that clarifies it and draws the listener or reader into that perspective on it. The text need not represent actual events or characters in order to perform this function, as indeed Jesus' parables indicate. What matters is our ability to identify with what is being related in the text, that is, whether we recognize something about our own lives in what is being represented there. By being drawn into the perspective that the text represents, the listener or reader finds her own life illuminated or challenged by that perspective. In that sense, mimesis involves not simply representation but also imitation. The text demands some response from us through our identification with it. What helps that identification is the particularity of the text matching the particularity of our lives. We live, not "in general," but here and now under these conditions, so a text that describes some aspect of life under certain conditions will evoke recognition in us, even if the conditions of the text are not identical to the conditions in which we live. To the extent that a particular text evokes recognition over and over again in human lives, it may communicate something that is "universal," in the sense that there is some pattern of living in which we all participate in our own unique ways.

Mimesis involves imitation, but because the conditions of the text will always be somehow different from the conditions in which we live, imitation should not, and perhaps never really can, be slavish. The text provides constraints because its language comes from a particular social and cultural world that existed in some period in history, and understanding the world of the text requires also understanding the world out of which its language comes. Entering and following the world of a text, though, do not mean replicating that world in one's own life. In fact, to recall a previously made distinction, imitation is not mere mimicry. To imitate, one must understand conventional use, but once understood, inventiveness becomes possible. Young speaks about the openness of mimetic imitation by drawing an analogy with music.[14] Performing a piece of music requires attending to the notes, having technical competence, and knowing something of the conventions of other performances, but it also requires knowing the acoustics of this particular room and the audience that will be listening. Performing under certain conditions means adjusting to those conditions. Even more, a "fresh" performance that captures and moves the hearts of the audience involves imagination and perhaps even improvisation. Similarly, responding to a text in the Bible entails not only attention to the conventions being used to communicate through the text but also attention to the conditions in which it will be interpreted and used. If we are not only to understand the text but to understand our lives in light of the text, then "our lives," including all the conditions in which we live, become essential ingredients for hermeneutics. Mimetic involvement with the text does not close off creativity; it in fact demands it because otherwise the text loses its connection with us.

I have spoken so far of "formation," but it is also the case that sometimes the growth that takes place in Christian understanding takes us so far from where we were before that we can speak of "transformation." Christian theological language is full of vocabulary that indicates this kind of deep and abiding change: repentance, conversion, justification, new creation. Christians often claim that they understand themselves differently than they once did or that they were once without God and now live with God. Indeed, the perspective that the Bible has on the world may contrast starkly with other perspectives, and giving them up in order to embrace the understanding of God that the Bible represents requires a dramatic change. One moves from living in, or finding meaning in, one narrative to another. For instance, living in a narrative that proclaims God's love for all people calls us away from any narrative that promotes prejudice. A change in narratives of this sort often has the kind of therapeutic benefits that we saw above in psychotherapy. By bringing traumatic details of our lives into a perspective that brings us into relationship with God, we may experience a change that can be described as healing. Other narratives do not always present us with a stark choice. We often live in multiple narratives at the same time. They may supplement each other, as when it is possible to hold multiple construals on a situation, but some do compete with one another when they offer conflicting construals. To the extent that Christian narrative offers an alternative horizon in which we integrate our diverse experiences to that offered by another narrative, it forms us in a way that changes us from what we might otherwise have been.

In some cases, some fundamental change could take place in a single recognition of what the biblical narrative means for one's life. Powerful experiences of conversion or justification often take place in this way. To be lasting, those dramatic experiences must be accompanied by the kind of continual formation that I have described above. Furthermore, sometimes one gains over time, instead of in a moment, a fundamentally new perspective as one gradually seeks and employs ways of thinking that challenge a former one or one that constantly presses for attention (take, e.g., how the continual pressure to accumulate possessions in a capitalistic society may be tempered by the call to give up one's possessions). Formation and transformation do not diverge sharply from one another. Rather, they are dimensions of coming to embrace a narrative that provides the contours for one's life, a narrative that may stand itself in contrast to other available narratives.

The ability of examples or texts to draw us in and involve us in ways that we grow conceptually is not restricted to religious examples or to religious texts. It is simply a quality of examples and texts of all sorts. How can this "communication" be considered communication by God, or revelation? In order to deal with that question, I will draw from a discussion by Grace M. Jantzen about religious experience and revelation. In her essay "Conspicuous Sanctity and Religious Belief," Jantzen first distinguishes between two kinds of religious experiences.[15] Some religious experiences are of a dramatic kind, for instance, ecstasy, visions, and voices. It would be fairly simple to connect these kinds of experiences with revelation when it is itself conceived as special communication of religious truths. If one were looking for that kind of revelation, then one would expect something like a voice to deliver it. What Christians most often mean by religious experience, though, is "the sense of the presence of God in their daily, ordinary lives, giving purpose to routine, providing courage, comfort, and hope, strengthening and deepening their moral commitment and sensitivity, leading them to worship and praise."[16] Experiences of this second sort have epistemological value that has not usually been recognized. Jantzen shows through an examination of Teresa of Ávila's *The Interior Castle* how even when some kind of ecstatic, dramatic, intense experience comes, it is tested by and supported by daily activities and experiences. Without them, the intense experience could be a matter of self-deception. For Teresa, the certainty that one has about God and who one is in light of God comes from a lifetime of putting into practice the values that one learns in meditation. Certainty, or what one knows to be true about oneself and God, comes, not from intense emotional experiences, but from "one's whole reflective self-concept," which is developed over time through the daily exercise of prayer, humility, and obedience. These kinds of experiences may not communicate new propositional truths, but they do contribute to knowing the loving presence of God. Salvation, Jantzen says, "is not primarily from 'hell-fire,' but from the fragmentation of a life not integrated in the whole-making love of God."[17] Bringing one's relationship with God to bear on the ordinary experiences of daily life is central to religious experience, and it has a forming and transforming effect.

All examples and texts invite us to attend to some aspect of human existence in a certain way. They offer a perspective on the world, and as we have seen, the sharing of a joint attentional scene is fundamental to human communication. What the Bible does through its examples and texts, embedded as they are in a larger narrative about God's involvement in the world, is to invite us to attend to God. We need something to call our attention to God because God is not an item in the world to be known as we come to know any part of the created order. That, after all, is the point of talking about revelation. Something is disclosed that we would not know otherwise. The Bible may not be the only way in which we are called to attend to God, but it has been a particularly effective way for Christians throughout centuries of its use. Through the collected texts that were brought together in this Bible, humans who authored, edited, selected, and transmitted these texts communicate with us by sharing a perspective on the world. In more traditional Christian language, they bear witness to us about God. Human communication itself may become a vehicle for God's communication. When we are invited to attend to God's activity in the world through the witness of others, then we put ourselves in the position of encountering God for ourselves, of coming into relationship with God, and of bringing that relationship to bear on our daily lives. What makes this communication different is, not intrinsically different texts, but the perspective that they invite us to share, namely, a perspective that brings to

our awareness God's involvement in the world and allows us the opportunity
to experience it.

When one thinks about God's communication to us in this way, the kind of
engagement with a text that I have described above helps explain the dynamic
character of revelation. Clearly, God's communication to us is connected to
the past, as we "hear" through biblical texts the witness of those who have
gone before, but God's communication through these texts *to us* requires that
we "hear" under different conditions. Particular biblical texts may highlight
particular aspects of human life in which attending to God has mattered in a
certain way, and from them, we may learn how to ask how we ought to attend
to God in our own particular location. If we are to bring our relationship with
God to bear on every circumstance of our lives, then we will have new insights
about how to do so as our circumstances change. We come to know God
through the Bible, which allows us to explore and test various insights about
how God works in different situations, but our understanding of God must
finally move beyond whatever situation is represented in the Bible to our own
situation. We grow conceptually in our understanding of God as we undertake this kind of engagement with the text, and the actual use we make of the
insights we have developed will constitute our living relationship with God.
Our understanding is not simply theoretical or abstract; it is enacted in
diverse ways under diverse conditions. This is exactly the kind of "newness"
that we spoke of in chapter 3 that revelation requires. It is ongoing, but not in
a way that replaces the witness of the Bible; instead, it continues that witness
in a new time and place.

NARRATIVE AS CANON

To allow that understandings of biblical texts may be diverse calls for a further
discussion about whether limits to that diversity exist. That question moves us
immediately into the notion of the Bible as canon, in the sense of "criterion."
The use of the word "canon" in this sense comes from the Greek *kanōn*, which
means "a straight rod used for measuring." The Greek may be translated as
"rule" or "standard," and the basic meaning may be extended to indicate a
"principle." The idea that a standard sets a limit also allows "canon" to designate a sphere or area of action or influence, in other words, the limits in which
some action or influence pertains.[18] The sense in which the Bible provides a
measure, or a limit, for its use is now the topic before us.

Wood reminds us that "measuring" itself can be more complex than it
might appear at first. "A canon is canon," Wood says, "only in use; and it must
be construed in a certain way before it can be used."[19] Even a straight rod, the
concrete implement that gives us the notion of canon, can be construed to
measure straightness or length. That implement, though, does not lend itself

to being used for some other kinds of measurement, such as the curvature of a surface or weight or the passing of time. In order to use a standard of any sort appropriately, one needs to know what it is a standard for. Wood describes the confusion that might arise if one were simply given a chunk of metal and told it was a standard without any further explanation. It could conceivably be a standard for length, weight, color, hardness, value, metallic purity, and conductivity. Furthermore, the item to be used as a standard will itself influence what kind of "rule" it can provide. If this chunk of metal were spherical in shape and had no noticeable markings on it, it would not make a good measure for length. As a result, one would be skeptical about any insistence by the person who handed it over that it ought to be used in that way. When thinking of the Bible as canon, then, Wood suggests that one must consider first its own form and content in order to determine what an appropriate construal of it as a standard might be.[20]

In addition, one also needs to consider how it actually is used. A ruler has actually been used for many things besides measuring straightness or length; I have seen rulers used to extend a person's reach when trying to retrieve an item that has fallen behind a chair, to swat a disobedient child, and to serve as a pretend sword or baseball bat in play. The inventiveness of the human mind allows for all kinds of activities that have nothing to do with using it as a standard, and one cannot determine its function as a standard simply by observing all the varieties of use to which a ruler may be put. Similarly, one cannot simply look at how the Bible is used and figure out what it means to use it as canon. On the other hand, if one observed a ruler's use long enough to begin to see a pattern, namely, that on many occasions it was used with great effectiveness to draw straight lines or to measure length, then one might have good reason to think that it made a good standard for those sorts of things. Conversely, if one never saw a ruler put to use to measure weight or color, one would have little basis for thinking of it as a standard for weight or color. In the same way, observing throughout its history a pattern of use for the Bible that seems to be effective under a variety of conditions might indicate something important about its use as a standard. Even a strong pattern of actual use does not determine by itself the appropriate use of the Bible (many Christians acknowledge that the Bible has been misused over and over again in Christian history), but a suggestion for the Bible's use as canon that does have historical precedent will have an advantage over a suggestion that does not.

Finally, Wood advises taking into consideration how it is possible to justify the Bible's role as canon. In other words, what makes the canon the canon? Wood explains three possible attempts to answer a question of this sort. One might reply that its content is consonant with Jesus Christ, but that answer only indicates that the Bible is itself normed by something else. One might reply instead that it is canon because it norms Christian witness, but that answer really just reminds us of its function rather than explains how it came to have that function. To answer why this collection serves as the criterion for Christian witness, one needs to know the history of how this Bible came to play that role. Knowing why this set of texts was taken in the past to be a measure for the life and thinking of the community will provide insight into how it ought to be taken as a measure for the life and thinking of the community now. In examining this history, distinguishing between the way the canon assumed its role and the way that people of the time understood and justified that role is important. For instance, as we have already seen, an apologetic theologian in the early church might appeal to the apostolic authorship of books we know not to be written by apostles. The explicit argument tells us less about what makes the canon the canon than why the theologian made that argument.

How might the understanding of the Bible as narrative inform these three considerations about canon? First, its character as a collection of diverse materials brought together to tell an overarching story should inform the way that the Bible can function as a standard. The diversity of materials present in the Bible's pages ought to make one skeptical about any simplistic, straightforward measurement that would be analogous to lining up a ruler next to a piece of paper that should be twelve inches long to see whether it matches up. Which text would one use, and what would count as "matching up"? To the extent that the text itself provides some constraints on legitimate interpretation, checking one's reading against the text is appropriate, but even with that kind of testing, a range of interpretations is possible. Second, the fact that these diverse texts were brought together in the Bible indicates that they have some sort of unity that ought to be considered also. The Bible itself functions as canon, not the texts within it as individual canons. While the parts have their own integrity and make singular contributions to our understanding, they have a place in the whole that we must take into account as well. Both diversity and unity have to be acknowledged, and the Bible will have to serve as a standard in a way that suits its complexity. Perhaps because of its complexity, thinking of canon in terms of a sphere or area of action or influence may be more suited to its own form than thinking of canon as a measure with a one-to-one correspondence, in the way that a yardstick works. The Bible, then, would serve as a standard by setting limits rather than working by straightforward conformity.

The actual use that Christians have made of the Bible will also be important. Christians have a long-standing history of using the Bible for the formation of Christian understanding, with the aim of knowing God. Through allegory, preaching, devotional Bible study, and other practices, Christians have sought to use the Bible to shape and transform their lives; and they have affirmed the Bible's effectiveness in doing so. This actual use highlights for consideration at least two points about the Bible as canon. First, the Bible functions as criterion primarily with regard to this knowledge of God. If the Bible is instrumental to God's self-disclosure, then it has a guiding function in helping us form what we know about God, and it has a normative function in that we may test what we think we know about God. Second, this knowledge of God also affects knowledge of ourselves as we live in the extratextual world. We have seen that biblical texts do not simply present to us static information gained in the past but invite us to engage in considering God's presence in the world. Because it helps to form and test our knowledge of God, the Bible then also functions to help identify God's presence in the daily experiences that are so important for our relationship with God. When we encounter difficult situations, Christians need to learn to recognize God's support through it. When we face an ethical decision, Christians need to struggle to imagine what God would have us do. When we hear a sermon preached, Christians need to have some sense of whether it proclaims the word of the God we have come to know. Furthermore, as Christians bear witness (in words or actions) to our experience of God, we turn to the Bible as a guide for how to do so. The Bible may not be all that needs to be considered in these matters, but it contributes to our understanding centrally and indispensably.

Very often when we turn to the Bible in these ways, Christians do not adequately distinguish between the Bible as source or resource and as canon. Just because a text is in the Bible does not make it by itself an adequate guide or test for belief or action. The presence of passages about slavery in the Bible, for instance, should not be taken to mean that the Bible endorses slavery. Because actual use (with the possibility of misuse) does not by itself determine canonical function, we also must take into account the other considerations I mention here. However, we can at least see a pattern in this actual use that Christians do seek to use the Bible as a guide for making judgments and for bearing witness (in its broadest sense). Whether we are engaged in discernment for critical or constructive purposes, Christians seek direction from the Bible, which calls us to take account of God in every situation, even if it does not give a precise formula as to how to do so in any situation.

Finally, what makes the canon the canon? We have already seen some of the influences on the shaping of the canon as a collection, and the Bible came to be what it was because of deep commitments about the one, true God who is present and active in this world through Jesus Christ. These commitments illuminate the Bible's function as a standard. Canon and identity emerged together so that canon provided definition to the community that came to be identified as orthodox Christianity. By accepting in its collection diverse perspectives on the way God was working in the world through Jesus Christ, this community was accepting a multifaceted standard. But by having a collection at all, it also set limits to acceptable perspectives. There were options this community did not take because something fundamental was at stake regarding the perspective it held on God and the world. Yet common use of Scripture did not end disagreements within the community that appealed to this Scripture. When individual passages were cited as evidence, the Bible was itself sometimes the source for ideas that were later deemed heretical. Where doctrines settled those disagreements, decisions were made according to the commitments that lay behind the canon's shaping in the first place. That is, those same problematic individual passages were read in light of the foundational perspective of the overarching story, which refused to separate God and the real world and saw in Jesus Christ their connection to each other. Because that perspective was embedded in the very shape of the canon itself, the Bible in that sense provided a standard for its own interpretation. That standard, though, has also allowed for a wide range of interpretations, for instance, different understandings of the atonement or of who Jesus Christ is (e.g., prophet, priest, king, friend, teacher, liberator), when they have not threatened this fundamental perspective. In other words, Christians have told about the significance of God's presence in the world through Jesus Christ in many different ways. These diverse tellings have not always rested comfortably together, and in some cases serious tensions have arisen, but the tellings fall within the scope of how faithful Christians have tried to understand the meaning of God's presence through Jesus Christ for their lives. This history, like the first consideration about the form of the Bible itself, suggests thinking about the canon as a sphere or area, inside of which appropriate communal reflection and living take place.

A construal of the Bible as narrative, then, informs its use as canon in important ways. Because it preserves in its very structure the commitments that formed the identity of the larger Christian community, it serves as the standard for the narrative perspective that identifies this community. It sets the limits within which our various interpretations about God's presence to the world through Jesus Christ ought to fall. Those limits, it turns out, allow for great diversity. Many interpretations have been and continue to be embraced, and the tension produced by that variety perhaps contributes to the vitality of Christianity because we can never simply rest easily with what has been said before. Creative adaptations to new situations can only take place when there is room to maneuver, a possibility that straight conformity precludes. Some interpretations, though, are ruled out because they threaten the fundamental perspective that Christianity has claimed as its own.

If the primary function of the Bible as canon centers on knowing God, we must keep in mind a further point. Human communication is instrumental to God's communication. The authors, compilers, editors, and interpreters of the Bible can make an effort to tell us about God, and we can make an effort to listen carefully to them in order to understand God, but finally we can only dispose ourselves to encounter the God whom we desire to know. One way of talking about this twofold communication is to speak, as Wood sometimes does, of letter and spirit.[21] This distinction, which has a long history in Christian thinking, helps in considering how the words of the text may or may not be revelatory in any given reading. If a text communicates when we understand how to make use of it, then it may fail and become "dead letter" if we have lost the ability to grasp the conventions needed for employing its concepts. On that level, even human communication breaks down. But further, the text may be "dead letter" unless the Holy Spirit, usually making use of our careful attention, has enlivened it to illumine our lives. When the text does come alive in letter and spirit, the text is "activated as canon," as Wood says.[22] In fulfilling its aim to enable knowledge of God, the text thereby can serve as guide and test for our daily experiences. This coincidence of letter and spirit is revelatory and is never finally under our control. Nor is it simply an intrinsic quality of the Bible itself. As Wood says, "Rather than saying either that scripture is the word of God or that it *contains* the word of God, we may say that scripture is *potentially* the word of God; it may become the word of God under certain circumstances."[23] Because that potential has been realized over and over again in the Christian community, the Bible continues to be regarded as the standard for the knowledge of God that we seek. Still, the Bible is really best thought of as a vehicle for its most important canonical function, a function that takes place when and where the lives of readers are touched by the life of God.

Because texts are instrumental to God's communication, nothing precludes God's ability to speak through any text in the Bible, no matter how problematic it may appear to us. Even the household codes, as Mary McClintock Fulkerson has demonstrated, illumine possibilities for Pentecostal women. Some texts may realize their revelatory potential more often than others because their human communication more easily coincides with God's communication. Some texts may be highly unlikely to become vehicles for God's word because of the nature of their human communication, and we ought to handle them with great care. To recognize the instrumental role that the Bible plays in knowing God means, though, that we cannot automatically disregard any text. It also means that no text in the Bible is above criticism in light of the ultimate context for our lives. The way the Bible tells its story is important for bringing us into relationship with God, but we may criticize the details of the story as we encounter them in individual texts for the sake of enabling the encounter with God, to which Christian understanding itself aims. Even as canon, the Bible is itself normed by God's own self-disclosure, the ultimate standard that is never finally in our grasp.

The distinction between letter and spirit, between human communication and God's communication, between the Bible's witness and that to which its witness points, will prove to be important when we consider more explicitly the ways in which the Bible may be said to have and exercise authority. Before we can go further in that explication, we need to consider the concept of authority itself, which is complex, just as the Bible and the notion of canon are complex. Authority can be held and exercised in a variety of ways for different purposes. Once we have clarified the concept of authority, we can more easily see how these notions fit together.

NOTES

1. For a list of books included in different canons, see Bruce M. Metzger, "Bible," in *The Oxford Companion to the Bible* (ed. Bruce M. Metzger and Michael D. Coogan; Oxford: Oxford University Press, 1993), 78–80.

2. David H. Kelsey, *Proving Doctrine: The Uses of Scripture in Modern Theology* (Harrisburg, Pa.: Trinity Press International, 1999), 89; repr. of *The Uses of Scripture in Recent Theology* (Philadelphia: Fortress, 1975).

3. Frances Young, *Virtuoso Theology: The Bible and Interpretation* (Cleveland: Pilgrim, 1990), 26.

4. See, e.g., Hans von Campenhausen, *The Formation of the Christian Bible* (trans. J. A. Baker; Philadelphia: Fortress, 1972); James L. Kugel and Rowan A. Greer, *Early Biblical Interpretation* (LEC 3; ed. Wayne A. Meeks; Philadelphia: Westminster, 1986); Jaroslav Pelikan, *The Emergence of the Catholic Tradition* (100–600) (vol. 1 of *The Christian Tradition: A History of the Development of Doctrine;* Chicago: University of Chicago Press, 1971).

5. Young, *Virtuoso Theology,* 31–43.

6. Frances Young, *The Making of the Creeds* (Philadelphia: Trinity Press International, 1991), 16–25.

7. Irenaeus, *Against Heresies,* in *The Apostolic Fathers: Justin Martyr—Irenaeus.* Vol. 1 of *The Ante-Nicene Fathers: Translation of the Writings of the Fathers Down to A.D. 325* (1868; repr. Grand Rapids: Eerdmans, 1993), 1.8.1; 1.9.4.

8. For a description of these differences, see Young, *Virtuoso Theology,* 48–53.

9. Many excellent discussions of these controversies exist. See, e.g., R. P. C. Hanson, *The Search for the Christian Doctrine of God* (Edinburgh: T & T Clark, 1988); William G. Rusch, ed. and trans., *The Trinitarian Controversy* (Sources of Early Christian Thought; ed. William G. Rusch; Philadelphia: Fortress, 1980); and Richard A. Norris Jr., ed. and trans., *The Christological Controversy* (Sources of Early Christian Thought; ed. William G. Rusch; Philadelphia: Fortress, 1980); Young, *Making of the Creeds;* Pelikan, *Emergence of the Catholic Tradition* (100–600).

10. The *Symbolum Romanum* of the second century included this triple affirmation, and descriptions of baptism that date from the second century recount a "baptism" after the

affirmative answer to each of three questions. See J. N. D. Kelly, *Early Christian Creeds* (London: Longmans, 1960), 35; and Bernhard Lohse, *A Short History of Christian Doctrine: From the First Century to the Present* (Philadelphia: Fortress, 1966), 32–36.

11. Charles M. Wood, *The Formation of Christian Understanding: Theological Hermeneutics* (Valley Forge, Pa.: Trinity Press International, 1993; repr., Eugene, Ore.: Wipf & Stock, 2000), 84.

12. Ibid., 75–81.

13. Young, *Virtuoso Theology*, 134–59.

14. Young uses this analogy throughout *Virtuouso Theology*, but a concentrated discussion may be found in chap. 8.

15. Grace M. Jantzen, "Conspicuous Sanctity and Religious Belief," in *The Rationality of Religious Belief: Essays in Honour of Basil Mitchell* (ed. William J. Abraham and Steven W. Holtzer; Oxford: Clarendon, 1987), 121–40.

16. Ibid., 122.

17. Ibid., 129.

18. An example of this use appears in 2 Cor 10:13, 15–16.

19. Wood, *Formation of Christian Understanding*, 93.

20. This and the following two considerations are found in Wood, *u* 94–99.

21. Wood makes this distinction in several of his works, including *Formation of Christian Understanding*. One particularly helpful discussion may be found in "Finding the Life of a Text: Notes on the Explication of Scripture," in *An Invitation to Theological Study* (Valley Forge, Pa.: Trinity Press International, 1994), 45–54.

22. Wood, *Formation of Christian Understanding*, 109.

23. Wood, *Invitation to Theological Study*, 100; italics in original.

CHAPTER SIX

※✕✕

The Concept of Authority

Feminist discussion of the authority of the Bible has a long and complicated history. Some of the struggle that reformist feminists have engaged in has been directed toward the Bible itself, namely, its interpretation, its harmful effects, and its androcentric character. But apart from specific problems associated with the Bible, even the notion of authority is problematic. Feminists of widely divergent disciplines mistrust authority for a variety of reasons, including the fact that historically it has been held and exercised almost exclusively by men and that it necessarily includes some element of hierarchy. Women who have been without authority often have resisted and subverted existing authority by various means, ranging from outright challenge to the development of alternative communities, languages, and support systems.

Feminists are not alone in questioning the notion of authority, though. Confidence in authority has been eroding since the seventeenth century, when the conflicts that emerged during and after the Reformation led to an increasing turn away from external authority toward some kind of internal test for truth. Yves R. Simon further observes how the idea of authority seems to conflict with other values that our society holds as important.[1] For instance, if one thinks of authority as coercion, particularly procuring things by force, then it opposes the idea of justice or fairness, in which everyone ought to have equal right to resources. Similarly, authority seems to violate creativity, freedom, and our spontaneous desires in that external rules or boundaries can limit our decisions and even our potential as vital human beings.

Despite all these objections, authority is not a completely expendable idea for feminist theology. Part of the feminist movement has included a claiming of women's authority, for instance, to speak in our own voices and to hold positions of influence. In short, we see difficulties with authority, but we also desire to have and exercise authority in some way.[2] Much of the discussion about the Bible reflects this tension, as women undermine the authority of the text itself and of male writers and interpreters by claiming authority for our own experiences and interpretations. Both Letty Russell and Kathryn Tanner have identified the need to reconceive authority as key to understanding our relationship to Scripture. How we conceive authority does matter, and "reconception" involves clarification and elimination of misunderstandings in popular usage of the term. A number of philosophers have already engaged in this sort of conceptual examination, and in this chapter, I want to explore in particular the work of one philosopher, Richard De George, in an effort to uncover a notion of authority that can help make sense of the complicated relationship reformist feminists have with the Bible.

SOME COMMON MISUNDERSTANDINGS

One of the first important steps in an analysis of authority is to distinguish it from other terms or ideas with which it is often confused. The first such distinction regards "power." Both "authority" and "power" have many usages and nuances and are thus difficult to define, but we should explore both their relation and distinction.[3] In general, "power" is the ability to do something, although this ability can manifest itself in a variety of ways that we call by different names, such as force, persuasion, influence, and manipulation. Since the capacity to accomplish something is in many cases an element of authority, it is easy to see why these two ideas are difficult to distinguish. There is good reason to do so, though, because power and authority do not always accompany one another. For instance, to say that Congress has the "authority" to declare war normally means that it has not only the right but also the ability to do so. If, however, some natural disaster rendered Congress unable to marshal the armed forces to go to the war that it had declared, then Congress would still have the right to declare war but not the power, or ability, to bring it about. One can also imagine the situation of a teacher in an unruly classroom. The teacher, both as a person knowledgeable in a field and as a duly certified official within the school, has the authority to guide students in learning but cannot actually do so without the requisite order that makes for a proper learning environment. In each of these cases, the right to act as an authority remains constant, though the ability to perform as one is either absent or greatly diminished. Conversely, it is possible to have the power to do something without having proper authority. Consider, for instance, the power that an armed robber has to take money from a victim, even though that robber has no right to do so. Proper authority to accomplish something involves more than sheer power.

The example of the armed robber introduces the idea of coercion, which is neither the exclusive meaning of power nor a necessary element of authority. At times, the exercise of authority involves coercion, whether actual or threatened. Drivers quite often obey speed limits only because of the threat of getting a ticket. When drivers disobey the speed limit, police officers have the authority to enforce the penalty that has been threatened. Other instances of the exercise of authority, though, do not necessarily involve coercion. At the site of a traffic accident, most people see the point of following the directions of a police officer who is directing traffic and will comply in voluntary recognition of the officer's authority to do so without either being actually coerced or threatened to be coerced. People may recognize and comply with authority for other reasons as well, for instance, when they follow the instructions for a task given by a more experienced person or when they accept the leadership of a charismatic or knowledgeable figure. While it may be ingredient to some kinds of exercise of authority, coercion is not a necessary element. In fact, the need for coercion may indicate that authority is not effective in the first place.[4] A police officer needs to use force to arrest a criminal, for instance, because the criminal has disregarded the authority of the law already. "Power" and "authority," then, have a complicated relationship to one another, but they are also sufficiently distinct that the two ideas should not be conflated.

Discussion of coercion leads to another term, "authoritarianism," that is distinguishable from "authority." In many cases, coercion is not only unnecessary but inappropriate to the exercise of authority, so coercion results in a misuse of authority instead of a genuine use of it. If, for instance, a police officer directed traffic by waving a gun at drivers, the officer's authority to direct traffic and to carry a weapon would be misused. Furthermore, even when coercion of some sort may be called for, as in an arrest, employing too much or an inappropriate means of coercion misuses authority. Excessive use of force by police officers in arresting a criminal is an abuse of authority, not a genuine use of it. Not all misuse of authority involves coercion, though. An authority figure, for instance, may deliberately use the authority that she or he has to mislead others with inaccurate or incomplete information or to influence decisions by persuasion. "Authoritarianism," the term given to the misuse of authority, can take the form of excessive use of authority, unjustifiable or illegitimate use of authority, or the use of authority for the good of the one who bears authority at the expense of the one subject to authority.[5] In any of these cases, misuse of authority occurs when the proper limits of authority are not respected and when some violation of the one subject to authority takes place.

E. D. Watt has pointed out, "When authority is frequently and gravely abused, critics may lose interest in the distinction between authority and the abuse of it. Nonetheless, the distinction is well worth preserving."[6] Without the distinction, anything that makes people obey becomes authority. One has no grounds, then, for asking whether authority is legitimate, whether particular means of exercising authority are appropriate, or whether any particular advice or command from the one in authority should be followed or obeyed. Feminists do well to keep in mind Watt's warning. Certainly, authority has been gravely abused with respect to women, and to deny all authority rather than distinguish appropriate from inappropriate forms of it is tempting, but the failure to make those distinctions actually works against our own best interests. If we fail to distinguish authority from authoritarianism, then we have no basis to speak of the authority we wish to claim for ourselves to perform certain critical tasks, such as the interpretation of Scripture. Ultimately, our concerns may lie more with misuse of authority than with the proper use of it.

AUTHORITY AND *AUCTORITAS*

The English word "authority" derives from the Latin *auctoritas,* and many studies of authority explore that ancient concept in order to shed light on the modern one. Theodor Mommsen is the source of much of the understanding about how *auctoritas* functioned in Roman society.[7] *Auctoritas* was distinct from *potestas* and *imperium,* the latter two terms referring to rights that were held by civil officials who issued lawful, enforceable commands. In contrast, the Roman Senate possessed only *auctoritas,* important in its own way because it was the role of giving counsel to those civil officials. Without being enforced by a magistrate, the counsel of the Senate had no legal effect, but the Senate's deliberations were not merely good advice. *Auctoritas* derives from the verb *augere,* which means "to augment," and as Hannah Arendt explains, the elders in the Senate played the role of augmenting or elaborating the wisdom of the founders of Rome for the current situation. Though the elders understood precedents in the past as binding, they recognized the need to explain them to fit the situation at hand. Civil officials were not bound to take the Senate's counsel, but they could not safely ignore the wisdom offered in such advice. Less than command but more than suggestion, *auctoritas* had a binding force in the sense that it bound every present decision to the sacred past, from which those decisions received approval or disapproval.

From this basic idea, *auctoritas* extended to other relationships—parents to children, tutors to pupils, and patrons to clients. On one side of each relationship was a person who had some wisdom or other asset that was shared in order to benefit the person on the other side of the relationship. Even the *auctoritas* of the gods was considered more approval, confirmation, or warning than commands to be obeyed. Ignoring counsel was always a possibility, but it could lead to serious peril. Over time, this advising role of *auctoritas* did take on the quality of command in imperial Rome, as emperors began to exercise *auctoritas* along with *potestas* and *imperium*. The distinction became very difficult to maintain, so weighty counsel from the emperor began to have the force of law. By the time the word "authority" began to be used in English, it often referred to command and obedience, although instances of its usage as counsel, testimony, and example still appear. "Authority," then, has come to have a range of meanings, and any reconception of it will have to consider its full scope.

Although the notion of authority has developed through time and is not exactly identical to the ancient notion of *auctoritas* on which it is based, Carl Friedrich looks to that original, core idea of augmentation to illumine the role of reasoning in authority across its range of meanings. For Friedrich, the core quality of authority is its "potentiality of reasoned elaboration."[8] In other words, decisions, opinions, commands, and advice are genuinely authoritative when it is possible to elaborate and understand the reasons for them if the need to do so arises. This potentiality gives authority a certain quality that is missing from a sheer exercise of power or even from an official title or position that simply designates someone as an authority. It provides authority with legitimacy by showing that it is worthy of acceptance. Acceptance can only happen, though, within some pattern of beliefs, opinions, and values that is shared both by the one in authority and those who are subject to that authority. Without such a shared pattern, reasons make no sense, and the rational component of authority disintegrates. Because opinions, beliefs, and values are subject to change, someone or something can "lose authority." Reasons that made sense in an old pattern may not be viable in a new one. If the ones subject to authority begin to operate within a new pattern, then communications from the authority figure who still operates in the old pattern will no longer be accepted as authoritative. Those communications no longer have the potentiality for reasoned elaboration in the new system. It is also possible for those who have authority in one community with a shared pattern not to be considered to have authority in another community with a different shared pattern. But within a shared pattern, Friedrich says, it is the potentiality, not the actuality, of reasoned elaboration that counts. Many relationships would be unmanageable if every decision, opinion, and command that was communicated from one person to another had to be accompanied with the reasons for it. The potentiality for giving those reasons if asked for them, though, is what makes it possible to accept those communications on the basis of authority.

Friedrich's description of the potential for elaboration begins to point to the social nature and the necessity of authority. *Auctoritas* originally referred to a specific way in which ancient Romans looked to the past for legitimation of present actions, and that way was quite different from the kind of legitimation used by the Greeks and probably also other cultures. The way the notion was expanded, though, as well as the way that it has been elaborated by Friedrich and others, points to a phenomenon that extends widely in human relationships. In ancient Rome, *auctoritas* was clearly a social concept. One person had *auctoritas* in relation to someone else—older to younger, tutor to pupil. That social element remains in the way that Friedrich develops the idea of authority. In fact, as social relationships become more extensive and complicated, the need for authority increases. Watt points out that authority is found and needed only where people together engage in an activity that depends on each playing some distinct, particular role.[9] Of course, such interaction fills human life. Both to integrate our different activities and to avoid the paralysis of having to consider every conceivable alternative in every decision, authority allows us to work together to accomplish a common goal. Doing without authority really does not seem possible. Because of the dependence that human beings have on someone else from birth onward, not simply for survival but even to become "human" at all, we cannot possibly opt out completely of this kind of social engagement. Even hermits have lived with and learned from others at one time or another. Unquestionably, authority has to be reasonable and legitimate in order to perform its role, and guarding against abuse is just as important as exercising authority. Both its indispensable character and the possibility of its distortion make it critical to our life together that we understand how it ought to be properly employed.

The Concept of Authority

De George, in *The Nature and Limits of Authority,* considers the concept of authority as it is found in social life in its myriad forms, and his analysis involves both empirical data (he reflects on the actual practice of authority that has been institutionalized) and conceptual inquiry (he makes clarifications, distinctions, and arguments about the theoretical frameworks within which that practice takes place). De George admits that authority may differ greatly in practice from what it should be in theory. In general, authority exists for, and is justified in part by, the benefit of those subject to authority.[10] Specific instances of the exercise of authority, or better of the misuse of authority, often thwart this purpose. He concentrates, then, on theory in order to uncover the ideal by which any actual implementation of authority might be tested.[11] His study is especially important for feminists for the following reasons. He understands authority as a relation rather than as a one-sided exercise of power, and he holds that this relation exists for the benefit of the one subject to authority rather than for the benefit of the one who exercises authority. He identifies types of authority beyond those to which feminists object, and he explores the proper use of executive authority, which presents the greatest problems for feminists. In particular, he shows that obedience or submission (to which women object so strongly) is not the appropriate response to many forms of authority. These features of his work make his ideas particularly suited to the feminist idea that authority should be understood as partnership rather than domination. His work holds promise, then, for developing an understanding of the authority of Scripture in a direction that addresses the kinds of concerns that feminists raise.

The Authority Relation

De George, like Friedrich, understands authority to be a normal and important part of social life. Despite its pervasive character in society, however, it is a much misunderstood concept. Authority takes many forms and serves many purposes in society, but too often these variations are missed because "authority" itself is mistakenly equated with political authority. Furthermore, the kind of political authority with which it is equated is quite often authority to command, which is itself a reductionistic understanding of political authority. Not only political leaders but also teachers, parents, doctors, businesspeople, and many others hold and exercise authority in some sense, and the authority that these persons hold and exercise is not primarily (although it may in some instances include) authority to command. When political authority to command becomes the paradigm for all authority, finding the needed concepts for evaluating authority that is exercised in other contexts and for resolving conflicts that arise in them becomes difficult. De George devotes a good deal of his attention to highlighting alternative types of authority so that their purpose and value in society may be understood and appreciated.

De George begins by analyzing the concept of authority as it emerges from the various forms of authority that exist in society. At this stage, he seeks what is common in the ordinary usage of the term, and later he deals with the diversity of the various forms themselves. He proposes a "working model," which he formulates in this way: "someone or something (X) is an authority if he (she, or it) stands in relation to someone else (Y) as superior stands to inferior with respect to some realm, field, or domain (R)."[12] Four elements compose this model: (1) the bearer of authority (X); (2) the one (or ones) subject to authority (Y); (3) a relation of inequality between X and Y; and (4) a particular realm in which this relation pertains. Authority, then, is fundamentally a relation between X and Y that is characterized by inequality in a particular field. Because "subject to," "superior," "inferior," and "inequality" are such problematic ideas for feminists, I will take special care as we proceed to explain the meaning that De George has for the relationship that those terms represent. I use this terminology here because it is his, although it may be an important task of feminist thinking to develop a vocabulary that is not so "loaded" that women cannot use it.

De George clarifies each element of this working model. First, the bearer of authority may be a person or a thing (such as a book, a law, or a tradition). If the bearer of authority is a thing, however, it has that authority because it is a product that represents the authority of the one who produced it. For instance, a dictionary represents the knowledge of its author or authors. Its authority, then, rests on the authority of the one or ones who wrote it.[13] Second, those subject to authority are not things but people. We own things, we use them, and we may even train animals to obey orders, but our relationship to these things, according to De George, is not properly a relationship that is characterized by authority. De George does allow, though, that classes of people and not just individuals may be subject to authority. The collective then is, not merely a "thing" in the way that an automobile is, but a group of individuals who are each singly and all together subject to authority. In this way, it is possible to talk about someone's authority over the nation or the church.[14] Third, the relation of inequality may be more evident in some cases than in others, but it is necessary to the concept of authority in any case. De George does not have in mind a fundamental inequality between classes, races, or sexes. No natural, permanent superiority of one person over another exists. Inequality pertains, as we shall see, to a particular realm or context in which authority is exercised, so it has limits and can change, and the inequality shifts as the realms and contexts shift. Political authority involves inequality because political authorities have the right and power to make certain decisions or give certain commands that others do not, although the relation of inequality need not be restricted to the political realm or to the giving of commands. Inequality exists even when talking about things such as expertise. An authority on a certain topic knows more about that topic than do any number of other people for whom the expert is an authority. A relation of inequality exists between X and Y in that X has knowledge that is superior to Y's. By talking about the authority relation in this manner, De George opens up the way for identifying types of authority that might otherwise go unrecognized. Finally, the authority relation applies in some realm. There is, says De George, no authority in general but only authority with respect to a certain field of knowledge or activity. The scope of one's authority depends on the realm or realms in which one has or is an authority. A professor of political science, for instance, may be considered an authority in the field of political science but not in the field of musicology. Her or his right to exercise authority, then, does not extend to the latter field. Each of these four elements is necessary to the analysis of the nature and limits of authority.

In some cases, context is a fifth element in the working model De George has proposed. Sometimes, he says, realm and context are the same, but at other times it is important to distinguish them. A professor of political science, for instance, may have more knowledge of the political process than many elected officials, but the professor does not, by virtue of that knowledge, have the authority to debate or vote on the floor of the Senate. Neither does a senator have the authority to walk into the professor's classroom and administer an exam. Though the professor and the senator may have overlapping areas of knowledge, they perform their functions in different contexts. A specific system defines who has authority in the Senate, and another system defines who has authority in the university. Having authority in one system does not mean having authority in the other. Both realm and context are important for defining the limits of authority, though in some cases one may take precedence over the other. This expanded working model provides De George with the basic structure of the authority relation he needs in order to examine the various types of authority that he identifies.

Executive and Nonexecutive Authority

De George adopts a basic division between two types of authority, *executive* and *nonexecutive,* each of which may be further subdivided. Executive authority, says De George, "in general is the right or the power of someone (X) to do something (S) in some realm, field, or domain (R)."[15] Executive authority, then, involves performing an action or actions of some sort, and the bearer of authority is the one who performs the action. Executive authority may be further subdivided according to the kind of action appropriate to it and the context in which that action is taken. With regard to action, De George distinguishes between *imperative authority,* which involves the right or power to command, and *performatory authority,* which involves the right or power to perform some action other than command, such as to perform marriages or to execute a will.[16] These two forms of authority differ with respect to those who are subject to authority. For imperative authority, Y is subject to X's command. For performatory authority, there may be no Y in the ordinary sense. When a justice of the peace (X) performs a wedding, the two people who are being married (Y) are not normally considered to be "subject" to the justice's authority. Rather, both X and Y are subject to the rules or laws of a political system that gives performatory authority to some (in this case, the justice of the peace) and requires others (the bride and groom) to make use of someone invested with this authority in order to achieve the benefits that the system provides to those who are married.[17] Since context (in this case, the framework of civil law) is very important for understanding executive authority, De George further specifies executive authority as *parental* (in the context of the family), *operative* (in the context of some organization, such as a club or corporation), and *politico-legal* (in the context of the structure of the state).[18] Both imperative and performatory authority may hold within any single context. For instance, in the context of the family, parental authority involves both the right and obligation to care for children born into the family (performatory authority) and the right to command those children, in certain circumstances, to do or not do certain things (imperative authority).[19]

Unlike executive authority, nonexecutive authority does not involve the right or power to perform any kind of action. Because of this, says De George, it is often overlooked or considered less important than executive authority, but it plays an important role in society, especially with regard to the transfer of knowledge, skills, and culture.[20] The primary type of nonexecutive authority in De George's model is *epistemic authority,* which is based on or related to knowledge. To bear epistemic authority involves having knowledge, that is, having greater knowledge of some field or realm than the one or ones subject to this authority. To be subject to epistemic authority involves believing what the bearer says on the bearer's say-so. This belief may be as strong as simply taking the statement to be true, or it may consist instead of taking the statement to be probably true. Even when the statement is only considered to be probably true, the acceptance of that probability indicates X's authority. Although epistemic authority extends to relationships other than teacher and student, we can see how epistemic authority works by thinking about a teacher/student relationship. Superior knowledge is essential to this relation because if the student knows what the teacher knows, then the student has no need for the teacher as an authority.

Epistemic authority is "substitutional" because its purpose "is to substitute the knowledge of one person in a certain field for the lack of knowledge of another." The teacher cannot, then, be an epistemic authority for anyone who has equivalent knowledge, for instance, another teacher. Furthermore, epistemic authority is "expendable" and "open to challenge" because the student may acquire knowledge independently of the teacher and thus may no longer have to accept what the teacher says on the teacher's say-so. When the student's belief is based on evidence instead of on the teacher's say-so, the student's belief is not based on authority. The student no longer needs to substitute the teacher's knowledge in place of the student's own lack of knowledge.[21]

In addition to epistemic authority, De George takes up *exemplary authority* as another kind of nonexecutive authority. Instances of exemplary authority include authority of competence and authority of personal authenticity or excellence. Competence and excellence both involve knowledge, but the appropriate response to them involves more than believing certain propositions. To learn a skill, whether skill for carpentry or skill for living an excellent life, Y must observe, follow instructions, and imitate.[22] For instance, a carpenter instructs an apprentice in what the apprentice must do to gain those skills, but such instruction is not a command to be obeyed. Rather, it is advice to be followed if the apprentice wants to learn. In some cases, nonexecutive authority may become the basis for executive authority. A person's knowledge in a field, for instance, is the basis for that person to hold a teaching position, and in that capacity as teacher, the person may exercise executive authority by giving exams to students.

De George asserts that, because instructions have the form of an imperative, nonexecutive authority of competence may be mistaken for executive authority. Doctors, for instance, may prescribe medicine or a course of exercise or diet for a patient. The patient might take this prescription as a command to be obeyed, but really, says De George, the doctor's imperatively formed statement, "Take these pills," is an abbreviated way of saying, "If you want to cure whatever it is you have, then take these pills." The patient is relying on the doctor's epistemic authority to diagnose what is wrong and on the doctor's authority of competence to know and suggest a remedy. But doctors have no right to treat patients without their consent, so their authority does not extend to issuing commands that patients have an obligation to obey or to forcing treatment upon a patient who resists.[23] The kind of authority that De George describes the doctor as having is similar to the kind of authority that Arendt, Watt, and Mommsen ascribe to the elders in Rome: it is advice that cannot safely be ignored. If the patient follows the doctor's advice, it is because the patient knows that the doctor is interested in the patient's health and will direct the patient in the proper remedy. The patient may not follow the doctor's advice for a number of reasons, and the doctor may well "threaten" the patient with the natural consequences of not following the prescribed course of action, but the doctor's "threat" is not punishment to be imposed on the patient for disobedience. Unlike a police officer who arrests or a judge who convicts a criminal, the doctor has no executive authority to act on the patient against the patient's wishes. Rather, the doctor, by informing the patient about the expected outcome of the patient's resistance to treatment, is still acting nonexecutively as an epistemic authority.

In many cases, a person may hold and exercise both nonexecutive and executive authority. For instance, a doctor may have executive authority to perform some action on the patient, such as surgery. She or he holds this authority, as a justice of the peace does, within the framework of a political and legal system that authorizes (or licenses) some people to perform operations on other people. Such certification, however, is authorization in general, and the surgeon has no right to force surgical treatment on any individual patient. In advising an operation, the surgeon still exercises nonexecutive authority of competence. However, to perform the actual operation if the patient heeds the advice, the surgeon must have executive performatory authority along with the permission of the patient (which De George calls "permissive authority") to perform the procedure. The situation is similar for lawyers, who are authorized to argue cases in court but may not force any particular person to go to court. In these cases, as well as others, executive authority empowers X to act on or for Y if Y accepts X's competent advice and grants X permission to do so. Nonexecutive authority and executive authority frequently go together, and both may in fact be necessary for the benefit of Y.

De Jure and De Facto Authority

With regard to the concept of authority, De George makes other important distinctions. One such distinction is between de jure and de facto authority. *De jure authority* is authority that is held or exercised "in accordance with a certain set of rules or specified procedures, which are frequently legal."[24] In other words, someone is a de jure authority (or has de jure authority) when she or he is officially designated as such within some framework, such as a set of laws or principles, by some title, position, or certification. *De facto authority* pertains to whether anyone actually accepts that person as an authority. X is a de facto authority (or has de facto authority) whenever some Y acknowledges and acts appropriately toward X as such. Being an authority in principle (de jure) and being an authority in fact (de facto) sometimes go together, but sometimes they do not. De jure and de facto authority coincide whenever a person has been duly designated as an authority within a system and when some other person acts appropriately toward the designated person as that authority. For example, they coincide when a person who is certified as a teacher (de jure authority) actually teaches in a class of students who are ready to learn (de facto authority), or they coincide when a person holding high rank in the military (de jure authority) issues a command that is obeyed by someone of lower rank (de facto authority). As these examples show, de jure and de facto pertain both to nonexecutive authority (the teacher) and to executive authority (the military commander). At times, though, de jure and de facto authority may not coincide. In the case of mutiny, for instance, the captain of the ship has de jure authority, that is, has been designated within a system as the leader of the crew, but the captain does not have de facto authority because the crew does not accept the captain's leadership. If in their rebellion the crew accepts the leadership of another crew member, then that crew member has de facto authority but not de jure authority.

Legitimate Authority

De jure authority, even though it is authority that is duly held and exercised in accordance with a system, should not be confused with *legitimate authority*. In order to be legitimate, authority must be grounded or justified.[25] That is, good reasons must exist for X to be or have this authority. The reasons given to show that authority is legitimate differ according to the kind of authority at issue and the context in which it is held and exercised. One can ask, for instance, whether someone who is considered an expert in a field really has sufficient and accurate knowledge in her or his field to be a nonexecutive epistemic authority. Consider a person's having been designated to hold a position of authority after having provided false credentials. In this case, she or he would not legitimately hold the de jure authority that goes along with that position. Another question is whether the framework within which a person is an authority or has authority is itself grounded. In a totalitarian government, a dictator has de jure executive authority, and probably de facto authority as well. That authority is not legitimate, however, unless totalitarian governments are themselves justifiable. Authority, then, may be either legitimate (grounded) or illegitimate (ungrounded). Unlike de facto and de jure authority, legitimate and illegitimate authority can never coincide. These latter terms are in opposition to each other. By saying that authority must be grounded in order for it to be legitimate, De George touches on Friedrich's concern for the potentiality of reasoned elaboration in the concept of authority. Neither De George nor Friedrich understands authority to be independent of reason, nor do they understand authority as something imposed on others in contradiction to their nature or well-being. Legitimate authority, as opposed to authoritarianism, must cohere with a system of values in which good reasons exist for having that authority.

De George discusses the grounding of epistemic authority at length, and the manner in which he considers epistemic authority enables him to ask questions about its legitimacy. Epistemic authority is legitimate, he says, if it meets four criteria: (1) the knowledge criterion, (2) the inductive criterion, (3) the relevance criterion, and (4) the trustworthiness criterion.[26] Again, let's consider the teacher/student relationship to see how these criteria work. The first and second criteria are closely linked. To meet the knowledge criterion, there must really be knowledge in a particular realm to be had, and the teacher must really have it. This criterion rules out epistemic authority for those who teach "false sciences" (such as alchemy), which do not have genuine knowledge of anything in our real experience, and it also rules out epistemic authority for those who claim to have knowledge that is genuine (such as physics) but who do not genuinely have it, either because the teacher just pretends to know or is mistaken about a large number of things. This first criterion deals primarily with the validity of epistemic authority, which I will explain further below.

For the student to know that the teacher meets the first criterion, the student must also use what De George calls the "inductive criterion," which means that there must be good reasons to believe that the teacher has the knowledge she or he purports to have. Those reasons might include certification by others who have equivalent knowledge (a license, a diploma) or one's own experience of knowing that the teacher has been right about certain things before. In either case, the student may infer that the teacher really has knowledge about a field. In both cases, the knowledge that the teacher has must be testable by someone else (whether other experts or one's own experience) in order for belief in what she or he says to be grounded. If no one besides the teacher possesses or has the possibility of possessing this knowledge, then the only possible ground for the teacher's authority is the teacher's own truthfulness. In other words, one has to take the authority's own word for being an authority on this subject. While trustworthiness is an important component of legitimacy (see the fourth criterion below), complete dependence on an authority that is not testable leaves the student vulnerable to believing misleading statements or outright lies. While not everything that a teacher says can or should be tested (an account of a private conversation with an important figure who is now dead may be very illuminating), the more things a teacher says that cannot be tested by others, the less her or his authority is grounded.

The third criterion, the relevance criterion, requires that the statements the teacher makes as an epistemic authority be related to the field of knowledge that she or he has. If the teacher is an epistemic authority with regard to art, the student is not justified in accepting a statement on the teacher's say-so about another field, such as politics. A statement about politics is not relevant to the domain in which the teacher may rightly be said to be an authority. It is possible, of course, to be an epistemic authority in more than one domain. The point is that the student is not justified in believing what the teacher says about a field unless the teacher is an epistemic authority in that field. Finally, the trustworthiness criterion requires that the student have good reason to believe that the teacher is telling the truth, or at least is stating what the teacher believes to be true, about a matter that does fall within her or his field. This criterion has to do with character, or the good will not to mislead or lie to another. Epistemic authority is legitimate only when all four of these criteria can be met.

Valid Authority

In addition to the term "legitimate authority," De George also uses the term "valid authority." It is not entirely clear how, or even whether, De George intends to distinguish these terms. Sometimes he seems to use the terms synonymously, but other times they seem to point to distinct elements under consideration. Though De George speaks at length about the legitimacy of executive (especially political) authority, it is primarily in his discussion of nonexecutive epistemic authority that the two terms appear together. His use of these two terms in this context provides an opportunity to develop a distinction that can and should be made. Though I have inferred from his use of the two terms a distinction that is not explicitly stated, I hope the distinction is not inappropriate to his study of authority. As I noted above, validity primarily refers to the first criterion for legitimacy, having real knowledge of a field. The other three criteria also have to be met in order for authority to be fully legitimate, but dealing with the first criterion at greater length on its own brings out some very important issues regarding epistemic authority.[27]

Although epistemic authority is not fully and finally legitimate unless the criterion of validity is met, distinguishing between legitimacy and validity helps makes sense of one area of authority that De George discusses briefly. He maintains that the epistemic authority relation is such that sometimes people understandably believe on authority things that are false.[28] This observation is pertinent to two situations. The first is a situation in which some false belief (e.g., that the earth is flat) is generally accepted as true by all the authorities of the day. In this case, X may meet the second criterion by being certified as knowing the science of the day (which includes the belief that the earth is flat). A person's own experience of walking on flat ground would also seem to confirm that belief. X may then make statements relevant to the field (e.g., describing the ends of the earth) and do so in a trustworthy manner (i.e., truly representing what X believes to be true), thus meeting the third and fourth criteria. In the absence of any way to test for the first criterion independently, ordinary people would understandably accept X as a legitimate epistemic authority. Of course, the weight of authority does not make this belief true, and the demonstration of counterevidence must finally show that it is false. When this happens, it is no longer reasonable for people to accept the false belief on authority. As Friedrich says, it is possible to lose authority when the potentiality of reasoned elaboration fails. De George does not describe this situation in order to defend the legitimacy of believing things that are not true. His concern is quite the opposite. He adopts the approach to epistemic authority that he does in order to raise questions about legitimacy and validity. Distinguishing between legitimacy and validity is an important step in this approach because the distinction makes it possible to show the grounds on which authority that has been considered legitimate may be questioned.

The second situation involves a relation with a single authority instead of with the consensus of authorities. De George maintains that epistemic authority may be legitimately held and exercised even if X is mistaken about some things, that is, even if some things that X says are not worthy of belief. Consider again the example of teacher and student. Epistemic authority is "substitutional" because the teacher supplies the student with knowledge that the student lacks. Students benefit by believing what the teacher says about some field because students would not otherwise have this knowledge of that field at all. Even if the teacher is wrong about certain particulars within a field, students still benefit most of the time from the teacher's superior knowledge of that field. It is reasonable for students to accept the teacher as a legitimate authority in that field. For example, a student may reasonably accept as true or probably true everything that a biology teacher says because the teacher has genuine knowledge of biology. Even if she is mistaken in some of her statements, the teacher is correct in most of them, and it is to the student's benefit to accept what she says on her authority.[29] She still has genuine knowledge of her field to share with her students and thus still meets the first criterion of legitimacy. In the absence of counterevidence, the student may legitimately accept even mistaken statements on her authority because the student knows only that she has genuine, superior knowledge of her field. Under those circumstances, it is reasonable for the student to believe what she says. Of course, if the student discovers the teacher's mistake, then it is no longer legitimate, or reasonable, for the student to accept that particular statement on the teacher's authority. Furthermore, the more particulars about which the teacher is wrong, the less benefit there is to the student and the less legitimate is the teacher's authority. That is, to accept what she says just because she says it is less reasonable. Possibly the teacher is mistaken about so much that one cannot say that she has enough genuine knowledge of the field to act as an authority in it. In that case, she no longer meets the first criterion of legitimacy. In most cases, though, teachers are not so incompetent as to fail to qualify as epistemic authorities for their students, but they can and do make mistakes. Distinguishing between validity and legitimacy in this case makes it possible to acknowledge X's mistakes without completely destroying the authority relation. For this reason, not conflating the two concepts is important.

Effective Authority

In addition to authority's legitimacy and validity, one may ask about its effectiveness. De George calls authority "effective" if there is an end or goal toward which X exercises authority and if that end or goal is achieved in an appropriate manner by X's exercise of authority. Authority is "ineffective" if there is an end or goal that either is not achieved or is not achieved in an appropriate manner. Clearly, in De George's view, the means by which the ends are achieved are important. One may have a legitimate authority to act toward a goal but exercise it inappropriately by using means that are not legitimate.[30] To measure effectiveness, then, it is necessary to know not only the end to be achieved but also the way in which it is appropriate to achieve that end. The realm and context of any instance of authority have bearing on both the appropriate means and end. For instance, in general, one may say that the goal of epistemic authority is learning, but that goal may be further specified according to the field or realm, such as learning about science or learning about literature. Methods for teaching may vary with the field. To illustrate, conducting experiments is an appropriate method to learn about science, but conducting experiments in a class on literature would be very strange indeed. Conversely, reading and analyzing poetry in order to learn about science would also be strange. Context also has important bearing on the end for which and the means by which one exercises appropriate epistemic authority. Exactly what level of understanding a teacher tries to bring students to depends at least in part on the setting. A teacher may have a very high goal for depth of understanding among students taking a course on poetry in a university, but the goal might be quite different if the teacher is invited to read poetry and discuss it with a book club. Similarly, the means to achieve those different goals would also vary according to context. While giving exams in a course offered at a university is appropriate, giving an exam to a book club would not be. To be effective, then, the one who has or is an authority must attend to a number of factors.

The Source of Authority

A final consideration regarding the concept of authority has to do with its source. One way that De George takes up this question is to ask about the source of authority itself. That is, why do some persons or things come to hold positions of authority at all? He lists four traditional answers to this question: (1) authority is divinely ordained by God; (2) it is inherent in nature; (3) it is accepted because of tradition; or (4) it is a social relation developed by human beings. De George seems to endorse the last answer, that authority comes from human beings, but remarks that it is not, therefore, mere contrivance. Authority arises from inequalities of intelligence, physical strength, talents, and so forth among human beings, together with the needs of individuals and of the community.[31] It exists to supply what is lacking for some with what others possess in order to achieve certain ends. In the case of religion, though, De George seems willing to entertain the possibility that authority comes from God. Not all religions claim God as their origin, but among those that do, God is considered the basis and justification for religious authority. De George is careful, though, to distinguish between divine authority, that is, the authority that God is or has by virtue of being God, and religious authority, that is, authority held and exercised by human beings in the context of a religion. Even though certain religions considered God to be the source for religious authority, De George maintains that religious authority itself is derived from divine authority, not identical to it. Religious authority is limited in a way that divine authority is not, and it is passed on by a formal structure that falls under human influence. Despite having a basis in divine authority, religious authority is exercised within an organization of human beings. It is subject, then, to the kinds of analysis and questions that can be raised about other forms of authority with regard to legitimacy and effectiveness.[32] A necessary, though not sufficient, condition for religious authority to be legitimate is that the religion itself must be legitimate. For religions that claim God as the basis for religious authority, God's existence is a necessary condition for that authority's legitimacy.[33] But God's existence does not by itself legitimate religious authority. Other conditions, such as the right of individuals to make free decisions, have to be met as well.

FEMINIST THEOLOGY AND AUTHORITY

Feminist theology characteristically appeals to some form of women's own internal authority as a foil to various kinds of external authorities that have exercised power over women in harmful ways rather than empowered women to act as full participants in society, church, and home. With regard to the authority of Scripture, this appeal usually translates to an emphasis on women's authority as interpreters. Though reformist feminist theologians typically do not deny the Bible's authority completely, they always in some way make its external authority dependent on women's own internal authority, whether this internal authority is based on universal women's experience or the unique experience of particular women. Russell's move from a monolithic authority to "multiple authorities" is a means of preserving the internal authority of individuals against the restrictive exercise of external authority over those individuals. At stake in this move for feminists is the ability of women to voice criticism of authority that has been oppressive.

The studies on the meaning of *auctoritas* are instructive for feminists considering the problems and value of external authority. The way that ancient Romans thought about *auctoritas* illumines how feminists often retain some sense of external authority even after Scripture's androcentrically based "authority" has been eroded. In Rome, the exercise of *auctoritas* by living elders linked the community to the past by binding it to the original vision of the founders. This authority need not shut off decision making and development, but it does help determine when and where the later community departs from the original vision. Feminists implicitly rely on this understanding of authority when they appeal to the prophetic vision or Jesus' own vision as the warrant for their own theology and for their criticisms of androcentric elements in the present community that has strayed from that vision. For all the emphasis on women's own authority as interpreters, feminists still acknowledge the Bible's role in providing access to this vision.

Friedrich's discussion of authority as "potentiality of reasoned elaboration" also illumines feminist claims about internal authority. Feminists argue that women's experience is a (if not *the*) crucial ingredient in the pattern of beliefs, opinions, and values in which authority may be considered to be reasonable. At least part of what is happening in feminist questioning of religious and biblical authority is that women who have had the "aha" experience of recognizing oppression no longer share the beliefs, opinions, and values that supported certain forms and exercises of authority based in an androcentric culture. According to Friedrich's description of authority, however, the erosion of these forms and exercises of authority eliminates neither the legitimacy of the concept of authority itself nor the need for authority. Our relationships, he says, would be unmanageable if reasons had to be given for every decision and command. Since authoritative utterances and actions will always have a place, the potential to elaborate the reasons for the authoritative utterances and actions within the new shared pattern of belief, opinions, and values must exist. Russell's statement that feminists consent to the authority of the Bible because it "makes sense" of life experiences suggests that such elaboration may indeed be possible within a feminist pattern. Women's internal experience, then, does not eliminate the need for external authority, though it provides a critical test for its legitimacy.

De George's philosophical analysis clearly indicates that the concept of authority is complex. Feminists, however, have not yet sufficiently taken the full scope of this complexity into account in their criticisms of the authority of the Bible. Even Russell's discussion of authority, which includes an identification of a few different kinds of authority, the source of authority, and other important factors, does not attend to all the aspects of the concept that De George has brought to light. De George's distinctions can help feminists articulate arguments with greater precision and avoid dismissing ideas that need to be retained. Consider, for example, how De George's distinctions illumine the contrast that Russell draws between authority of domination exercised over community (a paradigm based on hierarchy) and authority of partnership exercised within community (a paradigm based on mutuality). When she speaks about the authority of the Bible, Russell rejects the notion that consent should be coerced and argues instead for consent that is evoked from the Bible's ability to make sense of life experiences. She also rejects the idea that inclusion in the community should be a matter of assent to doctrine. In the feminist paradigm, inclusion is based instead on willingness to engage in community building and communal search for truth. De George's distinctions help reveal that in this contrast, Russell is proposing to replace the understanding of the Bible as executive authority (which has the right or power to make a norm binding and to exclude those who do not assent to it) with the understanding of the Bible as nonexecutive authority (which serves as a competent guide to make sense of life experiences). In doing so, she hopes to avoid the problems of coercion and exclusion that accompany the hierarchical paradigm of domination. Whether she is talking about the concept of authority in general or about the Bible's authority in particular, Russell seems to want to get away from certain elements associated with executive authority, in particular its right or power to command or act as a standard, and in consequence she shows a preference for nonexecutive authority.

While this contrast does bring out criticisms and values that are central to feminist thinking, De George's analysis also shows that other matters ought to be considered. It would be a mistake simply to pit executive and nonexecutive authority against each other. Coercion is not a necessary component of all forms or all exercises of executive authority, and its presence may well indicate a misuse of executive authority rather than a problem inherent in executive authority itself. Furthermore, nonexecutive authority is not immune to coercive misuse. Russell herself acknowledges that authority of knowledge, when used to indoctrinate others, falls under the paradigm of domination. Nor does executive authority alone involve hierarchy. De George has demonstrated that superiority is an essential element in any authority relation. This aspect of authority holds even in Russell's preferred paradigm. For instance, the only reason to turn to the Bible to make sense of life experience is if the Bible represents, to some extent at least, knowledge or competence that is superior to our own. It cannot answer questions or provide resources for understanding if it does not. Even our ability to be mutual authorities for each other depends on this relation. I cannot be an authority for you in some respect unless I have some knowledge superior to yours, and vice versa. Of course, this kind of superiority is quite different from the patriarchal hierarchy to which Russell rightly directs her criticism, but the contrast she draws between paradigms obscures the fact that even mutuality depends on inequality in a certain sense. One of the most valuable insights from De George's work is that when the full complexity of the authority relation is grasped, we all end up being authorities in some domains because we can each supply knowledge or skills that someone else lacks.

Finally, it is a mistake to think that a shift in emphasis to nonexecutive authority eliminates the need for executive authority altogether. Russell clearly wants to avoid excluding people from the community on the basis of conformity to normative doctrine, but she implicitly relies on a standard for inclusion herself and does not address the problem of how to handle those who do not conform to this norm. Her preferred paradigm bases inclusion on the willingness to build a community of wholeness. This willingness appears to be a standard, even though she has not labeled it as such. One can easily imagine how the community may need to exclude, or at least to identify as wrong and perhaps even protect others from, views that are not based on this willingness. De George has shown that nonexecutive authority sometimes becomes the basis for executive authority. Considering this connection may be important for identifying how a feminist vision can come to provide a standard for an inclusive community.

De George's analysis is important for feminist theology because it provides a sophisticated vocabulary and conceptual framework for characterizing both the problems and the possibilities that are associated with the authority of Scripture. It helps identify the relevance of certain issues and questions for the discussion. Does Scripture, for instance, have executive authority or nonexecutive authority or both? What are the legitimate grounds for the authority of Scripture for theology? What is its scope? What is the end or goal of its authority, and how is that end attained appropriately? All of these questions have bearing on the sense in which the Bible may be considered normative for feminist—or, for that matter, any—theology.

De George's analysis also provides categories that illumine questions about the authority of Scripture. Just as the examples we have already explored have nuanced, complex, and sometimes overlapping instances of authority, so Scripture's authority will need to be seen as multifaceted. Speaking about the Bible's authority is simply not an all-or-nothing matter, as it is sometimes taken to be, especially under the old Protestant orthodox doctrine of Scripture. As we move into the next chapter, we will have to consider not only feminist concerns about authority but also the description of how the Bible works narratively, which I developed in chapter 5. Central to our task will be the question of how we come to know God through this book.

NOTES

1. Yves R. Simon, *A General Theory of Authority* (Notre Dame, Ind.: University of Notre Dame Press, 1980), 13–22.

2. Feminist work outside of theology also exhibits this tension. See Lynne Tirrell, "Definition and Power: Toward Authority without Privilege," *Hypatia* 8, no. 4 (fall 1993): 1–34; and Carmen Luke, "Feminist Pedagogy Theory: Reflections on Power and Authority," *Educational Theory* 46, no. 3 (summer 1996): 283–302.

3. For an extensive discussion of the relations between the concepts of power and authority, see Michael D. Bayles, "The Functions and Limits of Political Authority," in *Authority: A Philosophical Analysis* (ed. R. Baine Harris; University, Ala.: University of Alabama Press, 1976). Others who urge making a distinction between these ideas include Hannah Arendt, "What Was Authority?" and Carl J. Friedrich, "Authority, Reason, and Discretion," in *Nomos I: Authority* (ed. Carl J. Friedrich; Cambridge: Harvard University Press, 1958).

4. This point is made by Arendt, "What Was Authority?" 82; and by Richard T. De George, *The Nature and Limits of Authority* (Lawrence: University Press of Kansas, 1985), 63.

5. See E. D. Watt, *Authority* (New York: St. Martin's, 1982), 1–25; De George, *Nature and Limits of Authority*, 56.

6. Watt, *Authority*, 25.

7. This discussion of *auctoritas* draws from interpretations by Arendt and Watt of Mommsen's findings.

8. Friedrich, "Authority, Reason, and Discretion," 35.

9. Watt, *Authority*, 105.

10. See De George, *Nature and Limits of Authority*, 38, 135, 234, 285.

11. De George pursues his task with an awareness of objections that might be made to it: first, that any position on authority is inevitably ideological, and second, that the process of analysis itself, by delaying action, tacitly defends the predispositions and commitments of the establishment. In response, De George admits that both criticisms are telling but maintains that analysis can be both neutral and useful. In the sense that analysis can be undertaken on any content, it is neutral. The use of reason is itself neutral, a fact that can be recognized when one observes that analysis is used to clarify concepts, expose inconsistencies, evaluate arguments, and so forth both by those who want to defend and by those who want to attack the same position. Analysis is useful because the clarifications, distinctions, and arguments that emerge from a study such as the one he proposes may be applied to specific situations in order to evaluate various models or various types of action or inaction. De George admits that any position about authority has certain values and makes certain claims, but this admission does not in his thinking amount to much. Some positions are still better than others, and the use of analytical reason shows their relative merits by uncovering which positions are best defended by argument and which best cohere with the basic values of society. He proceeds, then, with his study so that it, too, may be weighed on its merits or inadequacies. See his introduction.

12. De George, *Nature and Limits of Authority*, 14.

13. Watt agrees that the authority of a written text rests on the authority of its author. He adds that when a book or its author is called into question, appeal must be made to the knowledge that is the source of the authority of book and author alike. He also points out that written texts cannot explain their own meaning; they must be interpreted by living authorities (*Authority*, 45–46). Like Watt, De George realizes that a text must be interpreted, and he notes that Christians have been divided over whether interpretation of the Bible should be left to the individual or should follow some orthodox tradition.

14. De George, *Nature and Limits of Authority,* 16, 30.

15. Ibid., 62.

16. Ibid., 63.

17. Ibid., 67.

18. Ibid., 68.

19. Ibid., 72.

20. Ibid., 26.

21. Ibid., 36–37.

22. Ibid., 43.

23. Ibid., 43, 69.

24. Ibid., 19.

25. Ibid.

26. Ibid., 35–36. DeGeorge's full discussion appears throughout pages 34–42.

27. Though I have tried to represent what I think De George has in mind, this is my constructive interpretation of a distinction that is not stated explicitly. In my interpretation of his work, legitimate authority is related to, but distinct from, valid authority in the following ways. The two are related because legitimacy depends in part on validity. The first criterion for legitimate epistemic authority has to do with validity, that is, whether there is a genuine field of knowledge and whether X really does have knowledge of this field. Only when both requirements are met are the statements X makes about that field worthy of belief. But legitimacy and validity can and should be distinguished because legitimacy depends only in part on validity. Even if X really has knowledge of a field, other factors must be considered before accepting X's epistemic authority as legitimate. For instance, the statements must be relevant to X's field of knowledge, and X must be truly representing to Y what X truly knows. The relevance and trustworthiness criteria add grounds other than validity for showing that epistemic authority is legitimate. See De George's use of "valid" in *Nature and Limits of Authority,* 18–19, 29, 36, 41.

28. Ibid., 39, 42.

29. Ibid., 39.

30. Ibid., 19–20.

31. Ibid., 93–95.

32. De George discusses thoughtfully and at length the limits and proper use of religious authority, especially in Christianity, in his chapter entitled "Religion and Authority." He takes up issues, such as the authority of doctrine, of popes and bishops, and of theologians, that range beyond the scope of this discussion.

33. Ibid., 217–20.

CHAPTER SEVEN

The Authority of the Bible

If the Bible can be understood as narrative in the way that I have described, and if authority can be conceived in such a way as to serve feminist goals, then how do these insights help thinking about the authority of the Bible in a way that addresses feminist concerns about the oppressive and hurtful effects it has had on women? In this chapter, I will offer a proposal for how to understand the authority of the Bible that can be correlated with the authority of women to interpret the Bible. Only when both kinds of authority are kept together can we do justice to Christian claims about the Bible as well as feminist claims about women's experiences. To begin, I want to sketch the outline of an authority relation that I will expand through the rest of the chapter. Although the focus of this discussion will be the Bible's authority, it will become clear as we proceed that women may also be said in some way to have and exercise authority with respect to the Bible.

THE AUTHORITY RELATION

Talking about the Bible's authority at all requires the possibility of establishing an authority relation in the way that Richard De George has described it, namely, a relation of inequality between X and Y in a particular domain. For the first element of that relation, the bearer of authority is the Bible. This simple statement, however, needs to be explicated in order to avoid making a simplistic claim that the book itself, or the mere words on the page, is authoritative. First, since the Bible is a thing and not a person, its authority derives from someone else. Two possible sources of its authority exist: the humans who wrote, edited, and compiled this book, or God. Since the Bible works narratively both on the level of human communication and divine communication, we will need to uncover as we proceed how this distinction affects the way we understand the different kinds of authority that the Bible might have or exercise. For now, it is enough to keep in mind that as the bearer of authority, the Bible really stands in for someone else. Second, given the existence of several canons, even the designation "the Bible" is overly simple. Since the differences in these collections do not alter the fundamental narrative shape of the Christian way of viewing the world, I do not think these various collections are in competition with one another for authoritative status. The several canons do have some different material, and reflecting on that different material may have varying pedagogical import, but the way in which each canon works to bear authority is not fundamentally different. Third, the whole Bible and not merely portions of it may bear authority. Because the Bible stands in for someone else, it bears whatever authority this "someone else" bears. Every text has the potential to be used by God to communicate with us, even if the human communication has to be handled with care. To say the Bible "as a whole" can bear authority does not mean that everything must be taken as is. It means that just as no text is beyond criticism with regard to what its human authors have said, no text may be disregarded as having the potential to be used by God.

The second element of the authority relation, the matter of who is "subject to authority," is similarly complex. Although the simple answer is "human beings," the very existence of multiple ways of categorizing authority indicates that much more needs to be said. Clearly, for instance, the Bible does not have authority de facto for all human beings. Fewer people in the world actually accept the Bible's authority than do not. Whether any human should accept the Bible's authority depends on whether its authority is legitimate and valid. Furthermore, the question that most particularly concerns this book is whether women ought to accept the Bible's authority. Since both humans and God may communicate through this book, we must look at the question with each in mind. I think it is fair to say that just as the Bible as a whole has the potential to bear authority, any human being has the potential to be "subject to this authority." I see no need to rule out from the beginning the possibility that the Bible may form and transform any person's life, although whether or not the Bible actually does so depends on many factors. In this chapter, I will be concentrating on the way in which the Bible bears authority for Christians, those who actually seek to put themselves in this relation with the Bible, and the concerns of women in the Christian community will be my primary interest.

The third element of the authority relation is inequality. I have used the phrase "subject to authority" in quotation marks in the preceding paragraph because I want to use a different phrase throughout the rest of this book, one that more clearly indicates the kind of inequality I have in mind. I prefer to talk about those who *benefit from* authority rather than those who are *subject to* authority. Of course, "subject to" is the proper way to designate the relationship in some instances of the use of authority. For example, in the case of a criminal who is subject to the authority of the state, the direct beneficiary of authority is, not the individual criminal, but the citizens who are protected by having the laws enforced. Still, at the root of any authority relationship is the need in social relationships for mutual dependencies. In the above case, citizens depend on officers and judges to enforce the laws that protect them. Not all dependencies, though, are the same, and not all needs are met by coercion.

The way that the Bible has and exercises authority is quite different. If we keep in mind that the "superiority" or "inequality" at issue in mutual dependency is the ability to supply something lacking, then we may say that the Bible supplies Christians with what is necessary to form and guide the community. It does not supply everything that is needed, nor does it have to in order to retain its position of authority. Tradition, reasoning abilities, personal and corporate experiences, and more may contribute to formation and guidance, but the Bible provides access to the early self-understanding of a community that over time defined itself in a certain way. This community was, of course, made up of multiple communities, each undoubtedly with distinct characteristics, but they shared commitments that connected them together and that the Bible retains in its very structure. These are commitments that this community as a whole could not give up without becoming something else. In other words, they are foundational to its identity. Because of what it preserves, the Bible may also serve as a test for how well other activities make their contributions to the development of this community in all its diverse manifestations, that is, whether those developments are in keeping with its identity. Without the Bible, Christians would not have access to this foundation. It supplies what we otherwise would lack, so it plays an essential and irreplaceable role.

Finally, we need to establish the fourth element of the authority relation: domain. It is not possible to speak about the Bible's authority in general. Both authority and narrative belong to particular ways of understanding and interacting with the world. Although God is infinite, any finite person or thing, including the Bible, has particularity that we must recognize. Because human minds are finite, people need a finite instrument for coming to understand God; so, far from being a hindrance, the particularity of the Bible is crucial to its work. The Bible has and exercises its authority in a specific domain, and I want to suggest that this domain is "saving knowledge of God."

But what is saving knowledge of God? First, it does not mean all knowledge. The old distinction between what can be known by reason and what can be known by revelation shows that Christians have long recognized different domains of knowledge, even if the pressures following the Reformation began to obscure those differences. What we know in science, history, and mathematics falls in different domains, and the Bible is not the foundation for forming understanding and making judgments in them. In another sense, too, the Bible has specificity. Just as Christians know many things that they do not learn from the Bible, we also come to know ourselves through many narratives that are not formed by the Bible. For instance, any individual Christian may participate in a national narrative, an ethnic narrative, a family narrative, a professional narrative, and more. Some of these narratives may be influenced by the Bible (e.g., many ethnic narratives are connected to religious narratives), but they also have other influences. The point is that we are shaped in a variety of ways. We come to understand ourselves and our world through all these intersecting narratives. We do not learn everything that we are through the Bible, so in that sense, too, the Bible has limits.

Acknowledging the necessary limits of the Bible's particular domain, though, does not limit what may be encompassed under the perspective that is gained through it. Every item, all our thoughts and actions, may be illumined by the Bible's narrative. Because our relationship with God is the ultimate context for our lives, we gain through the Bible our most comprehensive sense of order. For a faithful Christian, it will provide the ultimate value pattern in which one understands everything else. Attending to God's involvement in the world will matter in how one makes use of knowledge gained in science, history, politics, business, parenting, and more. The faithful Christian understands the ultimate meaning of all these things through the narrative that the Bible tells. Establishing a specific domain for the Bible's authority, then, does not restrict its ability to address in some way all that matters to us.

Second, the adjective "saving" links the knowledge of God that the Bible provides specifically with what we come to know about salvation through Jesus Christ. While this knowledge provides ultimate meaning for Christians, the Bible is not the only possible way to seek ultimate meaning. Items in the world may be construed in different ways, and the Bible does not act as a resource for forming all these other construals. Salvation is a goal for human life that Christians seek, but, as several theologians have pointed out, not everyone shares that goal.[1] Other religions pursue other religious ends, such as enlightenment in Buddhism, and secular pursuits may also have very different understandings of what brings fulfillment. As I intend to use the phrase "saving knowledge," it has a distinct content even with regard to ultimate ends. Both Christian understanding of the human problem and Christian understanding of the fulfillment that God provides through Jesus Christ are shaped by the way that the Bible speaks of salvation. It offers through its narrative a way of viewing the world, and this perspective is the proper domain of the Bible's authority.

Accepting that this perspective is the domain for the Bible's authority does not predetermine the answer to important questions related to other construals of the world, such as the truth or relative value of other possible ways of coming to know God or of views of the world that do not explicitly refer to God. Certainly, for Christian faith, God is the universal ground of everything that is, ultimate reality itself, so having a relationship with God is not optional (under this view, even a rejection of God is really just a bad relationship with God). But humans live out that relationship in a variety of ways, and not all of them are shaped by the narrative rooted in the Bible. Many Christian theologians have been able to hold together knowledge of God that is gained through natural theology with knowledge of God that is gained through special revelation, and perhaps that coexistence can inform the way the Christian perspective can coexist with other perspectives on the world. Some of these may be compatible with Christian claims, and others may well be incompatible. However, the lengthy and careful examination necessary to make such judgments will not be a part of this discussion. For that matter, simply acknowledging the domain for Scripture's authority does not predetermine the truth and relative value of Christianity. We could know these things only after equally lengthy and careful examination of many issues, such as the existence of God, the uniqueness of Jesus Christ, the truth of other religions, and much more. Apologetics will always be an important part of Christian theology, and as important as those issues are to the subject of this book, I cannot begin to do justice to them here. By stating the Bible's proper domain of authority, I hope to clarify the appropriate arena for such discussion.

Third, saving *knowledge* of God calls to mind epistemic authority. Belief on say-so, though, is not exactly the right way to talk about how we come to have this knowledge. In fact, the idea that we believe what the Bible says simply because the Bible says it belongs to propositional revelation as it was developed by Protestant orthodoxy rather than to the understanding of revelation as God's self-disclosure that I have in mind. The need to believe the Bible on say-so led to expanding the scope of the Bible's authority to include much more than it could bear. What it said about history and science also had to be believed on say-so in an attempt to preserve the credibility of what the Bible said about salvation. Such an approach to the Bible's authority confuses domains of knowledge, and thus domains of epistemic authority. More importantly, this approach misses the Bible's own point, which is better captured in thinking about revelation as God's self-disclosure. Though this disclosure surely has a cognitive aspect, De George's category of epistemic authority does not exactly capture the kind of knowing that revelation brings about. As we proceed, we will have to expand the description of the authority relation that De George has provided. Some kind of nonexecutive authority will become very important as we develop a notion of Scripture's authority, but it will need to be informed by a model of pedagogy that aims, not at "knowledge about" God in the way that much teaching is directed to imparting knowledge about a field, but "knowledge of" God, that is, a knowing that belongs to personal relationship. That model of pedagogy will become important as we explore the authority of the Bible as teacher.

THE BIBLE AS TEACHER

To designate the domain of the Bible's authority as saving knowledge of God implies some kind of teaching function for the Bible. I want to consider that function and the authority it carries in light of how the Bible serves as resource and canon. I will not be examining all the possible ways in which the Bible may be used as a source of information, literary types, and language usage in history, literature, philology, or any number of other kinds of study. My concern is with the way the Bible is a source or resource for the Christian community as it informs, forms, and transforms Christian understanding. As this kind of resource, the Bible has and exercises some form of nonexecutive authority. It supplies a record of where the community of faith has been in its relationship with and its understanding of God, and that record includes decisions it has made about its identity. As De George has pointed out, nonexecutive authority often becomes the basis for executive authority. In this case, the record of the community's identity has also become the standard (or canon) for its ongoing development. In its role as both resource and canon, the Bible is the church's teacher. Teaching involves both nonexecutive authority (because the teacher has knowledge or skills that the students lack) and executive authority (because in order to share this knowledge the teacher may do things like provide direction and correction).[2] Let us consider how both kinds of authority might be employed in order for the Bible to lead us to saving knowledge of God.

First, just what kind of nonexecutive authority the Bible has deserves attention. Simply describing this authority as epistemic in the way that De George has defined that type is problematic. Instead, we might speak of how the Bible has and exercises authority of competence in showing us how to live. Or we might even say the Bible has exemplary authority because it is filled with examples and engages our thinking precisely through examples. Just as a doctor might say, "If you want to get well, then follow this prescription," which might range from taking medication to getting a certain kind of exercise, the Bible might be saying to us, "If you want saving knowledge of God, then follow the advice and examples you see in these pages." Women who have been convinced of feminist objections to the Bible, however, cannot simply follow what it says any more than they can simply believe what it says. Part of the feminist project has been to enable women to gain a voice, and that voice will need to speak, sometimes to criticize, "what the Bible says." In whatever way we need to recognize that knowledge, competence, and examples are important, the Bible's nonexecutive authority needs careful examination. How can the Bible teach us in any of these ways when it also needs to be criticized?

Answering that question requires a closer look at how authority actually works when people interact. When De George talks about nonexecutive authority, the relationship he describes is fairly (although not entirely) one-directional. For example, the doctor knows what the patient needs to do in order to be cured. The master carpenter knows the techniques that the apprentice needs to learn. The teacher has knowledge of a field that the student needs. Granted, since nonexecutive authority is substitutional and expendable, the one who benefits from this authority relation can have on her own experiences that confirm what the doctor says (the pill works), what the carpenter shows her (handling the tool in this way produces the right effect), or what the teacher tells her (certain chemicals do explode when mixed together). The patient, apprentice, or student contributes little to the process of learning.

Given that De George has aimed at analyzing a relation in which one person has greater knowledge or skill to share with another, it is not surprising that he would present things as he does. Relationships between real people, though, are rarely static, and we need to capitalize on the fluidity of authority relations in order to display the interaction between women and the Bible that will be helpful in thinking through the problems that feminist theology has uncovered. For instance, in a nonemergency medical situation that can be handled in different ways, a good doctor/patient relationship will involve the patient in the decision-making process about a course of treatment. The doctor knows various possibilities, and the patient chooses the one that fits best with her or his situation. If the patient discovers that this method is not working or if debilitating side effects arise, she or he reports back to the doctor, and another decision can be made. In a sense, the patient is the authority on the effectiveness of the treatment. The authority relation shifts as we each supply what the other needs to know or do. In this case, the patient tells the doctor what the doctor needs to know in order to make a good recommendation (this is also the case even in the initial diagnosis).[3] Good teaching also ought to involve the learner in the process, although De George's description of how epistemic authority functions does not do justice to that insight. I want to explore a model of pedagogy that can be helpful in opening up the kind of interaction that women need to have with the Bible in order for feminist concerns to be met.

Bryan P. Stone has discussed how different models of pedagogy affect the way that we understand revelation and biblical authority, and his approach fits well with the way that I have been describing revelation through narrative.[4] Stone stands, as I do, in that branch of Christian tradition that has its roots in John Wesley. He draws from that tradition in order to show that God's grace activates, rather than overrides, human freedom. God's own power and authority do not work by coercion. Instead, God exercises power and authority in persuasion and relationship as God's grace calls forth our response. We may resist that grace, but when we accept it, we gain freedom to live in new ways. Stone quotes Wesley as saying, in opposition to the Calvinism of his time, that God is "willing that all [humans] should be saved, yet not willing to force them thereto; willing that [humans] should be saved, yet not as trees or stones but as [humans], as reasonable creatures, endued with understanding to discern what is good and liberty either to accept or refuse it."[5] Stone argues that if God saves us "as humans" rather than "as trees or stones," then God's revelation will also come to us "as humans" rather than "as trees or stones." In order to reflect this commitment in the way he talks about revelation, he develops an understanding of divine pedagogy that honors our own involvement in learning.

Drawing from Paulo Freire's *Pedagogy of the Oppressed,* Stone discusses how "dialogical commitment to the learners as active human subjects rather than as passive inanimate objects" is central to liberation.[6] Freire is well known for his criticism of "banking" education, that is, a model of learning in which the teacher "deposits" information, which the student accepts. For those who already are entrapped by a situation that treats them as less than human, the passivity of banking education simply reinforces their oppression by presenting "reality" to them as given and unquestionable. What they need is to engage actively in their learning as full human subjects, and Freire proposes a model for pedagogy that allows this engagement to happen. The teacher encourages students to voice their own experiences and raise questions about what has always been taken for granted as an essential step in learning. Not simply accepting everything the students say at face value, though, the teacher also encourages critical thinking about their experiences. In that way, dialogue takes place, with both teacher and student playing a vital role in learning. What Freire has most in mind is critical thinking about situations of oppression, so that in the process of dialogue students' consciousness of their oppression is raised. As their understanding changes, they are also enabled to act to transform their situations. Reflection and action go hand in hand. Because they are educated "as humans," that is, as people who are capable of participating in their learning, they become increasingly free to think and act and live as subjects rather than objects.

Stone observes that Juan Luis Segundo has developed a way of thinking about the Bible that closely resembles the pedagogy proposed by Freire. Following Segundo, Stone suggests that the Bible exercises its authority as our teacher, "not at the level of learning 'things,' but at the level of our 'learning how to learn.'"[7] The Bible contains a rich diversity of material that does not fit easily together and that, in fact, may appear contradictory. The value of this material is, not in providing information that is simply to be accepted, but in pressing us to rethink our customary views of the world, that is, the "taken for granted" understandings of ourselves, our surroundings, and our relationships. The Bible itself contains a record of such rethinking, as the views of different times and places have been gathered together within its covers. This human process of reflection may contain significant errors, just as our own thinking undoubtedly will. As any good teacher knows, errors are often indispensable along the way to learning. For God to teach us "as humans," with all our potential and frailty, means that we will make mistakes even as we also come to profound insights. As both record of past reflection and prompter of continual reflection, Stone says, the Bible has

> the authority of a companion and fellow-sufferer who has "been there" before, who knows our situation, who respects our "subject"-hood, who is well-trusted in the community, but who, at the same time, without overwhelming or negating us, challenges us and calls forth in us more than we ever thought possible.[8]

If grace does not override our freedom, then the Bible's authority does not override our searching attempts to understand and come into relationship with God. Those who benefit from this authority do so, not simply by passively receiving "knowledge about" God, but by actively learning how to take God into account in every aspect of daily living.

Keeping in mind that the Bible really stands in for someone else, the "companion" described above really represents multiple companions, mostly anonymous and all conditioned by their historical contexts and social locations just as we are. On the level of human communication, the Bible makes their thoughts and experiences known to us so that we can learn from them or, better, so that we can learn *through* them. The Christian community, over time and for various reasons, has believed that these human accounts of life with God were worth preserving. The models of living, advice, principles, instructions, testimonies, laws, and other things contained in those pages have been found to be helpful in forming Christian understanding in past generations, and they continue to do so. In different ways, these materials share with us knowledge, competence, and examples. To emphasize "learning how to learn" instead of "learning about" does not mean that the content of what they have to say is unimportant. What they actually say becomes the topic for reflection, and they may have profound wisdom to share. But for us to learn through them "as humans" means that we have to enter into dialogue with them. Both the aim of feminist theology itself (to claim full humanity for women) and the nature of what we are to learn through the Bible (i.e., how to enter as humans into relationship with God) require us to do so. This dialogue is likely to be lively and often heated, but nothing less should be expected when the topic under discussion matters as much as it does.

Relationships change over time, and through the centuries, times have changed. Those who have come to see its harmful effects no longer share the customary view of the world that the biblical authors, editors, and compilers held about women. The potential for reasoned elaboration of many things the Bible says about women has broken down, and women who have come to see the problems with that view cannot accept its androcentrism as authoritative. Having differences between the views of the past and the views of the present is not, however, a new problem. Christians continually carry on dialogue with the past as worship practices adapt to new contexts, as ethical issues that could never even have been conceived centuries ago have to be addressed, as growing understanding of how the physical world operates raises questions about how to understand God's relationship to that world. We come to understand the relevance of knowing God in our daily lives precisely as we engage in how to think about these issues. Christians participate in this dialogue all the time, even if it is not always openly acknowledged. Does admitting that we are really doing something other than "what the Bible says" undermine the Bible's authority?

Let us consider this question in the context of narrative as a vehicle for revelation. Given the centrality of narrative in human cognition, being saved "as humans" will undoubtedly also have to include the way we understand our world and ourselves through stories. If we think of how the Bible, through the particular way in which it brings together all these accounts, presents to us a narrative about God's involvement in the world, then we have to enter into the world of the narrative in order to understand it. We have to approach our companion (or companions) as if there is something to be learned, as if there is a story to be followed. Being disposed to enter the narrative in order to follow it bears some resemblance to the way that a student is disposed to believe a teacher in De George's understanding of epistemic authority. A person can have expertise without sharing it with someone else, but no de facto authority relation exists without both a teacher who knows something and a student who is inclined to believe that the teacher knows something and who is willing to listen in the expectation that something is to be gained. In the case of the Bible, the reader has to be inclined to recognize that the Bible tells a story, that is, has to construe the Bible as narrative, and then further the reader has to be willing to follow the story. Upon entering a narrative, though, the hearer/reader is not preparing to accept items of information as true. Instead, she is preparing to engage in a world that this narrative creates in order to see where the story goes. Even on the level of human communication, this willingness to hear what is said is important. When one remembers that this human communication is potentially revelatory, being disposed to follow the story means also being willing to listen to God.

Being disposed to listen and learn, that is, entering into this de facto authority relation, does not mean simply accepting everything that the text says. Even in the way that De George describes epistemic authority, what the teacher says is always open to challenge, just as it is open to confirmation. The presence of an error does not automatically invalidate the teacher's authority. Errors only undermine authority when the student no longer benefits from accepting what the teacher says most of the time. In the case of narrative, the benefit to the hearer/reader is also important to consider, even if it has to be judged somewhat differently. Wrestling with a way of understanding God that is presented in the text, even an understanding that the hearer/reader comes to believe is wrong, can still contribute to her relationship with God. In order to see how that can happen, we have to consider how the Bible functions not only as resource but also as canon.

To see how such wrestling might take place, imagine the problems involved in reading Ps 137, which expresses despair about Israel's exile in Babylon and ends with a brutal, vengeful image of dashing the children of the Babylonian captors against a rock. To read this, or any, text in light of what the Christian community has taken it to be, that is, "as scripture" that tells about God's involvement in the world, means to listen for what this text has to say about God, as well as what God has to say through this text. It does not mean simply taking this text, or any other, by itself, apart from its canonical context. Since the canonical context I have in mind is the Christian canon, the following discussion will deal with how this text might be read by Christians, without presuming to say how it might be read in different contexts, for instance, as Jews might read it along with the Hebrew Scriptures, Mishnah, and Talmud.[9] How might one take this psalm as scripture in light of the narrative that Christians want to tell? How is this depiction of God followable and intelligible in a narrative that also includes, among other things, Jesus' words that we are to forgive our enemies?

Carol Antablin Miles observes that Christian discomfort with this psalm, the sense that it just does not "fit" with the Christian view of the world, has led lectionary readings of it to excise the final, offensive verses. Instead of excising them, Miles suggests that we can make use of them. She employs Charles Wood's hermeneutical suggestions to argue that when this text is seen in light of the whole canon, it can have a positive value within the canon.[10] It is not necessary to believe that this kind of vengeance is good or that God will carry it out in order to learn through this text. Rather than providing a model for how to treat one's enemies, or how to treat the children of one's enemies, this psalm places an expression of rage and suffering in the context of our relationship to God. By doing so, it forces us to think about those feelings and about who God is. Not only thanks and praise but also hurt and anger may be declared to God in the community of faith. Ps 137 is a resource for reflection on a moment in the community's tradition, but that reflection ought to involve more than just this psalm. The whole narrative that the community tells shows us how this psalm ought to be read. In that way, the canon (collection) becomes canon (standard) to help us know how to use this resource. An interplay between the nonexecutive authority of the resource and the executive authority of the standard directs our use of the resource so that God may teach us through this text.

We do not enter this narrative world simply because we think it is interesting or entertaining. The faith community turns to Scripture to make sense of life experiences, in this case powerful feelings of loss and anger. According to Stephen Crites, we try out various possibilities for our lives by seeing how those possibilities work in mundane stories, which are specific articulations of a sacred story. When we see that other things that the community says about God (creating and loving all humans, showing mercy and forgiveness) temper this psalm, our own vengeance may be tempered as well. We can be led to ask questions such as, What would my life be like if I sought vengeance for my own losses? What kind of God would I be worshiping if this God actually carried out my hateful desires? Does God really want me to think this way? The mundane story told in Ps 137 does not by itself resonate with the sacred story, the deep understanding of the contours of our existence, that Christians want to tell. Still, by articulating one possibility for our anger, the psalm allows us to test and reshape our understanding according to that sacred story as we struggle with the implications we discover there. What we gain from the narrative world that the Bible as a whole creates is a perspective on the world in which we live, which calls us to attend to God in all that we do.

Of course, we also gain this perspective through our engagement with other texts, and many of them contribute to our understanding more straightforwardly. The narrative world opens outward onto our own world, helping us order, understand, and find meaning in people, things, and events around us as we make decisions, face challenges, grow in insight, raise questions, and struggle to understand ourselves and our surroundings all in relation to God.

The very relevance of revelation through the Bible, the newness that is essential to ongoing relationship with God, depends on making this connection between the testimonies to God's involvement in the world of the past and God's involvement in our lives now.

Of course, it is always possible that psalm will be read as authorizing vengeance instead. Just because a text has the potential to be revelatory does not mean that it will actually be so. The Bible is instrumental to an encounter with God, but our own reliability in understanding what God would have us hear is always fallible. Dialogue with a text does not guarantee a particular outcome, and errors will continue to be a part of human reflection. Indeed, the possibility of error increases the importance of being in conversation with others as we interpret the Bible. The point here is that being disposed to listen and learn through a text does not mean accepting everything that it has to say exactly as it says it. The text exercises authority by prompting us to reflection, from which we may benefit when we open ourselves to the possibility that God can speak to us through it. When a coincidence occurs between our disposal to learn through the text and God's use of the text to teach, then that coincidence of letter and spirit enables even this text to be "activated as canon," as Wood says.[11] It becomes not merely a resource but also a guide, not a guide that is simply followed in itself but a guide that directs Christians to the one whom we ought to follow, Jesus Christ.

This description of the Bible's authority brings to mind the *auctoritas* of ancient Rome. The Bible connects us to the past by giving us access to the vision of God's involvement in the world through Jesus Christ that the Christian community formed itself around and committed itself to. It shares a perspective on reality so that by attending to God as we live in the world, knowing it to be God's, we may grow in a saving relationship. This vision has a normative function for the community, but it has to be brought into every present moment in order for revelation to continue to have meaning for us, because new situations call for new understandings of that vision. Elaboration and development do not undermine the Bible's authority; rather, they are essential to its extension into our lives. Its authority unfolds as the story of our lives unfolds. This elaboration requires dialogue with the text, though, in order for that vision to be employed properly. Just as a doctor needs to hear from a patient in order to offer good advice, the wisdom we gain from the Bible needs to fit to the circumstances that we actually face. In ancient Rome, living elders who knew the current situation interpreted the past to the present. The Bible, though, as Kathryn Tanner has pointed out, is now a fixed document that itself needs interpretation. For elaboration to take place, the role of the other partner in the dialogue has to be acknowledged. That is, the hearer/reader has knowledge of the conditions in which she or he lives. Since the conditions of the Bible do not exactly match the conditions of the person's life, she or he has to interpret the Bible in such a way that it has bearing on those conditions. In this sense, the interpreter supplies something that the Bible (or, perhaps better, the companions who speak in the Bible) does not itself have, namely, knowledge of these conditions. Expanding the narrative into one's life, then, involves both the wisdom of the Bible and the insight of the person. Without naming our own experiences, an essential part of entering dialogue "as humans," we cannot know how to make use of the wisdom that can be gained through the Bible.

Struggle with and criticism of specific texts belong to that process of elaboration. For women, naming our experiences will include naming how the androcentrism and patriarchy of the Bible have hurt us, how the humans who composed it have articulated the sacred story in ways that can hinder us from being the full persons God wants us to be. Where what the Bible says causes women to live in submission, marginality, and limited gender roles, rather than in the whole-making love of God, the Bible has not been a resource for saving knowledge of God. As it is possible to struggle with Ps 137, it is also possible to struggle with the ideas, images, and commands of texts that reduce women's possibilities to live fully human lives. Women supply knowledge about the effects of biblical texts on us and in that sense have and exercise a kind of nonexecutive authority. When we test those harmful effects against what we know that God wants for us, women also have authority to speak out about how androcentric and patriarchal texts fail to meet God's own standard. Fear of engaging in this dialogue comes from confusing human communication with God's communication. Women exercise the authority I have described with regard to humanly written texts and the socially conditioned views expressed there, but we are authorized to do so by God's own work in us. When we come to see how God values us, then we are able to challenge society and even the church community when they do not value us as God does. When we really grasp the perspective on the world that the Bible offers us, it allows us to question customary views about women, even those expressed by the human authors of the Bible, that have kept us from being fully human. To the extent that we criticize even the Bible in light of what we have learned about salvation through the Bible, we still can acknowledge it to be our teacher, and, in fact, such criticism frees the sacred story to be told in ways that it can be heard more clearly.

Grasping the value pattern that the Bible wants to display to us may also send us back to reexamine other areas of our own customary thinking, such as our views on race or wealth or relationships, areas in which we may need to be criticized ourselves. Insofar as the Bible calls us to attend to God in every situation, it directs us to the ultimate context in which we should understand all our thoughts and actions. When we test our lives against the all-encompassing love of God, we see how many ways we fall short. In the pedagogy that Freire describes, dialogue truly works two ways, which means the Bible never simply speaks to women, nor do women simply speak to the Bible. However important it may be for us to voice our own experiences, our voices are never exempt from criticism. It is always possible that we have not taken God fully into account in the things that we say. Women's authority to speak out, even in criticism of androcentric and patriarchal texts, does not cancel the authority of the Bible to act as standard. Although it is not identical to the Bible, a norm is gained through the Bible because it directs us to see the entire real world as belonging to God. This vision of how God values the world allows us, as valuable, to speak for ourselves, but that same vision may very well challenge us because we have failed to embody it in other ways. Genuine dialogue of this sort actually enhances the effectiveness of the Bible's authority.

Dialogue with the Bible involves dialogue with other people who interpret the Bible, because one way we learn through the Bible is by learning through others. No hearer/reader stands in isolation from other hearers/readers in the faith community, and we often come to understand the limitations of our own views by the encounters we have with people who have different views. Multiple interpretations of the way the Bible speaks to life today arise because, no matter what similarities may exist between people, every single person's situation is unique and thus will call for a unique dialogue and will produce unique insights. The history of feminist scholarship, which has had to learn to acknowledge the different insights of women who do not have white, middle-class, educated backgrounds, illustrates this point. Postmodern interest in the social location of concrete women continues to develop that idea. Part of what it means to be saved "as humans" is to recognize that others are saved "as humans" also, that is, as subjects who are mental agents who perceive the world and the Bible's meaning for their lives in different ways. In a community of people who see things differently (and these differences may be between individuals or gatherings of individuals, such as congregations or denominations) will inevitably be conflict and innovation that emerges from this conflict. Such is the nature of human existence. Not surprisingly, we find the same kind of interaction within the Christian community. The existence of multiple viewpoints is clearly a fact of life that will not disappear, and whether such multiplicity leads to division or creativity depends on how we handle our interaction.

To engage each other positively, we ought to remember at least two things. First, the Bible's authority is not at risk simply because its hearers/readers understand it in different ways. Variety is an inevitable and essential manifestation of the Bible's authority. Its narrative cannot open out onto our lives with less complexity than our lives actually have. At the same time, the Bible as canon does set some limits for its interpretation. The narrative structure of the Bible does not allow us to say anything and everything and still remain faithful to the understanding of God that Christians have had. Acknowledging limits may give comfort to those who fear a "new revelation" in feminist theology, but we should also keep in mind how even the views of those who never sought to question the tradition sometimes fail to interpret it adequately. For instance, Christians commonly speak of "the God of the Old Testament" and "the God of the New Testament," but the structure of the Bible itself calls that dual thinking into question. The New Testament was an addition to, not a substitute for, the older Scriptures. What often goes unrecognized is that even decisions about what would be included in the New Testament were in part guided by whether the new writings corresponded to what Christians knew about God from the older ones. Christians should not view whatever is new and important about Christian faith as denying or replacing that more ancient understanding. As the standard for Christian identity, the Bible has executive authority to serve as the test for the adequacy of our interpretations in this community even when they are widely held. The sphere of adequate interpretations, though, is much larger than most of us usually think it is. Taking that breadth seriously means taking each other seriously as we share what the Bible is saying to us.

Second, as we seek to determine the adequacy of our interpretations in light of the canon, we need to remember that we each have something that the other lacks, namely, information about what our lives are like, how God is working in our lives, and the conditions that prevent the fullness of life that God wants for us. As Letty Russell says, "multiple authorities" contribute to each other's understanding.[12] We each become resources for reflection about how the narrative world of the Bible opens out onto the world in which we live. As we take the rich complexity of human relationships into account, the Bible's relevance expands beyond what we by ourselves might be able to see. As H. Richard Niebuhr says, our patterns of beliefs and values become enlarged so that they more adequately (even if never fully) reflect God's own perspective. One person's view of the Bible or concept of God may need reexamination as she or he becomes aware of the impact that view has on someone else. In other cases, a view one person holds may help another person see a situation in a different, more helpful way. We pose problems for each other, as well as bear witness to each other about God's presence, when we share our stories. And the Bible calls us to attend to God while negotiating differences among ourselves. This kind of sharing is essential in helping us to see and correct authoritarian uses of the Bible so that its proper authority may be exercised effectively.

Dialogue with people outside Christianity can be as important as dialogue with people within Christianity in helping us to see the Bible's vision more clearly. As Niebuhr argues, those outside our own community can often point out things that we miss about ourselves. They can reflect back to us the ways in which we as a community fail to embody the standard that we acknowledge is ours, how we fail to be the people whom we understand God wants us to be. It is not necessary for another community to accept the Bible as its teacher in order for that community to help us learn through our teacher better. Given the realities of humans as historical creatures in finite times and places, we will not all have the same perspective or be shaped by the same stories. Observations about Christian identity and practice should not be ignored just because they come from people that have been formed in a different way. Those observations can be extraordinarily helpful in the kind of testing we have to do in order to remain faithful to the vision the Bible provides and to elaborate its meaning well.

CONCLUSION

Insofar as the church has collected these writings contained in the Bible to be the record of how the Christian community understands itself, the Bible has de jure authority to be a resource for Christian formation and a canon to test that formation. Since the resources the Bible provides for us can bring us to saving knowledge of God, it has nonexecutive authority, which becomes the basis for its executive authority in that gaining this knowledge supplies us with a standard for testing and judging all our attempts to articulate that knowledge. Because members of the church actually do make use of it in these ways, it also has and exercises this authority de facto.

Those who accept the Bible's authority do so because they believe its authority is legitimate. The first criterion for legitimacy is validity, and the Bible's nonexecutive authority is valid if it has real knowledge of its domain. To put it another way, the Bible's authority is valid if it really offers a perspective on the world that is a valid way of seeing the world. The validity of that perspective does not depend on our acceptance of it. Rather, it depends on whether God really is offering saving knowledge through the Bible. Still, in order for us to benefit from that knowledge, we need to dispose ourselves to learn from it, that is, to accept its authority de facto, and we need to have good reasons for doing so. The other criteria for legitimacy address those reasons.

To meet the second criterion, the knowledge that the Bible offers to us must be testable. As long as Christians engage in open dialogue with people who hold other perspectives on the world, such testing may take place. Perhaps more important for individual Christians, though, is that salvation through Jesus Christ is testable in one's own experience; that is, one knows personally and intimately the wholeness that entering into relationship with God through Jesus Christ brings. Because women have had experiences that confirm the life-giving, sense-making power of the Bible, feminists have reason to believe that at least in some sense, its authority is legitimate authority.

The third criterion for legitimacy, that of relevance, is very important for feminists. In other words, the Bible exercises its authority legitimately when it acts as a resource and canon within its proper domain. Use of it outside that domain fails to meet this criterion. The Bible plays an irreplaceable role in forming a distinct perspective on the world, but it should not be used to form every perspective. For instance, to use the Bible as a resource for forming scientific thinking would be an illegitimate use of its authority. Similarly, to use the Bible to test scientific judgments would be illegitimate. What constitutes the domain of the Bible is, not a body of knowledge about a field, but rather a narrative that brings us to knowledge of God. Telling this narrative has a goal, namely, sharing a perspective on reality so that by attending to God as we live, we may rightly orient ourselves toward God and grow in a saving relationship. The Bible's authority is exercised properly within its relevant domain when it is exercised for this purpose.

Patriarchy distorts our understanding of the way we ought to be and act before God and thus hinders the proper exercise of the Bible's authority. Unfortunately, this way of thinking pervades biblical texts. Socially located human beings cannot tell stories apart from what they know of the social reality in which they live, but the relationship with God to which their stories point needs to be distinguished from the conditioned character of those stories themselves. Customary views such as patriarchy are not the point of the Bible's story. The point of that comprehensive narrative, namely, to make all things intelligible in light of their relationship to God, may in fact challenge the customary ways of understanding the world that permeate the actual texts. Any appeal to the Bible's authority to support patriarchy is illegitimate, and any contribution that biblical texts make to patriarchal thinking needs to be criticized. The Bible exercises its authority within its proper domain when it brings us into saving relationship with God, not when it supports the very social structures that keep us from realizing that relationship fully. Criticizing illegitimate uses of the Bible's authority, though, does not undermine its legitimate authoritative function to bring us into saving relationship with God.

To meet the fourth criterion for legitimacy, trustworthiness, the Bible depends on the trustworthiness of those it represents. Human trustworthiness is always open to question. Even if individual authors, compilers, and editors did not intend to deceive, they have been wrong about many things. By collecting and using these materials in the way that it has, the church has intended to bear witness to God, but the church has not always been faithful to that intent. Instances of authoritarian use of the Bible abound in the history of the church, and those have to be acknowledged. Still, because the community has also made use of the Bible over and over again as a resource for saving knowledge of God, there is reason to trust that the narrative it tells can in fact enable us to gain that knowledge ourselves. More important for this purpose than the trustworthiness of the humans involved is God's trustworthiness. The Bible is potentially revelatory because God can make use of it for self-disclosure, and that potential may be realized as we dispose ourselves to learning through it.

By recognizing the Bible's potential as a teacher, we do not surrender our own ability to make contributions to the process of learning through it. In fact, the kind of learning that we need to do depends on the exercise of our own proper authority. As we do so, we need to remember that our own reliability to receive accurately what God would have us know is not greater than that of other humans. If the Bible is not revelatory simply because of who wrote it, then neither is it revelatory simply because of who reads it. We need to test our understandings and actions against the Bible itself, against other interpretations of the Bible, and against the observations of outsiders in order to see whether we are receiving God's disclosure accurately. However, when we actively seek to make use of the resources the Bible has to offer in order to reflect on God's involvement in our lives, and when God uses those resources to illumine our lives so that we are made whole in God's love, the Bible's authority is effective.

If the above description of the Bible's authority is accurate, then the Bible's authority and women's authority are not necessarily pitted against each other. Feminists can acknowledge the way that the Bible encourages our faith in God while at the same time working to uncover its harmful impact on women. When conceived as narrative in the way I have described, the Bible plays an indispensable role in revelation for the Christian community, even when the human communication there needs to be criticized. We grow cognitively, we broaden our understanding of God's relationship to our specific circumstances, as we wrestle with the very texts that have been so problematic. The feminist struggle with Scripture, far from denying the authority of the Bible, is crucial for making real its authority in our lives.

Recent developments in feminist theology have been critical of essentialist views of the self, the Bible, and even communities. I have tried to show that it is possible to talk about processes of formation and still acknowledge the authority of the Bible. The multiplicity of communities, narratives, selves, and texts is inescapable, but the Bible points to the ultimate context in which all this multiplicity may be understood—God. Through its varied texts, it provides a way of viewing the world that forms our identity as Christians. We gain that identity as we engage the Bible and each other in thinking about what it means to attend to God in every aspect of our lives. Because life is so complex, different issues arise for different people in different ways. The task of seeing how this rich diversity is intelligible and followable is not easy and will never be completely finished. Clearly, Christians disagree on many, many things, but to the extent that we share a commitment to understand our lives in light of how God has been revealed in Jesus Christ, we have a basis for dialogue among us. As Christians, we are committed to finding the order of all things in connection to God, and that means further that we should attempt to order our own lives in such a way that we value things as God values them. Appealing to the vision that may be gained through the Bible as the point of contact for our discussion clearly acknowledges Scripture's authority and provides grounds for us to talk with one another despite our differences. Feminists need such a shared ground in order to persuade other Christians of the need to work for justice for women. Where women have been disvalued, we can call others within the Christian community to acknowledge that mistake and reevaluate ideas and practices in light of our common commitment. The norm that may be gained through the Bible is never completely at anyone's disposal, and yet it may be shared and used in important ways.

Through the narrative that the Bible tells, the hearer/reader comes to understand better the way that she and others stand in relation to God. Her actions, attitudes, and convictions are shaped as she interacts with the story, and that shaping is never fully finished because the story is told so richly and diversely that it intersects with her life in a multitude of ways. Learning through the story includes learning to live in accord with the story, that is, living in the real world in a way that acknowledges through actions and attitudes that this world belongs to God. When we live in this way, we clearly acknowledge the point of the notion of the doctrine of Scripture that was developed after the Reformation, namely, that the end of Scripture is salvation. In their own way, Protestant orthodox theologians were trying to preserve an insight about Scripture that is very ancient. As they put the point, the Bible exercises causative authority as it actually brings about our faith in God and thus enlivens our relationship with God. As these theologians also saw, all human endeavors are fallible, so we are left to trust and rely on God alone for that salvation. The truth of the Bible is confirmed in one's own experience of coming to know God, and that experience can then be used for testing and interpretation (its canonical authority) as the Christian community works to draw out the implications of God's love for us. Although feminists cannot accept the specific way in which that doctrine was worked out, we do share some of the concerns that lie behind it. The very struggle that feminists have with the Bible, far from threatening Christian commitments about Scripture, actually brings them to light. I have tried to show that the shift from propositions to narrative provides a way of talking about those commitments in a new and more helpful way.

My hope is that this way of understanding the Bible's authority will be useful beyond the feminist conversation. The way we work through other issues can also be informed by thinking of the Bible as revealing God to us through our participation in its narrative. The process of conversation will not be easy and likely will not produce clear-cut results, but our very engagement with each other matters. Through it, the Bible's vision finds new expression. When the witness of the past meets our present circumstances in our creative appropriation of its vision, the Bible performs its task of revealing God to us with authority.

NOTES

1. For a good discussion of the diversity of religious ends, see S. Mark Heim, *The Depth of the Riches: A Trinitarian Theology of Religious Ends* (Grand Rapids: Eerdmans, 2001), pt. 1. His footnotes can also direct the interested reader to others who make this point. I find Heim's analysis more compelling than his conclusion.

2. For a good description of how teaching involves a complex interaction of types of authority, and how that model can be instructive as we think about the Bible's authority, see Charles M. Wood, "Scripture, Authenticity, and Truth," *The Journal of Religion* 76 (April 1996): 189–205.

3. De George points out that the advantage of his approach to epistemic authority is that people we do not ordinarily think of as authorities, for instance, children, can in fact be recognized as such. He uses an example of how a doctor believes what a child says about her or his pain. We are all, he says, "potential authorities on certain aspects of ourselves." See *Nature and Limits of Authority,* 28.

4. Bryan P. Stone, "Wesleyan Theology, Scriptural Authority, and Homosexuality," *Wesleyan Theological Journal* 30 (fall 1995): 108–38.

5. Ibid., 119. The original quotation comes from John Wesley, "Predestination Calmly Considered," in *John Wesley* (ed. Albert Outler; New York: Oxford University Press, 1964), 450.

6. Stone, "Wesleyan Theology," 121.

7. Ibid., 125.

8. Ibid., 126.

9. By using Ps 137 as an example, I do not mean to imply that Hebrew scriptures are inferior to the Christian scriptures that were added to them. Such an implication would conflict directly with my main argument. I mean only to take a text that is particularly difficult for Christians, and, in fact, I want to encourage a reading of it that acknowledges that it is really scripture for us. We learn from other Hebrew scriptures about God's love for all people, and because those texts are also in our canon, they, along with texts in the New Testament, ought to inform how we read this psalm.

10. Carol Antablin Miles, "'Singing the Songs of Zion' and Other Sermons from the Margins of the Canon," *Koinonia* 6 (1994): 151–75. Although I am using Miles's work on a particular psalm, I should note that Walter Brueggemann recommends this kind of reading for psalms of vengeance in general. See *Praying the Psalms* (Winona, Minn.: Saint Mary's, 1982).

11. Charles M. Wood, *The Formation of Christian Understanding: Theological Hermeneutics* (Valley Forge, Pa.: Trinity Press International, 1993; repr., Eugene, Ore.: Wipf & Stock, 2000), 109.

12. Letty M. Russell, *Household of Freedom: Authority in Feminist Theology* (Philadelphia: Westminster, 1987), 33.

Bibliography

Arendt, Hannah. "What Was Authority?" Pages 81–112 in *Nomos I: Authority.* Edited by Carl J. Friedrich. Cambridge: Harvard University Press, 1958.

Bayles, Michael D. "The Functions and Limits of Political Authority." Pages 101–11 in *Authority: A Philosophical Analysis.* Edited by R. Baine Harris. University, Ala.: University of Alabama Press, 1976.

Berger, Peter L. *The Sacred Canopy: Elements of a Sociological Theory of Religion.* New York: Anchor, 1969.

Berman, Ruth A., and Dan Isaac Slobin. *Relating Events in Narrative: A Crosslinguistic Developmental Study.* Hillsdale, N.J.: Lawrence Erlbaum, 1994.

Bird, Phyllis A. "What Makes a Feminist Reading Feminist? A Qualified Answer." Pages 124–31 in *Escaping Eden: New Feminist Perspectives on the Bible.* Edited by Harold C. Washington, Susan Lochrie Graham, and Pamela Thimmes. Sheffield: Sheffield Academic Press, 1998.

Bloesch, Donald G. *The Battle for the Trinity: The Debate over Inclusive God-Language.* Ann Arbor: Servant, 1985.

Brenner, Athalya, and Carole Fontaine, eds. *A Feminist Companion to Reading the Bible: Approaches, Methods, and Strategies.* Sheffield: Sheffield Academic Press, 1997.

Brueggemann, Walter. *Praying the Psalms.* Winona, Minn.: Saint Mary's, 1982.

———. "What Is a Narrative Fact?" Pages 17–27 in *The Future of Fact.* Edited by Jeffrey J. Strange and Elihu Katz. Vol. 560 of *The Annals of the American Academy of Political and Social Science.* Edited by Alan W. Heston. Thousand Oaks, Calif.: Sage Publications, 1998.

Bruner, Jerome, and Joan Lucariello. "Monologue as Narrative Recreation of the World." Pages 73–97 in *Narratives from the Crib*. Edited by Katherine Nelson. Cambridge: Harvard University Press, 1989.

Bultmann, Rudolf. "New Testament and Mythology." Pages 1–43 in *New Testament and Mythology and Other Basic Writings*. Selected, edited, and translated by Schubert M. Ogden. Philadelphia: Fortress, 1984. Translation of "Neues Testament und Mythologie." In *Kerygma und Mythos* 1. 2d ed. Hamburg: Herbert Reich-Evangelischer Verlag, 1951.

————. "On the Problem of Demythologizing." Pages 95–130 in *New Testament and Mythology and Other Basic Writings*. Selected, edited, and translated by Schubert M. Ogden. Philadelphia: Fortress, 1984. Translation of "Zum Problem der Entmythologisierung." In *Kerygma und Mythos* 2. 1st ed. Hamburg: Herbert Reich-Evangelischer Verlag, 1952.

————. "Science and Existence." Pages 131–44 in *New Testament and Mythology and Other Basic Writings*. Selected, edited, and translated by Schubert M. Ogden. Philadelphia: Fortress, 1984. Translation of "Wissenschaft und Existenz." In *Glauben und Verstehen*. Vol. 3. Tubingen: J. C. B. Mohr, 1965.

————. "Theology as Science." Pages 45–67 in *New Testament and Mythology and Other Basic Writings*. Selected, edited, and translated by Schubert M. Ogden. Philadelphia: Fortress, 1984. Translation of "Protokoll der Tagung 'Alter Marburger' 2." *Hofgeismar* (January 1979): 1–23.

————. *What Is Theology?* Minneapolis: Fortress, 1997.

Campenhausen, Hans von. *The Formation of the Christian Bible*. Translated by J. A. Baker. Philadelphia: Fortress, 1972.

Chemnitz, Martin. *Loci Theologici*. Translated by J. A. O. Preus. St. Louis: Concordia, 1989.

Cheney, Emily. *She Can Read: Feminist Reading Strategies for Biblical Narrative*. Valley Forge, Pa.: Trinity Press International, 1996.

Christ, Carol P., and Judith Plaskow, eds. *Womanspirit Rising: A Feminist Reader in Religion*. San Francisco: Harper & Row, 1979.

Cottrell, Jack W. "The Nature of Biblical Authority: A Conservative Perspective." Pages 21–40 in *Conservative, Moderate, Liberal*. Edited by Charles R. Blaisdell. St. Louis: CBP, 1990.

Crites, Stephen. "The Narrative Quality of Experience." *Journal of the American Academy of Religion* 39, no. 3 (September 1971): 291–311. Repr. pages 65–88 in *Why Narrative? Readings in Narrative Theology*. Edited by Stanley Hauerwas and L. Gregory Jones. Eugene, Ore.: Wipf & Stock, 1997.

Original edition, Grand Rapids: Eerdmans, 1989. (Page citations are to the reprint edition.)

Curry, David. "Inclusive Language Liturgies: The Renunciation of Revelation." *Churchman* 105 (fall 1991): 54–70.

De George, Richard T. *The Nature and Limits of Authority.* Lawrence: University Press of Kansas, 1985.

Dulles, Avery R. *Models of Revelation.* Garden City, N.Y.: Doubleday, 1983. Repr., 1985. 2d ed. with a new introduction. Maryknoll, N.Y.: Orbis, 1992. (Page citations are to the 1985 edition.)

Farley, Margaret A. "Feminist Consciousness and the Interpretation of Scripture." Pages 4–51 in *Feminist Interpretation of the Bible.* Edited by Letty M. Russell. Philadelphia: Westminster, 1985.

Frei, Hans W. *The Eclipse of Biblical Narrative: A Study in Eighteenth and Nineteenth Century Hermeneutics.* New Haven: Yale University Press, 1974.

Friedrich, Carl J. "Authority, Reason, and Discretion." Pages 28–48 in *Nomos I: Authority.* Edited by Carl J. Friedrich. Cambridge: Harvard University Press, 1958.

Fulkerson, Mary McClintock. *Changing the Subject: Women's Discourses and Feminist Theology.* Minneapolis: Fortress, 1994.

———. "'Is There a (Non-Sexist) Bible in This Church?' A Feminist Case for the Priority of Interpretive Communities." *Modern Theology* 14, no. 2 (April 1998): 225–42.

Geertz, Clifford. *The Interpretation of Cultures.* New York: Basic, 1973.

Gonçalves, Óscar F., and Paulo P. P. Machado. "Cognitive Narrative Psychotherapy: Research Foundations." *Journal of Clinical Psychology* 55, no. 10 (1999): 1179–91.

Guignon, Charles. "Narrative Explanation in Psychotherapy." *American Behavioral Scientist* 41, no. 4 (January 1998): 558–77.

Hanson, R. P. C. *The Search for the Christian Doctrine of God.* Edinburgh: T&T Clark, 1988.

Hauerwas, Stanley, and David B. Burrell. "From System to Story: An Alternative Pattern for Rationality in Ethics." Pages 15–39 in *Truthfulness and Tragedy: Further Investigations in Christian Ethics.* By Stanley Hauerwas with Richard Bondi and David B. Burrell. Notre Dame, Ind.: University of Notre Dame Press, 1977. Repr. pages 158–90 in *Why Narrative? Readings in Narrative Theology.* Edited by Stanley Hauerwas and L. Gregory Jones. Eugene, Ore.: Wipf & Stock, 1997. Original edition, Grand Rapids: Eerdmans, 1989. (Page citations are to the reprint edition.)

Hawthorn, Jeremy. "Narrative." In *A Glossary of Contemporary Literary Theory.* New York: Oxford University Press, 1998.

———. "Story and Plot." In *A Glossary of Contemporary Literary Theory.* New York: Oxford University Press, 1998.

Heim, S. Mark. *The Depth of the Riches: A Trinitarian Theology of Religious Ends.* Grand Rapids: Eerdmans, 2001.

Henry, Carl. "Inerrancy and the Bible in Modern Conservative Evangelical Thought." Pages 53–65 in *Introduction to Christian Theology: Contemporary North American Perspectives.* Edited by Roger A. Badham. Louisville: Westminster John Knox, 1998.

Heppe, Heinrich. *Reformed Dogmatics: Set Out and Illustrated from the Sources.* Foreword by Karl Barth. Edited by Ernst Bizer. Translated by G. T. Thomson. London: George Allen & Unwin, 1950.

Hermans, Hubert J. M. "Self-Narrative as Meaning Construction: The Dynamics of Self-Investigation." *Journal of Clinical Psychology* 55, no. 10 (1999): 1193–1211.

Howard, George S. "Culture Tales: A Narrative Approach to Thinking, Cross-Cultural Psychology, and Psychotherapy." *American Psychologist* 46, no. 3 (March 1991): 187–97.

Humm, Maggie. "Authority." In *The Dictionary of Feminist Theory.* Columbus: Ohio State University Press, 1990.

Irenaeus. *Against Heresies.* In *The Apostolic Fathers: Justin Martyr—Irenaeus.* Vol. 1 of *The Ante-Nicene Fathers: Translation of the Writings of the Fathers Down to A.D. 325.* 1868. Repr., Grand Rapids: Eerdmans, 1993.

Jantzen, Grace M. "Conspicuous Sanctity and Religious Belief." Pages 121–40 in *The Rationality of Religious Belief: Essays in Honour of Basil Mitchell.* Edited by William J. Abraham and Steven W. Holtzer. Oxford: Clarendon, 1987.

Kelly, J. N. D. *Early Christian Creeds.* London: Longmans, 1960.

Kelsey, David. H. *Proving Doctrine: The Uses of Scripture in Modern Theology.* Harrisburg, Pa.: Trinity Press International, 1999. Original edition, *The Uses of Scripture in Recent Theology.* Philadelphia: Fortress, 1975. (Page citations are to the reprint edition.)

Kugel, James L., and Rowan A. Greer. *Early Biblical Interpretation.* Edited by Wayne A. Meeks. Library of Early Christianity Series 3. Philadelphia: Westminster, 1986.

Leith, John H., ed. *Creeds of the Churches: A Reader in Christian Doctrine from the Bible to the Present.* 3d ed. Atlanta: John Knox, 1982.

Lichtenberg, Judith. "The Will to Truth: A Reply to Novick." Pages 43–54 in *The Future of Fact*. Edited by Jeffrey J. Strange and Elihu Katz. Vol. 560 of *The Annals of the American Academy of Political and Social Science*. Thousand Oaks, Calif.: Sage Publications, 1998.

Lohse, Bernhard. *A Short History of Christian Doctrine: From the First Century to the Present*. Philadelphia: Fortress, 1966.

Luke, Carmen. "Feminist Pedagogy Theory: Reflections on Power and Authority." *Educational Theory* 46, no. 3 (summer 1996): 283–302.

MacIntyre, Alasdair C. "Epistemological Crises, Narrative, and Philosophy of Science." Pages 453–72 in *After Virtue: A Study in Moral Theory*. Edited by Alasdair C. MacIntyre. Notre Dame, Ind.: University of Notre Dame Press, 1981. Repr. pages 138–51 in *Why Narrative? Readings in Narrative Theology*. Edited by Stanley Hauerwas and L. Gregory Jones. Eugene, Ore.: Wipf & Stock, 1997. Original edition, Grand Rapids: Eerdmans, 1989. (Page citations are to the reprint edition.)

McFague, Sallie. *Metaphorical Theology: Models of God in Religious Language*. Philadelphia: Fortress, 1982.

———. Models of God: *Theology for an Ecological, Nuclear Age*. Philadelphia: Fortress, 1987.

Melanchthon, Philip. *Commentary on Romans*. Translated by Fred Kramer. St. Louis: Concordia, 1992.

Metzger, Bruce. M. "Bible." In *The Oxford Companion to the Bible*. Edited by Bruce M. Metzger and Michael D. Coogan. Oxford: Oxford University Press, 1993.

Miles, Carol Antablin. "'Singing the Songs of Zion' and Other Sermons from the Margins of the Canon." *Koinonia* 6 (1994): 151–75.

Mink, Louis. "Narrative Form as a Cognitive Instrument." Pages 129–49 in *The Writing of History: Literary Form and Historical Understanding*. Edited by Robert H. Canary and Henry Kozicki. Madison: University of Wisconsin Press, 1978.

Mishara, Aaron L. "Narrative and Psychotherapy—The Phenomenology of Healing." *American Journal of Psychotherapy* 49, no. 2 (spring 1995): 180–95.

Moore, Stephen D. *Literary Criticism and the Gospels: The Theoretical Challenge*. New Haven: Yale University Press, 1989.

Muller, Richard A. *Prolegomena to Theology*. Vol. 1 of *Post-Reformation Reformed Dogmatics*. Grand Rapids: Baker, 1987.

———. *Holy Scripture: The Cognitive Foundation of Theology*. Vol. 2 of *Post-Reformation Reformed Dogmatics*. Grand Rapids: Baker, 1993.

Niebuhr, H. Richard. *Faith on Earth: An Inquiry into the Structure of Human Faith.* Edited by Richard R. Niebuhr. New Haven: Yale University Press, 1989.

———. *The Meaning of Revelation.* New York: Macmillan, 1960.

Norris, Richard A., Jr., ed. and trans. *The Christological Controversy.* Sources of Early Christian Thought. Edited by William G. Rusch. Philadelphia: Fortress, 1980.

Novick, Peter. "(The Death of) the Ethics of Historical Practice (and Why I Am Not Mourning)." Pages 28–42 of *The Future of Fact.* Edited by Jeffrey J. Strange and Elihu Katz. Vol. 560 of *The Annals of the American Academy of Political and Social Science.* Thousand Oaks, Calif.: Sage Publications, 1998.

Nussbaum, Martha. "Narrative Emotions: Beckett's Genealogy of Love." *Ethics* 98, no. 2 (January 1988): 225–54. Repr. pages 216–48 in *Why Narrative? Readings in Narrative Theology.* Edited by Stanley Hauerwas and L. Gregory Jones. Eugene, Ore.: Wipf & Stock, 1997. Original edition, Grand Rapids: Eerdmans, 1989. (Page citations are to the reprint edition.)

Origen. *On First Principles.* Edited and translated by G. W. Butterworth. 1936. Repr. Torchbook edition. New York: Harper & Row, 1973.

Pelikan, Jaroslav. *The Emergence of the Catholic Tradition* (100–600). Vol. 1 of *The Christian Tradition: A History of the Development of Doctrine.* Chicago: University of Chicago Press, 1971.

Popkin, Richard H. *The History of Scepticism from Erasmus to Spinoza.* Berkeley: University of California Press, 1979.

Preus, Robert D. *The Theology of Post-Reformation Lutheranism: A Study of Theological Prolegomena.* St. Louis: Concordia, 1970.

Pui-lan, Kwok. *Discovering the Bible in the Non-Biblical World.* Maryknoll, N.Y.: Orbis, 1995.

Pui-lan, Kwok, and Elisabeth Schüssler Fiorenza, eds. *Women's Sacred Scriptures.* Maryknoll, N.Y.: Orbis, 1998.

Ruether, Rosemary Radford. "Feminism and Patriarchal Religion: Principles of Ideological Critique of the Bible." *Journal for the Study of the Old Testament* 22 (1982): 54–56.

———. "Feminist Interpretation: A Method of Correlation." Pages 111–24 in *Feminist Interpretation of the Bible.* Edited by Letty M. Russell. Philadelphia: Westminster, 1985.

———. "Is Feminism the End of Christianity? A Critique of Daphne Hampson's *Theology and Feminism.*" *Scottish Journal of Theology* 43 (1990): 399.

————. *Sexism and God-Talk: Toward a Feminist Theology.* Boston: Beacon, 1993.

————. *Womanguides: Readings toward a Feminist Theology.* Boston: Beacon, 1985.

Rusch, William G., ed. and trans. *The Trinitarian Controversy.* Sources of Early Christian Thought. Edited by William G. Rusch. Philadelphia: Fortress, 1980.

Russell, Letty M. "Authority and the Challenge of Feminist Interpretation." Pages 137–46 in *Feminist Interpretation of the Bible.* Edited by Letty M. Russell. Philadelphia: Westminster, 1985.

————. *Household of Freedom: Authority in Feminist Theology.* Philadelphia: Westminster, 1987.

————. *Introduction to Feminist Interpretation of the Bible.* Edited by Letty M. Russell. Philadelphia: Westminster, 1985.

Schmid, Heinrich. *The Doctrinal Theology of the Evangelical Lutheran Church Exhibited and Verified from the Original Sources.* Translated by Charles A. Hay and Henry E. Jacobs. 3d ed. Minneapolis: Augsburg, 1961.

Schneiders, Sandra M. *The Revelatory Text: Interpreting the New Testament as Sacred Scripture.* San Francisco: HarperSanFrancisco, 1991.

Scholder, Klaus. *The Birth of Modern Critical Theology: Origins and Problems of Biblical Criticism in the Seventeenth Century.* Translated by John Bowden. Philadelphia: Trinity Press International, 1990.

Scholes, Robert, and Robert Kellogg. *The Nature of Narrative.* London: Oxford University Press, 1966.

Schottroff, Luise, Silvia Schroer, and Marie-Theres Wacker, eds. *Feminist Interpretation: The Bible in Women's Perspective.* Translated by Martin and Barbara Rumscheidt. Minneapolis: Fortress, 1998.

Schüssler Fiorenza, Elisabeth. *Bread Not Stone: The Challenge of Feminist Biblical Interpretation.* Boston: Beacon, 1984.

————. *In Memory of Her: A Feminist Theological Reconstruction of Christian Origins.* New York: Crossroad, 1984.

————. *Sharing Her Word: Feminist Biblical Interpretation in Context.* Boston: Beacon, 1998.

————. "The Will to Choose or to Reject: Continuing Our Critical Work." Pages 125–36 in *Feminist Interpretation of the Bible.* Edited by Letty M. Russell. Philadelphia: Westminster, 1985.

Simon, Yves R. *A General Theory of Authority.* Notre Dame, Ind.: University of Notre Dame Press, 1980.

Soskice, Janet Martin. "Can a Feminist Call God 'Father'?" Pages 81–94 in *Speaking the Christian God: The Holy Trinity and the Challenge of Feminism*. Edited by Alvin F. Kimel Jr. Grand Rapids: Eerdmans, 1992.

———. *Metaphor and Religious Language*. Oxford: Clarendon, 1985.

Stiles, William B., Lara Honos-Webb, and James A. Lanji. "Some Functions of Narrative in the Assimilation of Problematic Experiences." *Journal of Clinical Psychology* 55, no. 10 (1999): 1213–26.

Stone, Bryan P. "Wesleyan Theology, Scriptural Authority, and Homosexuality." *Wesleyan Theological Journal* 30 (fall 1995): 108–38.

Stout, Jeffrey. *Flight from Authority: Religion, Morality, and the Quest for Autonomy*. Notre Dame, Ind.: University of Notre Dame Press, 1981.

Tanner, Kathryn E. "Scripture as Popular Text." *Modern Theology* 14, no. 2 (April 1998): 279–98.

———. "Theology and the Plain Sense." Pages 59–78 in *Scriptural Authority and Narrative Interpretation*. Edited by Garrett Green. Philadelphia: Fortress, 1987.

———. *Theories of Culture: A New Agenda for Theology*. Guides to Theological Inquiry. Minneapolis: Augsburg Fortress, 1997.

Tirrell, Lynne. "Definition and Power: Toward Authority without Privilege." *Hypatia* 8, no. 4 (fall 1993): 1–34.

Tolbert, Mary Ann. "Protestant Feminists and the Bible: On the Horns of a Dilemma." *Union Seminary Quarterly Review* 43 (1989): 1–17.

Tomasello, Michael. *The Cultural Origins of Human Cognition*. Cambridge: Harvard University Press, 1999.

Trabasso, Tom, Nancy L. Stein, and Lucie R. Johnson. "Children's Knowledge of Events: A Causal Analysis of Story Structure." Pages 237–82 in *The Psychology of Learning and Motivation: Advances in Research and Theory*. Edited by Gordon H. Bower. Vol. 15. New York: Academic, 1981.

Turretin, Francis. *The Doctrine of Scripture*. Edited and translated by John W. Beardslee III. Grand Rapids: Baker, 1981.

Via, Dan O. *The Revelation of God and/as Human Reception*. Harrisburg, Pa.: Trinity Press International, 1997.

Ward, Keith. *Religion and Revelation*. Oxford: Oxford University Press, 1994.

Washington, Harold C., Susan Lochrie Graham, and Pamela Thimmes, eds. *Escaping Eden: New Feminist Perspectives on the Bible*. Sheffield: Sheffield Academic Press, 1998.

Watt, E. D. *Authority*. New York: St. Martin's, 1982.

Wesley, John. "Predestination Calmly Considered." Pages 42–72 in *John Wesley*. Edited by Albert Outler. New York: Oxford University Press, 1964.

Wood, Charles M. "Finding the Life of a Text: Notes on the Explication of Scripture." Pages 45–54 in *An Invitation to Theological Study*. Valley Forge, Pa.: Trinity Press International, 1994.

———. *The Formation of Christian Understanding: Theological Hermeneutics.* Valley Forge, Pa.: Trinity Press International, 1993. Repr., Eugene, Ore.: Wipf & Stock, 2000. (Page citations are to the original edition.)

———. "Scripture, Authenticity, and Truth." *Journal of Religion* 76 (April 1996): 189–205.

Young, Frances. *The Making of the Creeds.* Philadelphia: Trinity Press International, 1991.

———. *Virtuoso Theology: The Bible and Interpretation.* Cleveland: Pilgrim, 1990.

Zikmund, Barbara Brown. "Feminist Consciousness in Historical Perspective." Pages 21–29 in *Feminist Interpretation of the Bible*. Edited by Letty M. Russell. Philadelphia: Westminster, 1985.

Index